D1064180

Charles Chauncy at eighty-one. By an unknown artist.
Reproduced by permission of the Massachusetts Historical Society.

OLD BRICK

Charles Chauncy of Boston,

1705-1787

By

Edward M. Griffin

Department of English
University of Minnesota

UNIVERSITY OF MINNESOTA PRESS □ MINNEAPOLIS

Published by the University of Minnesota Press,
2037 University Avenue Southeast,
Minneapolis, Minnesota 55455

The University of Minnesota Press gratefully acknowledges
the financial assistance of the Graduate School and
the College of Liberal Arts of the University of Minnesota
in the publication of this book.

Library of Congress Cataloging in Publication Data
Griffin, Edward M.   1937–
     Old Brick, Charles Chauncy of Boston, 1705–1787.
     (Minnesota monographs in the humanities; v. 11)
     Bibliography: p.
     Includes index.
1. Chauncy, Charles, 1705-1787. 2. Congrega-
tional churches—Clergy—Biography. 3. Clergy—
Massachusetts—Boston—Biography. 4. Boston—
Biography. I. Title. II. Series.
BX7260.C527G74   285.8′32′0924 [B]   79-27203
ISBN 0-8166-0907-1

To **Edward J. Griffin** and the Memory of **Margaret Koessler Griffin**

Preface

Jonathan Edwards brought me to Charles Chauncy. Some years ago, when I began to read Edwards and think about his work, I discovered that behind many of his writings lurked some opponent, some advocate of a dangerous position whom Edwards needed to correct or defeat. The Great Awakening of the 1740s, of course, gave him his most dramatic opportunity to defend a position and attack his adversaries. His chief antagonist in that controversy, I soon learned from the histories of the Awakening and from studies of the life and thought of Edwards, was the Reverend Charles Chauncy of Boston. Clearly, I thought, if one wanted to understand what Edwards was saying, one should see what Chauncy was saying; so I began looking into Chauncy's life and works.

I thought for a time that the commentators on Edwards had done my work for me, because they dutifully told me about Chauncy's opposition to the Great Awakening and to Edwards's defense of the movement. Yet to judge from their accounts, not only was Chauncy an intellectual adversary, he was an out-and-out villain in Edwards's life: narrowminded, mean-spirited, cold-hearted, double-dealing, self-centered, he emerged as a nasty "heavy" out of a nineteenth-century melodrama. One could almost hear the scholars and critics hiss each time they brought him into their pages. I yield to no one in my admiration for the mind of Jonathan Edwards. But such a depiction aroused my suspicions, for I knew the temptation to write melodramatic history. The attacks on Chauncy also stirred my curiosity to learn more about this man who had inspired such a strong response from Edwards and such an impassioned reaction from my fellow students of the great theologian.

A few trips to the library, however, taught me how hard it was to learn more about Charles Chauncy. His name appeared in all the histories, but neither a biography nor a full-scale study of his works had been published. His works had not been collected, and none of the individual works had been printed in a modern edition. Clifford Shipton's 1942 biographical sketch in *Sibley's Harvard Graduates*, along with a chapter on Chauncy in Williston Walker's 1901 study, *Ten New England Leaders*, appeared to be the published sources for most of the subsequent commentary. Edwin Scott Gaustad had also written a good bibliography of Chauncy's writings during the years of the Great Awakening. The dissertations of Harold Bernhard (Chicago, 1945), Norman Brantley Gibbs (Duke, 1953), Barney Lee Jones (Duke, 1958), Charles H. Lippy (Princeton, 1972), and Harold B. Wohl (Iowa, 1956) touched on Chauncy's life.

I thought then of doing a biography of Chauncy. The need for such a study pressed upon me as I continued my study of Edwards and New England in the eighteenth century, for I soon discovered the truth of a truism in American colonial studies: the importance of Charles Chauncy. He kept turning up everywhere. For sixty of his eighty-two years he had been a pastor at the First Church of Boston (known in the eighteenth century as the "Old Brick"), the oldest Congregational church in Boston and one of the most important in New England. In that capacity he had played a role in the major events of his time: not only the Great Awakening, but also the French and Indian wars, the controversy over the proposed establishment of the Anglican episcopacy in America, political events from the Stamp Act through the Revolution, the rise of the Enlightenment, the growth of "liberal Protestantism," social changes in Boston, the development of Unitarianism—the list continued to grow. Here was a man whose importance transcended that of spokesman for the opposition in the Great Awakening or antagonist to Jonathan Edwards. He was a significant figure in his own right. His story was in many ways the story of eighteenth-century America. It deserved to be told.

All biography requires considerable detective work, and, as Paul Murray Kendall has observed, the biographical detective follows a paper trail.[1] In Chauncy's case, surprisingly, the trail proved unusually faint and the detective work particularly challenging. Unlike many colonial New Englanders he left very little by way of personal papers. Chauncy took great pride in his systematic temperament, but if he submitted himself to the discipline of a diary or a journal, these documents have not yet turned up. Edwards and Franklin wrote classics of personal narrative; for Chauncy, however, we have no "spiritual relation" or memoir. (Chapter Twelve of this book contains a possible explanation for the odd absence of Chauncy's private papers.) Still it has been possible, through following the clues left in such sources as the scattered surviving correspondence, the diaries and journals of his contemporaries, the records of Harvard College, the First Church, and Boston, and a wide variety of other manuscript and published documents, to piece together the events of his life both private and public.

Like all biographers I have tried to create my subject as a character; I wanted not only to set the events of his life in order, but also to capture his personality, portraying the private life of Chauncy the man as well as the public life of Chauncy the spokesman for this or that controversial position. In doing so, however, I have proceeded cautiously because so much of the available evidence is indirect and circumstantial, dictating restraint in the face of strong and frequent temptations to press Chauncy into a particular psychological pattern or to guess at the psychological forces working behind his actions. One wishes that Chauncy had left better records of the stirrings of his heart; in the absence of such records one should probably resist inventing them for him. But one should not conclude from their absence that if he had a heart it was never stirred. Although I reject the traditional caricature of the cold-blooded Chauncy, the evidence has not led me to counterbalance tradition by writing Chauncy into the calendar of saints. I have tried, in short, to bring the picture of his personality into focus without reaching beyond what my evidence reasonably suggests.

Many clues to Chauncy's personality, of course, lie in his expository and hortative writing, a great deal of which was published in his lifetime. Precisely because he commented so frequently and forcefully on the issues of his times, he has served historians conveniently as a spokesman. As I studied his writings, both in print and in manuscript, I realized how rich an intellectual life Chauncy led. Surely a major task of his biography must be the concise, critical presentation of his thought, and I hope I have stitched such a presentation into the narrative fabric of this study. I have tried to give a sense of the way the man's thought and temperament connect with his life and times.

Research for this study took me to many libraries. I thank the staffs of the following institutions for their assistance, and for permitting me access to their valuable collections: the American Antiquarian Society; the American Philosophical Society; the Boston Athenaeum; the Boston Public Library; Boston University Libraries; the Congregational Society Library; University of California Libraries; Forbes Library; Harvard University Libraries; the Historical Society of Pennsylvania; the Massachusetts Historical Society; University of

Minnesota Libraries; the New York Public Library; Princeton University Libraries; University of San Francisco Library; Stanford University Libraries; and the Sutro Branch of the California State Library.

The publications of the Massachusetts Historical Society, the American Antiquarian Society, and the Colonial Society of Massachusetts, along with the riches of the *New England Historical and Genealogical Register*, have proved invaluable. The recent publication of the complete records of the First Church of Boston by the Colonial Society of Massachusetts (*CSM Pubs.*, 39–41) was especially welcome. Of course every student of early America is aware of the immense value of Clifford K. Shipton's *Sibley's Harvard Graduates*, but only one who has turned to these volumes as often as I have can appreciate the skill and scholarship they represent.

I have been aided in the preparation of this study by the Danforth Foundation, which gave me the graduate fellowship that started it all long ago, and by the University of Minnesota, which provided me with a Graduate School summer research grant and a travel grant through the Putnam D. McMillan Fund. I owe thanks to many people who gave me encouragement and criticism as I worked through several versions of this book. David Levin, William A. Clebsch, and the late Claude M. Simpson read my work in its earliest version. I have profited from their advice and from the critiques of Everett Emerson, Roland A. Delattre, Gordon O'Brien, and Richard Warch. I owe a special debt to Professor Levin, whose guidance on many matters has been so reliable. Dorothy Snyder typed the manuscript cheerfully and skillfully. To Jean Chisholm Griffin I owe my greatest debt, for even though she never mustered much affection for Charles Chauncy, she always had plenty for me.

Contents

OLD BRICK

Charles Chauncy of Boston, 1705-1787

Introduction

Frequently historians studying the intellectual life of the eighteenth-century Anglo-American colonies and of the young United States have emphasized the evangelical wing of Congregationalism on one hand and secular Deism on the other. The great representative of the former is Jonathan Edwards; of the latter, Benjamin Franklin. As Perry Miller has put it: "The intellectual history—or, if you will, the spiritual history—of the United States has been dramatized by a series of pairs of personalities, contemporaneous and contrasting, which have become avatars of the contradictory thrusts within our effort to find or to create a national identity." Such pairs, Miller points out, as John Smith and William Bradford, Thomas Jefferson and Alexander Hamilton, Robert E. Lee and Abraham Lincoln, serve as major examples. "But of all these, and of several lesser pairs, the pre-eminently eloquent linked antagonists in American culture will always be Jonathan Edwards and Benjamin Franklin."[1] Chauncy, however, belonged to neither the school of Jonathan nor the school of Ben. He was caught in the middle, linked with Edwards only as an opposer but not an antagonist so extreme as to rival Ben Franklin; linked with Franklin only because, like him, Chauncy also found some of the dogmas of Puritanism "unintelligible, others doubtful."[2] If he has been placed in anyone's school, it has been at the doorstep of that of William Ellery Channing, the great nineteenth-century Unitarian, for the tendencies Chauncy supported led eventually to the highly rational Unitarian Christianity of which Channing was the major early representative.[3] Yet Chauncy was not a Unitarian, and he would hardly have

3

found many of Channing's basic beliefs Christian in the sense in which he understood the word.

It is actually deceptive to divide the eighteenth century between Edwards's evangelicalism and Franklin's Deism. The middle ground that Chauncy defended was a vast and well-populated territory with a long history of its own. A great many eighteenth-century Americans held ideas similar to Chauncy's. In religious terms, he spoke for a long-standing tradition that in the seventeenth century is best represented by Richard Baxter and in the eighteenth by a movement that has been described as the "supernatural rationalism of such men as Locke, Tillotson, and Clarke."[4] Although like the Deists these thinkers affirmed "Natural Religion"—the belief that humans, using only their unaided reason, could arrive at such basic doctrines of religion as the existence of God, the necessity of divine worship and love of neighbor, and the existence of a future state in which they would be rewarded or punished—they did not thereby exalt natural reason over revelation. Instead they denied the adequacy of Natural Religion, insisting on the necessity of divine revelation for a genuine, complete view of religion. Their sentiments, Conrad Wright points out, were "far more sharply defined, prevalent, and significant" in eighteenth-century America "than any of our scholars, whether philosophers or historical theologians or church historians, have ever intimated."[5]

Although Chauncy was a major American figure—perhaps *the* major figure—in this tradition, "supernatural rationalism" is not a term he would have applied to himself. He considered himself simply a good Congregationalist, true to his own heritage of dissent and free inquiry. After about 1750 he did not consider himself a traditional evangelical Calvinist. Neither, however, did he consider himself an Arian, Arminian, Pelagian, or Deist. He defended the Christian tradition. He honored the native powers of the mind, but he denied the efficacy of unaided reason and confirmed the primacy of Scripture, asserting that he educed his theological opinions from a close examination of the sacred writings. He did not deny the doctrines of the covenants of works and grace, but he stressed the divine role of Christ in atoning for sin and earning the merits of salvation for humankind, insisting, in fact, that traditional Calvinism had not strongly enough emphasized Christ's redemptive sacrifice. Chauncy believed that man entered the covenant of grace only by faith in Christ. He consistently maintained his allegiance to the Congregational principle of covenanted church organization. He insisted, even in his most "heretical" works, that he was conducting his speculations within the framework of reformed Protestantism. In doing so, he firmly believed, he was pledging allegiance to the true spirit of the ancient New England Way.

4

Indeed, if there is one theme governing his thought and behavior over the long period of his life, it is his defense of the New England Way. He is true to the myth that God had entered into a special covenant with the favored people of New England to redeem the world. He distrusted New-Lights, Anglicans, and Deists about equally because he saw them as threats to this great mission. The Great Awakening persuaded him that New-Light rigidity would inevitably pit New Englander against New Englander, destroy New England's sense of itself, and throw into disarray the basic social order that had come down from the Puritan founders. By insisting so relentlessly that the colonists were inherently miserable, worthless creatures, hopelessly and helplessly damned by an angry God, the New-Lights influenced the people to define themselves as unworthy of the great task before them. When this stark Calvinism took hold during the Awakening, the colonists' sense of common purpose—their sense of themselves as a redeemer nation—crumbled, never, despite Chauncy's efforts, to be perfectly repaired. The threat, in the 1760s, of Anglican control provided Chauncy with a chance to unite the descendants of the Puritans once more in a common effort—to rekindle in them the zeal, which they had lost in the 1740s, for their special redeeming mission. The Revolutionary War offered the same chance in the political order and seemed to Chauncy the natural extension of his religious principles. But if political action came to mean a challenge by secular leaders to Protestantism's traditional place or an attack on organized religion generally—as Deism's emphasis upon natural reason seemed to portend—then Chauncy withheld allegiance and rose to the defense of revelation and sound doctrine.

Precisely this intermixture of revision and defense in Chauncy's life makes him a more interesting character than the stock figure of the stony Great Opposer of the Great Awakening will allow. Just as we can hardly get a true picture of Benjamin Franklin by concentrating solely on the young rationalist's pretentious "bold and arduous Project of arriving at moral Perfection,"[6] so we can hardly get a true picture of Chauncy by looking only at the Great Awakening—even if we are willing to grant that Chauncy took the job of Great Opposer for more complex reasons than sheer villainy. The Chauncy of the Great Awakening was a complicated fellow—and the Great Awakening was hardly all there was to Chauncy. The story of his life is not that of a static character, flat and unchanging. It is in fact one of steady change. He found the basic rhythm of his life in the beat laid down by the old Puritan reformers, and from this he tried not to vary; but for the better part of a century he played over that base a number of new melodies in a wide range of keys. And his personality was not frosty

5

and mean-spirited. Bezaleel Howard knew him as an old man; his description sums up Chauncy as well as any: "He was, like Zaccheus, little of stature. God gave him a slender, feeble body, a very powerful, vigorous mind, and strong passions; and he managed them all exceedingly well. His manners were plain and downright,—dignified, bold, and imposing. In conversation with his friends he was pleasant, social, and very instructive."[7] We might not agree that Chauncy always managed his body, mind, and passions exceedingly well, but this is hardly a portrait of a coldhearted monster.

Chauncy's chief aim in life was not the destruction of Jonathan Edwards. The caricature of the villain will not serve. Instead, believing himself obliged by his New England heritage to do so, he was trying to work his way through a set of problems that he knew he shared with many colonists but that, for all their brilliance, Edwards and Franklin were spared. Perhaps a glance at Edwards's "Personal Narrative" and Franklin's *Autobiography* will illustrate this point.

As a young man, Edwards once recalled, he had suffered over the doctrine of God's sovereignty "in choosing whom he would to eternal life, and rejecting whom he pleased; leaving them eternally to perish, and be everlastingly tormented in hell." His mind, he said, "had been wont to be full of objections against the doctrine" and it "used to appear like a horrible doctrine to me."

> But I remember the time very well, when I seemed to be convinced, and fully satisfied, as to this sovereignty of God, and his justice in thus eternally disposing of men, according to his sovereign pleasure. But never could give an account, how, or by what means, I was thus convinced; not in the least imagining, in the time of it, nor a long time after, that there was any extraordinary influence of God's spirit in it; but only that now I saw further, and my reason apprehended the justice and reasonableness of it. However, my mind rested in it; and it put an end to all those cavils and objections, that had 'till then abode with me, all the preceding part of my life. And there has been a wonderful alteration in my mind, with respect to the doctrine of God's sovereignty, from that day to this; so that I scarce ever have found so much as the rising of an objection against God's sovereignty, in the most absolute sense, in showing mercy to whom he will show mercy, and hardening and eternally damning whom he will. God's absolute sovereignty, and justice, with respect to salvation and damnation, is what my mind seems to rest assured of, as much as of any thing that I see with my eyes; at least it is so at times. But I have often times since that first conviction, had quite another kind of sense of God's sovereignty, than I had then. I have often since, not only had a conviction, but a *delightful* conviction. The doctrine of God's sovereignty has very often appeared, an exceeding pleasant, bright and sweet doctrine to me: and absolute sovereignty is what I love to ascribe to God.[8]

6

As a Boston-born lad, Franklin also struggled with the fundamentals of Puritan doctrine. "I had been religiously educated as a Presbyterian," he recalled (his parents had "early given me religious Impressions, and brought me through my Childhood piously in the Dissenting Way"),[9] but, "tho' some of the Dogmas of that Persuasion, such as the Eternal Decrees of God, Election, Reprobation, &c. appear'd to me unintelligible, others doubtful, and I early absented myself from the Public Assemblies of the Sect, Sunday being my Studying-Day, I never was without some religious Principles; I never doubted, for instance, the Existance of the Deity, that he made the World, and govern'd it by his Providence; that the most acceptable Service of God was the doing Good to Man; that our Souls are immortal; and that all Crime will be punished and Virtue rewarded either here or hereafter. . . ."[10]

Edwards enjoyed a two-stage conversion from repulsion at the doctrine of sovereignty to delightful acceptance of it. After his mind was opened to the reasonableness of the doctrine, the Holy Spirit then provided him with enough divine and supernatural light to pass from mere speculative understanding of it to a holy affection for it. Franklin's mind also balked at the doctrine. He did not come to see its reasonableness. For him, moreover, what ran counter to reason was false, and he turned instead to those religious principles that did seem to him reasonable and certain, troubling himself little thereafter with the dogmas of Presbyterianism.

Chauncy, however, continued to trouble himself with doctrinal "cavils and objections." He left us no personal narrative or autobiography to dramatize his own intellectual struggles, but a lifetime's worth of writings testifies that he had them. His mind, unlike that of Edwards, did not receive an "extraordinary influence of God's Spirit" that enabled him to "rest assured" in "delightful conviction" about troublesome dogmas. A New-Light might consider his failure to be so favored as evidence of his damnation after all. At any rate, an anxious Chauncy was left to spend his life wrestling with his problems instead of confidently defending the old orthodoxy. Unlike Franklin he would not turn away from the faith of his fathers when he found some of their ideas "unintelligible, others doubtful." For although Franklin could say, "Revelation had indeed no weight with me,"[11] Chauncy could not. Revelation carried great weight with him, and he set himself the task of reconciling what it told him with what his mind told him. A philosophe of the Enlightenment might smile at his wasting his effort in such a fatuous exercise. (Franklin, three months before his death, slyly wrote Ezra Stiles that he had never studied the question of Christ's divinity, "and think it needless to busy myself with it now, when I expect soon an Opportunity of knowing the Truth with less Trouble.")[12] For Chauncy, as for many Americans like him, it was worth the trouble.

Furthermore, as Michael Kammen has pointed out in *People of Paradox*, a religious position such as supernatural rationalism, especially in a Congregational vein, was thoroughly congenial to the colonial cast of mind. From the beginnings Americans have been pushed and pulled between contradictory tendencies in the culture; they have resolved the tensions between these tendencies, if they have resolved them at all, by taking a middle position that mixes elements of each. This has been the national "style," as Kammen puts it, and that style was particularly manifest in the colonial period. Religion was characterized by "fatalistic optimism," which combined a belief in the omnipotence of God with "hope in human striving"; "practical piety," "in which religion becomes a useful instrument of social order and underpins a crusade for benevolence"; and "reverent unbelief," a distrust of form coupled with intensity of devotion. In the eighteenth century this kind of piety took the form of supernatural rationalism. In politics "several sorts of biformities" prevailed: "pragmatic idealism, conservative liberalism, orderly violence, and moderate rebellion." In manners and morals, colonists displayed "practical moralism," "humble pride," "ostentatious austerity," and "prurient prudishness."[13] The hybrid position—at its best the paradoxical position—prevails throughout the culture.

Probably no colonial figure embodies all Kammen's categories perfectly, but Chauncy comes very close. Few others were so active on so many fronts. Unlike many political leaders, he was heavily involved in the day-to-day affairs of the churches; unlike many religious leaders, he was deeply involved in politics on a day-to-day basis. He was moreover a visible, public arbiter of manners and morals. And he lived long enough to struggle through the great crisis of the American style, the Revolutionary War. We shall see in each arena his tendency to adopt the paradoxical and uncomfortable middle position between contradictory tendencies. With all the hedging, accommodation, confusion, deformity, irony, creativity, courage, and complexity that were his style, it was the colonial style; it may be, if we are indeed a people of paradox, the American style.

Chauncy, then, can fairly be seen as a Representative Man. If we must arrange the intellectual scenery of eighteenth-century America in a tableau, Edwards and Franklin should surely stand in honored places at front stage, right and left, for they were truly giants. But in fairness we must also allow a place for Chauncy and the tradition, the style, he represents—some paces toward the backdrop and at the edge of the shadows, to be sure, so as not to steal the limelight from the stars, but at center stage nonetheless.

8

Prologue

Cotton Mather, at sixty-four a year away from his death, but still sturdy and imposing, stepped forward and clasped the right hand of young Charles Chauncy of Boston. For Chauncy, small, thin, and only twenty-two, it was a moment of great importance. In accepting the traditional right hand of fellowship from the venerable Mather, he was stepping into the ranks of Congregationalist ministers—ranks whose number had included his famous great-grandfather, the second president of Harvard College. He was placing himself in association with men of stature and responsibility—men of God—such as those gathered around him in Boston's First Church: Mather, Benjamin Colman, Peter Thacher, and the senior pastor of the oldest church in Boston, Thomas Foxcroft. More important even than these associations was the fact that he had been called to preach God's word to a congregation of his own.

The appointment to the post as Foxcroft's assistant at the First Church had been a long time coming. It had been nearly three years since Chauncy had taken his Master's degree at Harvard; he had competed regularly for this and other positions since that time. Finally the First Church had chosen him, and at last, on Wednesday, October 25, 1727, ordination day had arrived.

The ceremony followed the traditonal format. Foxcroft began with prayer; then Chauncy mounted the pulpit to preach his ordination sermon on a text from Matthew, "Lo, I am with you always." Clearly he was expected to perform in a manner that did honor to the memory of his great-grandfather, whose biographer, Cotton Mather, was in front of him, listening carefully. Everyone present had heard of President Chauncy, and many had known Chauncy's father when he was alive—fellow merchants, members of the Old South Church, fellow officers in the Ancient and Honorable Artillery Company. Because his mother had died the year before, she was not there to see the resemblances between the young man and his forebears; but as he spoke, such resemblances may have occurred to Mather and Judge Samuel Sewall. After Chauncy brought his sermon to a close, Peter Thacher of the New North prayed. Benjamin Colman, then in his twenty-eighth year as pastor of the Brattle Street Church, delivered the traditional charge to the young minister: a message of welcome, caution, and exhortation enlisting the young man in the ministry. And finally, in the name of the Boston ministers, Cotton Mather extended the right hand of fellowship, welcoming him to their brotherhood. The parishioners expressed their welcome in the lavish entertainment that followed the ceremony.[1]

On October 29, 1727, the fourth night after Chauncy's ordination, the people of Boston were shaken from their beds by one of the most violent earthquakes in New England history. The next morning Cotton Mather's meetinghouse was full to hear him interpret the event as an omen and call for repentance to assuage the "Terror of the Lord." A few hours later the congregation of the First Church met by candle-light at the Old Brick as Foxcroft branded the earthquake a sign of God's anger and a clear demand for repentance throughout New England. In the hubbub probably only Chauncy remembered that October 29 was also the day of his admission to the First Church as a member. He must have paused to consider what significance he might draw from the fact that the commencement of his ministry virtually coincided with the most terrifying night in the history of Boston. Whatever omen he drew at the time, it is likely that later in his life he had occasion to look back on the coincidence and find it haunting. For he was that week in Boston setting forth on a career destined to continue at the First Church for the next sixty years. Few who had gathered at his ordination, or had been awakened in the night by the rumblings of the earth, would be there to gather at the close of his life and ministry. These were to be eventful, stormy, revolutionary years, and Charles Chauncy was to be caught up in nearly every storm and event, even in the Revolution. He was to become an unsettling clergyman, one of the most influential of his time; he was to espouse views radically different from those of Mather and his own great-grandfather. Finally he was to become so closely associated with the church in which he had been ordained that he was to be given its nickname: for most of his life he would be known by antagonists and friends alike as Charles Old-Brick, the fiery pastor from Boston.

10

CHAPTER ONE

A Boston Lad

Every November fifth young Bostonians from the South End of town snakedanced through the early evening chill to the beat of drums and the accompaniment of bells and whistles. The torches they carried through the streets flickered on their wildly painted faces and sent shadows across their ragged and brightly patched costumes. It was Pope's Day, an annual event to celebrate the foiling of the attempt by Catholics in 1605 to blow up Parliament in the so-called gunpowder plot. At the center of the procession the men and boys dragged "the pope's carriage"—a long wagon supporting a large platform. On a throne at the center of the platform sat a huge grotesque effigy of a fat pope in a red gown, adorned with a flowing white wig and crowned with a hat of gold lace. Toward the front of the platform was mounted an effigy of James III—the "Pretender" to the throne of England; behind the pope loomed a gigantic devil, holding a trident in one hand and a lantern in the other, and curling an enormous tail about him. Invisible inside each figure was a long rod, extending under the stage, where a team of small boys manipulated the rods to make the Pope bow, the Pretender cringe, and the Devil dance. As the people weaved through the streets, the revelers ran to the houses, demanding money and food and frequently taking anything burnable that they could pry loose from the premises. For a similar procession was marching down from the North End. When the two mobs met in Union Street the young men and boys scrimmaged as each side tried to capture the effigies of the other. If the North-Enders outbattled the South-Enders, they tossed their captured prizes onto a fire at Copp's Hill. If the

South-Enders won, they raced to their own bonfire at Boston Common. Although many boys paid a price in bloody noses and broken bones, they never lost their enthusiasm for the autumn scuffle.[1]

Of all the lively events—from shooting fireworks on the Governor's birthday to attending the public execution of a pirate—available to a Boston boy when Charles Chauncy (and such neighbors as Benjamin Franklin) were growing up, he took a special interest in Pope's Day, not only because a boy loves action and excitement, but also because he had been taught from early childhood that November fifth carried special meaning in the traditions of the Chauncy family. His great-grandfather, who became President Charles Chauncy of Harvard, had been obliquely involved in the gunpowder affair, and his adventure had become a staple of family history. President Chauncy was a grammar-school student at Westminster school, adjoining the House of Parliament, on the day of the gunpowder plot, "and must have perished," his great-grandson later recalled, "if the Parliament house, as was intended, had been blown up." Fortunately for the Chauncy line, the plot failed, but the Chauncys never forgot this narrow escape. "I particularly mention this fact," wrote Charles in a letter late in his life, "because it is an emphatically important one as relative to myself, and strongly points out the special obligation I am under to set an asterism on the 5th of November, which, to this day is commemorated in the colonies, as well as mother country, as I hope it always will be, with expressions of joy and gratitude. My existence, with all its connections in this world and another, which were then only possible futurities, were absolutely dependent on this deliverance by an extraordinary interposition in God's all governing providence."[2]

After this stroke of Providence Chauncy's great-grandfather went on to set a memorable example for his descendants. An accomplished scholar, especially in languages, he also became so effective a Puritan minister in England that he ran afoul of Archbishop Laud. He escaped in 1637 to the New World and ministered at Plymouth and Scituate until 1654, when he was named president of Harvard, a position he held with distinction until his death in 1671. Always remorseful over the single instance, in 1635, when he had submitted to Laud's order to recant his beliefs, in his will he left his posterity a solemn directive to keep faith with Puritan doctrine and "not to conform (as he had done) to rites and ceremonies in religious worship of man's devising, and not of God's appointing." Like the story of his providential deliverance, this charge was passed down through the generations; throughout his life Charles, as the eldest son of President Chauncy's eldest grandson, paid special heed to the challenge, just as he set an "asterism" next to Pope's Day on his calendar.[3] His heritage was Protestantism of the most vigorous Puritan stamp. From his infancy, militantly Protestant attitudes and practices dominated his family, as indeed they still dominated his town. Colonial Bostonians of the early eighteenth century identified the Pope, the Pretender, and the Devil as their symbolic enemies, and fought for the first chance to pitch them into the flames. Chauncy would have gladly added to that unholy trinity another effigy—the Archbishop of Canterbury.

But he was not a minister's son. His father, also named Charles, was a successful businessman, and the Chauncy family was connected with commerce, politics, and civic affairs as well as with the church. Born in England (where his own father, Isaac, had emigrated after graduation from Harvard in 1651), this Charles Chauncy had become a merchant. Making his way to Boston as a young man, he established himself as an agent for the Jamaican business of John Taylor. In 1699 he married Sarah Walley, the daughter of Judge John Walley of the Massachusetts Supreme Court. Charles, their first son, was born January 1, 1705 and was baptized six days later at the meetinghouse of the Third Church, now known as the Old South.[4]

Charles and Sarah Chauncy probably reared their children pretty much the way their neighbors Josiah and Abiah Franklin reared theirs. In his *Autobiography* Benjamin Franklin, born the year after Chauncy and in the very shadow of the Old South meetinghouse, recalls affectionately how his parents "by constant labour and industry"[5] maintained their large family. He also recalls the hospitality and vigor of family life in Mr. Franklin's Puritan household: His father liked to have at his table, "as often as he could, some sensible Friend or Neighbour, to converse with, and always took care to start some ingenious or useful Topic for Discourse, which might tend to improve the Minds of his Children. By this means he turn'd our Attention to what was good, just, and prudent in the Conduct of Life."[6] One might speculate that the Chauncys were numbered among such "sensible friends" who visited the Franklins. At any rate Josiah Franklin's practices were probably common enough. A generation later, when young Charles Chauncy had children of his own, he treated them in much the same way.

A Puritan father also used more formal means to turn the attention of his children to goodness, justice, and prudence. Prayer, attendance upon the Word, both through the reading of Scripture and careful attention to sermons and catechetics, still shaped a Boston childhood in the early eighteenth century. Like generations of New Englanders before him, young Charles and his brothers probably learned to read by studying a primer that included the Westminster *Shorter Catechism* as well as the familiar rhymes used to teach the alphabet. Even as a

13

young child he listened to the sermons of the Reverend Ebenezer Pemberton at the meetinghouse.

In May 1711 Charles attended the funeral of his father there. The young merchant died on May 4, leaving Sarah Chauncy a widow with three sons: Charles, then seven, and his younger brothers, Isaac and Walley. The Honorable Samuel Sewall described the funeral in his diary: "Mr. Chauncy buried; Bearers, Mr. Daniel Oliver, Mr. Francis Clark; Mr. Wm. Welsteed, Mr. Grove Hirst, Mr. Oliver Noyes, Mr. Anthony Stoddard. Many of the Council there."[7]

Family friends came to Sarah Chauncy's assistance in her widowhood. The men who bore her husband's coffin were important and controversial figures in Boston commerce and politics, for the merchant had recently become an increasingly powerful force in community affairs. Since the 1690s Boston, like the other major colonial settlements, had changed from a big village to a good-sized town, and now "the events of town life were enacted on a constantly widening stage."[8] After the revocation of the Massachusetts charter in 1684 and the establishment of the colony's new status as a royal province in 1692, the "townspeople, royal officials and merchants competed to dominate the political, social and economic affairs of the town."[9] Charles Chauncy the elder had worked actively with the merchant bloc. Naturally his chief allegiances were with the shipowners, but he also counted other commercial and political leaders among his friends, and he achieved a position of some importance in the community. Business and marriage connected him with Andrew Belcher, Nathanial Byfield, Elisha Cooke, Oliver Noyes, Daniel and Nathaniel Oliver, and Samuel Sewall. Judges Sewall and Byfield were especially close to the family. Eighteen years after his father's death, when Charles was twenty-five, he published a work acknowledging that he had "reason to love and reverence" Judge Byfield "as a Father"; it is likely that the judge was a father to Charles at this time, precisely when he needed one.[10]

The year after his father died Charles, probably helped by such family friends, went off to school. On the death that same year of Judge Walley, Sarah Chauncy's father, she received enough property and income to enable her to live comfortably and to continue Charles's education.[11] John Taylor, for whom Mr. Chauncy had been Boston agent, was in Jamaica when he received word of his associate's death. Later in 1711 he returned to Boston, where his wife owned a house near the Old South meetinghouse. He brought along his son John, just five months older than Charles Chauncy, and arranged to enter the boy in the Boston Public Latin School. When his father returned to Jamaica young John was put to board with Benjamin Wadsworth, the pastor of the First Church, whose careful accounts of John Taylor's school expenses still survive.[12] John became young Charles Chauncy's

14

closest chum. They were "playmates when little boys, went to school together, were classmates at college, and all along till death in close friendship and acquaintance with each other," Chauncy was to recall many years later.[13] His remark that he and Taylor attended school together lends substance to Boston Latin's traditional claim that Chauncy was one of its illustrious graduates. The boys started school in 1712.[14]

Boston Latin instructed youngsters in the elementary subjects and also prepared them to meet the admissions requirements of Harvard College. Nathaniel Williams, who also served as deacon at the South Church, was Master during the four years Charles spent there; Edward Wigglesworth, later to have great influence on Chauncy, served as Williams's assistant, or "usher."[15] Charles's most famous schoolmate was the dropout Benjamin Franklin, who entered in 1714 and made startling progress for a year. After that his father, Franklin remembers in the *Autobiography*, "from a View of the Expence of a College Education which, having so large a Family, he could not well afford, and the mean Living many so educated were afterwards able to obtain . . . altered his first Intention, took me from the Grammar School, and sent me to a School for Writing and Arithmetic kept by a then famous Man, Mr. Geo. Brownell, very successful in his Profession generally, and that by mild encouraging Methods."[16]

Charles Chauncy, John Taylor, and the other boys persevered, however, in "a pretty stiff and thorough classical course."[17] The 1712 curriculum at Boston Latin has been preserved; it outlines the kind of training to which Chauncy was exposed. The curriculum was Latin, Latin, and more Latin, and included three years of intensive drill on vocabulary, grammar, and translation, along with readings of Corderius's colloquies and Aesop's fables. Later the students read Erasmus's colloquies, Ovid's *de Tristibus* and *Metamorphoses*, Cicero's *Epistolae, de Officiis* and Orations, Virgil's *Aeneid*, Justin, Horace, Juvenal, and Persius. In addition they worked hard on Latin prosody and composition, and wrote dialogues, verse, and Latin prose essays. When they were not studying Latin they were learning Greek, using texts that included Homer, Isocrates, Hesiod, and the New Testament.[18]

Such a course of study prepared a boy for college. To gain admission an applicant was to satisfy the president or one of the tutors of the college that he possessed "an ability to read Cicero or some such classical author extempore, to 'make and speak true Latin in verse and prose *suo, ut aiunt, Marte*,' and decline the paradigms of Greek nouns and verbs."[19] All this by the age of fifteen. In 1716, when Charles was eleven, Sarah Chauncy married Francis Willoughby, a widower from Salem; that same year Charles went over to Cambridge and passed the examination. He began his studies at Harvard in June 1717.[20]

CHAPTER TWO

The Young Harvard Scholar

Chauncy went to Harvard during troubled times at the college. Starting in 1717, the year he entered, John Leverett, the college president, was "in almost continual hot water." The Boston press became critical of the college and the misbehavior of its students. Serious discontent had developed among the faculty, and Leverett had to deal with growing dismay among powerful New England political and religious leaders over the liberal tendencies they accused the school of fostering.[1]

Elected president in 1708, Leverett had managed early in his administration to put the school on sound financial footing, but he suddenly saw his position threatened because so many students were slipping over to Boston for such mischief as horse races and pirate hangings, or, when they stayed in Cambridge, were disturbing good order by "profane swearing," "bringing Cards into College," window-breaking, and other "riotous Actions." Leverett's worries increased markedly when James and Benjamin Franklin began publishing *The New-England Courant* in 1721, for the president and his frivolous students became the frequent target of Franklinian satire and public laughter.[2]

But his troubles were hardly confined to the rowdiness of students and the potshots of the Franklins. His most serious challenges came from the camp of Cotton Mather. Since the turn of the century Mather and many of his colleagues had feared that the college was slipping away from the Puritan orthodoxy of its founders. Leverett's election to the college presidency had been unpopular with the Mathers; Cotton Mather had grumbled that they might just as well have turned the school over to the bishop of London. During the first decade of

16

Leverett's administration Mather's forces gained strength in Boston, for while Leverett was getting started, several young pro-Mather ministers were finishing at Harvard. By 1717 Mather's adherents held many Boston pulpits. That year they joined battle with Leverett and continued until the president died in 1724. Both sides boxed nicely but relied on infighting to score their most telling blows.[3]

In 1717 Leverett gained a sympathetic majority on the Harvard Corporation by having the liberal ministers Nathaniel Appleton and Benjamin Colman named fellows to that body, which, along with the board of overseers, governed the college. The next year Harvard refused the usually automatic Master's degree to Ebenezer Pierpont, a 1715 graduate who had been teaching in Roxbury. According to tutor Nicholas Sever, Pierpont was not qualified, for his students were coming to the college poorly prepared. Pierpont, backed by an odd syndicate including the Dudleys and the Mathers, promptly sued Sever. Both Governor Shute and the local Cambridge court heard the arguments and dismissed the case. The Mather faction did not take this lightly. Judge Samuel Sewall became furious with Leverett during an overseers' meeting, and Cotton Mather and the Reverend Thomas Prince worked hard that year to divert Elihu Yale's money to the young college in Connecticut. They also tried, unsuccessfully, to convince the wealthy London merchant Thomas Hollis to establish his divinity professorship not at Harvard, as he intended, but at Yale.[4]

If 1717, 1718, and 1719 were stormy years, 1720 and 1721 were positively tumultuous. In 1720 tutors Henry Flynt, Thomas Robie, and Nicholas Sever launched "one of the most famous controversies in Harvard history by addressing to the Board of Overseers a memorial demanding as of right their fellowship in the Corporation." Resident tutors had once held membership as fellows of the corporation, but during the presidency of Increase Mather (1686–1701) the fellowships went predominantly to nonresidents, chiefly Congregational ministers. Sever and his colleagues, trying to gain some influence in college decision-making, wanted the original practice restored. They saw the board of overseers—who represented the community and whose membership was drawn from the conservative local clergy and magistrates —as their greatest support against Leverett. Samuel Eliot Morison describes what happened: "From the time that Sever's memorial was presented, there began a contest which somewhat resembles a bitterly solemn game of chess. The Board of Overseers, in which the sectarian party had a majority, took Sever's part. For, if his claim were allowed, Colman and Appleton, the two noted liberals on the Corporation, must go."[5]

The game continued until 1723. In 1721, while this controversy was reaching its peak, a number of other important events took place in Boston and its environs. *The New-England Courant* began ruffling ministerial as well as collegiate feathers; at the same time, the town was deeply involved in disagreement over a proposed land bank; and in June Boston was visited by a serious, fast-spreading epidemic of smallpox.[6] In the midst of all this the power struggle at Harvard continued, this time centering on the Hollis chair of divinity. When Hollis, a Baptist, had finally endowed the professorship, it was with the stipulation that it should not be closed to Baptists. The corporation readily agreed to the gift, and on June 28, 1721 appointed Edward Wigglesworth, who had taught Chauncy at Boston Latin, to the post. The overseers, however, were not so ready to accept the gift on these terms; they insisted on reinterpreting Hollis's stipulation in order to restrict the chair to Congregationalists. They then insisted on examining Mr. Wigglesworth to see if he were "sound and orthodox." It turned out that he was, although, as Perry Miller says, "Wigglesworth was capable of swearing allegiance to Ames's *Medulla* and to the divine right of infant baptism without allowing such un-catholic impositions to interfere with his moderate and civil instruction."[7] It took a year to settle the matter; Wigglesworth was not installed as Hollis professor until October 23, 1722. The question of making resident tutors members of the governing board dragged on until the tutors' proposal finally met defeat in 1723.

During the course of these squabbles Chauncy was pursuing his undergraduate education. From the first day each class was placed in the charge of a tutor, who carried the class through each subject in the curriculum for all four years. The responsibility for Chauncy's class of thirty-six youngsters—the largest class to enter the college up to that time—fell to Thomas Robie, who had held a tutor's position since 1712.[8] Although troubles on and off campus, including Robie's own quarrel with the corporation, must have complicated academic life immensely, Robie could take some comfort in having an especially able group of students. Years later Ezra Stiles, president of Yale, remembered them as "the learned class," many of whom were to achieve prominence of one sort or another.[9] Among them were Ebenezer Pemberton, one of the founders of Princeton; Harvard's first Hollis professor of mathematics, the unhappy Isaac Greenwood; Judge Stephen Sewall; the poet John Adams; Thomas Hubbard, the pious man who was to become treasurer of the college, commissary general of the province, and a member of the General Court; the controversial doctor, financier, and soldier Colonel Robert Hale; the equally controversial clergymen, Ebenezer Turell and Ebenezer Parkman; and John, the first of a long line of Harvard's Lowells. John Taylor and Stephen Sewall, nephew of Judge Samuel Sewall, became Chauncy's closest friends.[10]

This group of young scholars followed a program of study strikingly similiar to that of the great Renaissance humanists. As a freshman Chauncy spent a year reviewing the classical authors and working on his Greek. The same year he began Hebrew grammar and the formal study of logic. He went on to advanced Greek grammar and poetry in his second year, continued his Hebrew, and studied natural philosophy (physics) along with his logic. (Tutor Robie was particularly strong in science—he was elected a fellow of the Royal Society in 1725—and instilled in Chauncy a lifelong interest in the subject and in "philosophical apparatus.") During the next year he continued with more natural philosophy and added metaphysics, ethics, and divinity. In his final year he continued the latter two subjects and took up geometry and astronomy. The year concluded with a general review. Basic to all four years, and a continuing study for each class, was rhetoric. If the other liberal arts—grammar, logic, mathematics, geometry, astronomy, history—could be studied within the confines of a term or two, rhetoric could not: the art of speaking and writing clearly and persuasively was considered fundamental to the education of a Christian gentleman—and essential to the training of a minister.[11]

Of course Chauncy, like everyone else in the college, was as interested in the struggles for power in the school as he was in memorizing classical paradigms. He had personal connections with many of the disputants on both sides. Thomas Robie was his friend as well as tutor; Henry Flynt was another friend. Judge Sewall was a family friend from the Old South Church. He knew Cotton Mather and the other ministers. There is no record that as a young student in his early years at Harvard he took any particular side in the disputes, but in his final year, when the issue of the Hollis professorship of divinity crystallized, Chauncy's sympathies were clearly engaged on the side of the corporation's nominee, Edward Wigglesworth. Tutor Robie surely helped mold Chauncy's mind, but the strongest intellectual influence on him during his Harvard days must have come from Wigglesworth.

The appointment of the first Hollis professor caused such controversy because it carried great symbolic weight. If the appointee were not a "sound and orthodox" Congregationalist, believed the overseers, it would surely signify that Harvard had (as was widely feared) abandoned its Puritan heritage. Even if a Congregationalist with a tolerant and "catholic" attitude were certified as orthodox, such certification would suggest that Harvard had gone soft. It was an issue that many were to raise about Chauncy himself in later years. He believed that one could remain a genuine Congregationalist and heir of the Puritan fathers without rigid adherence to a particular doctrinal scheme.

Wigglesworth, the son of the famous poet Michael Wigglesworth, became Chauncy's model of such a person. Although as time passed

Wigglesworth drifted toward rationalism, in the 1720s he was not a wild-eyed liberal. He was engaged then in the defense of traditional Puritan thinking in favor of the eternal punishment of the wicked and the spiritual inefficacy of mere works; he was also writing in defense of Congregational polity against the attacks of such Anglicans as John Checkley.[12] Chauncy surely found his own anti-Anglican persuasion buttressed by Wigglesworth's research and writing. There is little reason to believe that he had strayed far from traditional theology at this time, although he was obviously speculating on the question of eternal punishment, for he defended as his Master's thesis the affirmative position on the question of whether Christ would be a mediator forever—a question figuring prominently in his final, major works on the salvation of all men.[13]

What Chauncy probably took most forcefully from Wigglesworth was a quality praised by generations of the professor's students: the habit of meeting difficult issues by presenting both sides of an argument and requiring the young men to exercise their judgment. He encouraged debate and discussion. Chauncy, forty-five years after his college days, could still recall keenly the temperament of his former teacher: "He is highly deserving of being remembered with honour, not only on account of his character as a man of learning, piety, usefulness in his day, strength of mind, largeness of understanding, and an extraordinary talent at reasoning with clearness and the most nervous cogency, but on account also of his catholick spirit and conduct, notwithstanding great temptations to the contrary. He was one of the most candid men you ever saw; far removed from bigotry, no ways rigid in his attachment to any scheme, yet steady to his own principles, but at the same time charitable to others, though they widely differed from him. He was, in one word, a truly great and excellent man."[14]

Wigglesworth was nominated to the Hollis professorship in June 1721, the month that Chauncy graduated, but it took the overseers more than a year to confirm his appointment.[15] By then, after a year spent traveling, visiting relatives, studying independently, and, probably, keeping a winter school, Chauncy had returned to Harvard to work for the Master's degree as a graduate student in divinity.[16] As an undergraduate he had of course studied divinity, but only as much "as was supposed to be requisite for an educated Christian layman; and that of course was a great deal, according to our standards. It included the careful study and analysis of the Bible in the original tongues, a short handbook of Protestant divinity (Ames's 'Medulla' or Wolleb's 'Abridgement of Christian Divinity'), taking notes on two long sermons every Lord's Day, and being quizzed on them subsequently."[17] Graduate study was more intense but less formal. Graduate students undertook a "review of undergraduate lectures, and more or less independent reading, guided or not, as the student chose, by president and professors."[18] Chauncy, his previous class rank finally restored, and assisted by college scholarships,[19] chose Wigglesworth as his guide and thereafter had "the pleasure of being many times in a week in company with him" from June 1722 until June 1724.[20]

Less than three months after graduate student Chauncy settled into his chambers in Cambridge, there took place in Connecticut "possibly the most dramatic event in the ecclesiastical history of the American colonies." Timothy Cutler, Harvard graduate and Rector of Yale College, along with several of the faculty, used the Yale commencement of September 12 to disclose that they had gone over to the Church of England.[21] Their defection was seen as perfidy by such Congregationalists as Cotton Mather, who had considered Yale an orthodox antidote to the dangerous tendencies at Harvard; it was also considered evidence of a grand Anglican plot to establish bishops in America and take over American society. To counter this threat the Congregationalist pastors sounded the alarm in the press and among the people: "Sly allusion, insinuation, sarcasm, and ridicule, coupled with countless hours of pulpit denunciation of the New Haven apostates, provided the rank and file of Yankees with a delectable fare of human interest such as had never previously been set before them; and they ate it up greedily."[22]

Perhaps because he had spent considerable time in Connecticut the previous year, and perhaps because he had connected himself with the controversial Wigglesworth, rumors circulated that Chauncy had joined the Anglican converts. To those who knew him, however, these reports were astonishing indeed, for his entire heritage and temperament had been anti-Anglican. Joseph Green, who graduated a year ahead of Chauncy at Harvard, testified to his own credulity and Chauncy's orthodoxy by commenting on the apostasy: "we have with admiration Surprize & Astonishment heard many things about it; what the Event of this will be God only knows Mr Chaunceys Conversion was to me the most surprizing of all. . . ."[23] There was nothing to such scuttlebutt. The Congregationalist-Anglican feud was to worsen year after year until it reached a vicious stage in the 1760s, and by mid-century Chauncy had established himself as the foremost opponent of the Anglican attempt to establish episcopacy in America. If Chauncy entertained suspicious views, they were not in the realm of ecclesiology. He never forgot his great-grandfather's solemn will.

His temperament was that of a debater, however. A month after the scandal of apostasy broke at Yale, Chauncy, with his friends, organized a debating club known as the "Society in Harvard Colledge." The forerunner of this group was a more imaginatively named society, the Spy Club, which they had formed while undergraduates and which even published the college's first periodical, *The Telltale*—a newspaper in the *Spectator* manner. The new club seems to have been more pious, aiming to "profit" as well as "Divert," by disputing any "Difficulty" which "may be propos'd to the Company." Some of the issues the members debated were theological ("Whether Heathens can be Sav'd according to the Terms of the Gospel"; "Whether any Sin is Unpardonable"); others were ethical ("Whether it be Fornication to lye with ones Sweetheart [after Contraction] before marraige"); or philosophical ("Whether humane Souls are Equal"; "Whether the Souls of Brutes are Immortal"; "Whether sight is made by the reception of Species"). In addition to debates, members presented lectures upon such topics as "Regeneration"; "Upon Light, a Phisico-Theological Discourse"; "Upon Transubstantiation & Predestination" and "Upon the fear of God." The meetings continued until at least January 1724.[24]

In June 1724, having completed the customary three years waiting period after the Bachelor's degree, Chauncy was awarded the Master's degree. He was nineteen. By then he had already decided to follow a career in the ministry.

That summer he was accepted into membership in the Old South Church.[25] Here his father and mother had worshipped, and now his mother and stepfather had a pew in the church; here he had strong ties. Both the pastors, Joseph Sewall and Thomas Prince, were his friends. Also in the congregation was a young lady named Elizabeth Hirst, for whom Chauncy had special regard. Elizabeth was the granddaughter of Judge Samuel Sewall and had lived with the Sewalls since 1717.[26] The Judge's son Joseph, who knew Elizabeth well, described her in his diary as "prudent, modest, courteous, and . . . pious"—a clergyman's description, to be sure, but these are also qualifications that would appeal to a serious young minister launching a new life.[27]

Any thought of marriage at this time was premature, of course; it remained for Chauncy to be "settled" in a congregation before he could take a wife. The "settling" process was delicate and often time-consuming. From time to time a church would seek a replacement for a pastor who had died, or an assistant for a senior minister. It would invite aspirants for the post to demonstrate their talent and promise by preaching as visitors, often in rotation, for a number of Lord's Days. After hearing the candidates, the church members picked the man they wanted and invited him to join the church as minister. Meanwhile the candidate was also appraising the situation. If he were lucky he had a choice among a few offers and could weigh one against the other. If the prospect seemed mutually agreeable he "settled" at the church, in many cases for life. An important decision on both sides, it was not taken lightly.

During the selection process a young man had to provide for himself. New Master Chauncy returned to Harvard, where he won an appointment as "Scholar of the House," beginning in September 1724.[28] This award, a kind of "work-scholarship," was ordinarily given to "the more responsible" and "older students" or to M.A.'s such as Chauncy who were exercising their graduates' privilege of residence.[29] Chauncy's award carried a stipend of four pounds, eleven shillings.[30] In return, he was to "take a strict Account of all the buildings, Chambers, Studyes, and fences belonging to the College and shall give an account quarterly to the Treasurer what dammage the Colledge hath susteyned in any of the aforementioned particulars and by whom. No Schollar shall enter into or leave the possession of any Chamber or Study untill Some one of the Schollars of the house have viewed the State thereof, which they shall represent unto the Treasurer."[31] The "Scholar" award not only provided him with some money, it also gave him a chance to continue his studies and association with the college while he was riding out to preach at nearby churches. His friend Joseph Sewall lost little time getting him into the pulpit at the Old South—thus giving him experience and exposure.[32] Soon the congregation at Ipswich asked him to try for the newly vacant post there. His classmate Nathaniel Rogers won that place, however, soundly defeating both Chauncy and William Welsteed.[33] Closer to home, Chauncy visited the New Brick in Boston. After a period of trial there during the summer of 1725 he was found "very Agreeable to the Generality of the People," and the congregation asked him to assist its pastor, William Waldron, for half a year.[34] But this was only stopgap. Early in 1726 Chauncy was still looking for a permanent position. Because of events at Harvard a place became available that year at Boston's First Church.

As Chauncy was preparing to leave the college after more than eight years there, its affairs were scarcely more settled than they had been at his entrance. President Leverett had died in May 1724. The presidency remained vacant for over a year as the corporation offered the post first to Joseph Sewall, who declined, and then to Benjamin Colman, who did likewise. Cotton Mather would have been delighted to accept, but he was not asked. Finally, in June 1725 the choice fell to a compromise candidate, Benjamin Wadsworth, at that time pastor of the First Church. Wadsworth—reluctantly—accepted the presidency and moved to Cambridge. His assistant pastor at the First Church, a serious, orthodox young man named Thomas Foxcroft, became the pastor. In July 1726, a year after Wadsworth's departure, the church decided to obtain an assistant for Foxcroft. They "had their Eyes principally upon" Chauncy and William Welsteed, and asked the pair to "preach frequently" at the Church.[35] In August a dozen church members came to Foxcroft with the request that Samuel Dunbar be added to the list of candidates.[36] As winter came on the people of the First Church grew accustomed to seeing a different face in the pulpit nearly every week, for the three men continued to preach in turn.

They were still coming in the springtime, for the church had not decided on its man. In May 1727 Foxcroft noted in the church records that Colonels Townsend and Byfield, Captain Green, and Mr. Cooke had been asking for a church meeting to choose another minister. And in the margin he wrote, *"and signify'd an Uneasiness and Dissatisfaction that it was delayed so long."*[37] If the Colonels and the Captain were uneasy, it is not hard to imagine how Chauncy, Welsteed, and Dunbar felt.

The general uneasiness made its impression upon Foxcroft, and, two weeks later, the church met to choose a junior pastor. In a close vote (64–43) Chauncy was elected over Welsteed. Dunbar received one vote. The church then chose Deacon Williams and Captain Langdon as "Messengers of the Church to wait on Mr. Chauncey (now at York) and acquaint him that we had made Choice of him, etc."[38] After conferring with these "messengers," Chauncy drafted a letter of acceptance and sent it off to the pastor and congregation. On the evening of August 27 the church members met to hear the letter. Apparently they were pleased, for they voted to allow the new minister "out of the Contribution Box, for the present Three pounds per Week Salary."[39] With this munificent sum coming to him as interim pay, Chauncy moved from Cambridge to quarters in Boston while preparations for his ordination were afoot.[40]

Once the First Church decided to act, it could move with dispatch. At a church meeting on October 2, 1727 several measures arranging for Chauncy's ordination were passed. As a first step Chauncy was asked to procure a dismission from the South Church. The date for the ceremony was settled on as Wednesday, October 25, 1727. ("God willing," Foxcroft noted.) It was then voted "that the several associated Churches in Boston together with the Church in Cambridge be desired by Letters in the Name of this Church to afford their Presence and Assistance by their Elders and Delegates on that solemn Occasion." Foxcroft was asked to give the "charge" at the ceremony, but bowed to a senior, Benjamin Colman of Brattle Street, "in Consideration of our more special Communion" with that church. The church members wanted Wadsworth, the former pastor, to "open the Solemnity with Prayer," and the senior pastors of Boston, Cotton Mather, Peter Thacher, Joseph Sewall, Colman, and Foxcroft, "to impose hands in the Ordination." Finally it was voted: "That a publick Contribution be asked, and Notice on the next ensuing Sabbath be given thereof, to the Congregation, by one of the Deacons, in order to defraying the Expences of the Entertainment on the Ordination-day."[41]

If they considered the matter, old-time New Englanders could point with pride to Charles Chauncy as his ordination day approached. The young man was orthodox and pious. His keen intelligence had been carefully trained and sharpened by more than a decade of study. He came from a family with a distinguished past and gave promise of a useful future. He was, in short, a first-class product of the Puritan tradition which had for a century produced ministers for New England by combining piety and education. His manner may have been a trifle too cool and detached to suit every taste, and he *was* rather young—but the First Church was already favored with an orator of renown in Foxcroft, and besides, as a new man he would not be very important for a while.

CHAPTER THREE

A "Godly, Faithful Man"

Chauncy spent the morning of January 1, 1730 at the deathbed of Judge Samuel Sewall. Death was a daily visitor to the affairs of an eighteenth-century minister. To read the journal of any of them is to travel from sickbed to sickbed, prayer to prayer, funeral to funeral. A young pastor quickly came to know most of the ways men die—his daily rounds took care of that part of his education. During the first three years of his ministry Charles Chauncy had stood at many death-beds and attended the funerals of many men, but few were so dear to him as Judge Sewall, the father of one of his closest friends and for many years the guardian of Elizabeth Hirst, who was to become his wife. Three days after Sewall's death Chauncy preached to the congregations of the First Church and the Old South, assembled at the Old Brick meetinghouse. Recent events obviously determined his choice of text: he spoke from John xi. 25: "He that believeth in me, though he were dead, yet shall he live," and Joseph Sewall was moved to record in his diary that Chauncy "made an honorable mention of my father." Judge Sewall's death, however, had more than a personal significance for Chauncy. Following less than two years after the pass-ing of Cotton Mather, it helped mark for New England the end of a mighty generation. Sewall died as Boston was beginning its second century; on that same day Charles Chauncy marked his twenty-fifth birthday.[1]

In 1730, while Massachusetts took stock of its first hundred years, Chauncy himself could very well take stock of his first quarter-century. He had grown in experience and maturity since his ordination, and he had begun to gain a measure of respect and stature in Boston. If he had reckoned himself a young man of modest accomplishments and great promise, he would have judged well. Within ten years he was to be thrust, chiefly by circumstance, into a position of power and prominence from which he would conduct the first major battle of an embattled life—opposition to the Great Awakening.

Early in 1730, however, he was getting used to being a husband and father as well as an eager young assistant pastor. He and Elizabeth Hirst had set their wedding date for early in the spring following his settlement, and they were married in Boston on May 9, 1728.[2] With a wife to support, Charles needed more money and a new place to live. The parishioners played musical chairs to satisfy the housing requirement. The church owned two minister's houses, one on Treamount Street, as it was then known, and the other on Summer Street. When Wadsworth moved to Harvard he left the Treamount Street residence vacant. Foxcroft, now the senior man, promptly moved his family into it, thus vacating the house on Summer Street. The First Church deacons then rented the vacant quarters to a Dr. Dolhonde, who lived there until May 1728, when the deacons repossessed the house for the Reverend Mr. Chauncy and his bride. Shortly after the couple settled into the minister's house, the church raised Chauncy's salary to £4, 10s per week and gave him £40 per year for firewood.[3]

Elizabeth Chauncy promptly became pregnant. Although this circumstance was assuredly counted a blessing from God, it also made four pounds a week seem a little thin. Foxcroft, moreover, had first priority on salary increases, not merely because he was senior, but also because he had a large family (six children by 1729) that gave every sign of growing larger (a dozen children by 1740).[4] In January 1729 Foxcroft reported that he was finding the "present weekly allowance not sufficient to answer his necessary expenses." The church met to consider the matter and declined to raise the weekly salary, but suggested instead an "occasional Collection, and this for the Use of the Senior Pastor, as apprehending the Circumstances of his Family call for such a special Relief." In the church records Foxcroft describes the scene following upon this suggestion: "Upon hearing this I thanked the Brethren for their kind Willingness to do for my Relief; yet withal told them I would chuse that my Brother Chauncey should divide the intended Contribution with me. Upon which Mr Chauncey stood up and declared himself freely willing, that the Church should act their own Judgment and Inclination in the matter, and that I should receive the Whole, as being sensible that the weekly Allowance is not sufficient for the Support of my Family."[5] A month later a collection, amounting to just over eighty-nine pounds, was finally taken up and given in its entirety to the senior pastor.[6] With Elizabeth five months into her pregnancy, the "Circumstances" of Chauncy's family were also becoming obvious to everyone, but the junior pastor did without a share of this "occasional Collection." It is doubtful that Chauncy begrudged Foxcroft the money: the two men entertained high regard for each other throughout their lives, despite occasional and serious differences of opinion.

Three months later, on May 16, 1729 (almost exactly a year after his marriage), Chauncy became the father of a son. Two days after his birth the boy was baptized at the First Church and named Charles—the name given for generations to the eldest sons in the Chauncy family.[7]

While Chauncy was shouldering important new family responsibilities, Foxcroft was giving him his share of pastoral duties, and the town was calling on him for occasional civic functions. Of course he was expected to help with the preaching, but he also devoted much of his time to services marking the waystations of his parishioners' lives: baptisms, marriages, funerals. The earthquake that had welcomed Chauncy to the First Church had caused an "awakening" there as in most of Boston. Following the tremor, and the sermons that interpreted it, the number of infant baptisms in some parishes jumped to thrice the yearly average, and church memberships also rose as stricken sinners sought admission.[8] Chauncy, who made his place in American history by opposing the Great Awakening, began his career by ministering to just such "awakened" souls. He performed his first baptisms on December 10, 1727, when he baptized Joseph Millar, George Rushton, and Joseph Cooke at the Old Brick.[9] That same month a crowd of new members—mostly women—sought admission to the church (in the margin of the church records next to their names is the cryptic notation: *In the time of the Earthquake*), and the influx of new members continued for the next few months before the awakening dwindled.[10]

In addition to his ministerial duties Chauncy also began to take part in affairs outside the church. One of his chief interests, of course, was Harvard College; now, since he was a minister of the First Church, he was ex officio member of the Harvard Board of Overseers. He must have taken great delight in attending his first overseers' meeting on February 13, 1728.[11] Another duty that Chauncy was called upon to perform was to open the Boston Town Meeting with prayer. This task, chiefly honorary, was by the invitation of the selectmen only, and was not offered lightly. Probably as a gesture of welcome to the new minister in town, the selectmen invited Chauncy to the meeting on March 11, 1728. In later years they were to call upon him for more political and practical reasons.[12]

Thus the young minister Chauncy was organizing his life around his family, the church, and the town, but for many other young people in Boston—and for many of their parents—the church was no longer a focal point of life. During the year 1730 the several pastors who tried to sum up the first century of American experience and look into the future struck a familiar, and dominant, theme: the great experiment begun in the wilderness of New England a hundred years before had been, thanks to the presence of God, gloriously successful at the start; but New England—the new Canaan of God's chosen people—had fallen on evil days. "ALAS!" exclaimed Foxcroft in a sermon celebrating the centenary of the settlement of the First Church, "*there is among us a visible Decline of Religion* in the power and practice of it, and not the ancient Success of Gospel-Ordinances."[13] As Perry Miller has shown, the jeremiad—a bewailing of the decline of religion and denunciation of the wickedness that had brought about the displeasure of the Lord—had been a traditional kind of sermon in New England for three generations. Foxcroft, however, was not only producing the expected excoriation when he spoke to his church in Boston; he was also reflecting a hard fact that could be verified daily. Church membership had dwindled, despite the brief flurry following the earthquake. Interest in the affairs of the church, let alone the affairs of the soul, was on the wane. These matters seemed less and less vital in the bustling seaport town of Boston.[14]

Under such circumstances, Chauncy believed, people easily drifted into Anglicanism. The Yale apostasy had left as strong an after-shock as that of the 1727 earthquake. By 1731 Chauncy felt its rumblings close to home, for his brother-in-law and sister-in-law converted to the Church of England, and his brother-in-law, Addington Davenport, went to England for ordination by a bishop. This defection jolted Chauncy and triggered a nearly compulsive drive to defend the Congregational system and to attack the Episcopacy on every front. Chauncy's preoccupation with this subject during his late twenties and early thirties established his reputation among New England Anglicans and Congregationalists alike. Consequently, when in a few years defenders of the old New England way of church government needed a champion, they knew where to turn.

Chauncy had officiated at the 1730 wedding of Addington Davenport and Jane Hirst, Elizabeth's sister. He had known Addington since college, where Davenport was a member of Harvard's class of 1719, and where he had taken his second degree in 1722. Davenport had entered the law; he quickly made a name for himself. By 1728 he had prospered well enough to turn down the House of Representatives when it elected him attorney general. Jane Hirst was twenty years old and still living with Judge Sewall's family when Addington began his courtship, and of course Chauncy knew her well. In November 1732 Davenport sailed for England to be ordained. He returned in 1733 as a missionary to St. Andrew's in Scituate, and he later became rector of Boston's Trinity Church.[15] Davenport had made his decision, Chauncy believed, "upon this pretence, that it was a certain fact, that Episcopacy, in the appropriated sense, was the form of government in the church from the time of the Apostles and down along through all successive ages."[16] Chauncy's Puritan temperament bristled at this "pretence," but he knew that his lawyer-brother-in-law would be able to argue the point when the occasion arose. Family ties were so close that the issue would not lie still for very long even if one wanted it to. With typical understatement he later recalled his feelings: "I imagined that my connection with him would naturally lead me into frequent conversations upon this point; and, that I might be thoroughly qualified for a debate with him or others he might be connected with, on this head, I entered upon this study and went on in it at the expense of much more time and pains than I imagined it would cost me at first."[17] It was a thorough investigation. "I spent four years of harder study than ever I went through in any part of my life in reading the Fathers, and all the books I could find upon the Episcopal controversy, on both sides, in all the libraries in town, and that at Cambridge."[18]

Two years after he began his research he apparently thought he had the subject well in hand, for the *Boston News Letter* advertised that "A Compleat View of the First Two Hundred Years After Christ, Touching Episcopacy," by the Reverend Charles Chauncy of Boston, was being prepared for the press and would be published by subscription.[19] The very idea of such a project enraged Timothy Cutler, former Yale Rector and apostate, now Anglican rector of Boston's Christ Church, who sent a letter to England denouncing the proposal as "a doughty Performance" of an "Insidious Person," who "has but a little time agoe begun his Enquiries, and not above a month before the Publication of his Proposals profess't himself to a churchman as an Enquirer then." Cutler was relieved, however, that the book would probably not see print after all. "I am heartily glad That Subscriptions do not come in near enough." This was lucky, because "thro the Inability and Indisposition of the Laity here, we should not defray the Charge of an answer; and so our Adversaries would triumph."[20] Subscriptions lagged, and Chauncy was left with a lifelong interest in the question, a pile of notes, and the itch to publish his findings. He kept the notes handy for years, adding to them occasionally. He told Ezra Stiles in 1768: "I have by me extracts from all kinds of writers upon this subject; and could write folios upon it, was it needful."[21] With much satisfaction he finally found the proper time to bring out his massive volume, *A Compleat View of Episcopacy*, in 1771, thirty-nine years after he started his research and twenty-five years after the death of Addington Davenport.

Preoccupied as he was with his study of the Episcopacy issue, Chauncy also devoted himself to other problems during these early years of his ministry. By 1732 his sermons were finding enough favor to be printed. Recurring in them are two themes: a challenge to young people to replace the mighty generation passing away before their eyes, and an examination of the character of the "Godly, faithful man."

He not only bewailed the spiritual sluggishness of the times and the danger of Anglican inroads, he also insisted on the obligation of young people like himself to revive and continue the noble heritage of their forebears. In a sermon upon the death (at seventeen) of Elisabeth Price, Chauncy identified himself with the young people gathered for the funeral and exhorted them:

> O our young people! We are the hope of this Church of our Lord Jesus. It's increase; it's glory, it's very continuence in being is in a measure dependant on us. If we should rise up in our father's stead a generation that know not God; what is like to become of the *gospel* worship and ordinances in this place? . . . Let us then give our hearts to God;—seek FIRST his kingdom and righteousness;—repent of our sins;—believe in Christ;—and yield up our selves absolutely and intirely to him, in an everlasting covenant. And O! let us this day chuse our fathers God for our God; and know and serve him with a perfect heart and a willing mind. . . .[22]

A year later, in a sermon on the death (at eighty) of his good friend Judge Byfield, he worked from a different point of view but sounded the same alarm:

> We now heartily joyn, in lifting up our prayer to the GOD who dwelleth in the heavens, that showers of divine blessings may descend upon the *children's children*! And may you sincerely chuse your *father's* and *grand-father's* GOD, for your GOD! So will he be your never-failing friend of all sufficient portion.—
>
> AND may the breaches which a righteous GOD is making in this church of our LORD JESUS, whereby he is thinning our glory, and weakening our strength, be happily repair'd! And let there be no reason for that complaint, *the righteous perisheth, and no man layeth it to heart.*
>
> AND as our aged and venerable fathers go off the stage, O holy LORD GOD, *pour out thy Spirit from on high*, upon the *Sons* of NEW-ENGLAND, that they may be qualified to adorn and fill up their places!—that we may have *our Judges as at the* first, and *our Councillors as at the beginning*; all our *Officers peace*; and *our Exactors righteousness.*[23]

There are elements of the jeremiad tradition in these sermons, of course, but underneath the formulary listing of the degeneracies of the present day there is a real concern for the state of the church. As a young man trained to reverence his elders and acutely aware of his

Puritan heritage, Chauncy winced to see laxity prevalent among his generation, especially when he was working so hard to model his own life on the old Puritan pattern of piety and disciplined faith.

This attempt to define "the good man" and to understand the kind of life such a person must lead is the second major theme of Chauncy's early sermons. In these years he was clearly grappling with his idea of himself, working out the values he would embrace, the goals he would seek. He knew that he wanted to be a "good man," a "Godly, faithful man." Throughout his childhood and school days he had heard innumerable sermons on the problems of attaining goodness in an evil world; he had watched many try to solve these problems with varying degrees of success; and he had attended the funerals of many of them. Now, preaching funeral sermons himself, and commemorating men at their burials, he faced the same problems in trying to express his vision of the Christian life. As a mature man he tried to apply his theoretical standards to his own experience.

At this time Chauncy was working out his ideas about human nature within the frame of traditional Congregational theology. He viewed human beings as frail creatures, caught up in the grand scheme of God's salvation and utterly dependent upon him. We are corrupted by the fall and further corrupted by our own sins. Chauncy believed in the absolute necessity of faith in Christ for salvation; he counted the Bible his sole authority. But his humanistic training, as well as his Puritan background, also affected his view of humankind: although we are enfeebled, we do retain some rational faculties. We are capable of thinking and acting morally; we are therefore obliged to do so. Later, as Chauncy tried to cope with the challenges of the Great Awakening and the Enlightenment, he would carry his emphasis on human abilities further than a seventeenth-century Puritan would have been willing to go, but at the start of his ministry he was well within the traditions of Puritan thought.

In his first published sermon, *Man's Life Considered Under the Similitude of a Vapour* (1730), Chauncy pointed out that we can and must live a good life for two reasons: as a preparation for the saving grace of God, or as evidence of regeneration.[24] In *Early Piety* he considered the importance of living rationally. In *Nathanael's Character* he concentrated on sincerity as a vital characteristic of the good person. His most complete statement of the idea of the "Godly Man" during these early years came in his 1737 sermon, *Prayer for Help*. The "foundation-stroke" of such a character is faith—not only a speculative power, but "an active living principle . . . exciting and moving the several *passions and affections* of his mind" to a "due regard" for God. Thus the godly person, *believing* in God's majesty, is *moved* to awe; believing in His veracity, he is moved to trust; believing

32

in God's beauty and amiability, he is moved to love him; believing in God's goodness, he is moved to hope for salvation; believing in God's sovereignty, he is moved to acquiesce in the will of God.[25] Chauncy insisted that these "religious affections" are essential to true faith. And the godly person *expresses* these affections, this awe, trust, love, hope and acquiescence, in *action*, in outward reverence and obedience. In short, Chauncy said, "He aims at the glory of God; and what gives him the finishing stroke in his character, constantly endeavours to be as *like him* as possible."[26]

The godly person, then, is a faithful person—a person of active faith who expresses his belief and regard for God in his daily life. *Faithful*, Chauncy says, means veracious and truthful and trustworthy; in a larger sense the term applies to one who employs himself "with *fidelity in the whole work of religion*. . . . His concern is, to fill up his time with work and labour; *doing with his might whatsoever his hand findeth to do*: considering there is *no work, nor device, nor knowledge, nor wisdom in the grave, whither he goeth*."[27] Thus the godly person "improves" his time, uses his talents, and accepts his state in life.

In all Chauncy's considerations of the character of the godly person he returned often to the close relationship between saving faith and faithfulness, sometimes stressing the sense of honesty and veracity, at other times emphasizing the sense of fidelity to religious duty, often combining the two by insisting on utter sincerity in the performance of religious duties. From the start Chauncy had small patience with those who went through the motions of piety for the sake of appearance. As he said in *Nathanael's Character*, hypocrisy is "the most odious sin."[28]

It has sometimes been thought that Chauncy denied the importance of the "affections" in religious experience. On the contrary, he believed that true faith necessarily calls them up, and that the truly faithful person must *act* on his faith and its accompanying affections. If, however, his actions arise from true faith, they will be in accordance with God's word and with the noblest aspect of human nature. Thus, as he said in *Early Piety*, we are "endowed with the noble powers of reason and understanding."[29] Let us act accordingly. "If we would become truly religious, we must *take heed to our way*, i.e., We must not live at random; without care or caution: but must advise with our reason & conscience; make a pause before we act, and not enter upon any course heedlessly; without tho't or consideration."[30] With this as a fundamental position, it is small wonder that Chauncy tangled with itinerant preachers and religious "enthusiasts" three years later. And with their differing views of psychological "faculties," it is not surprising that he and Jonathan Edwards never actually made intellectual contact during their famous dispute in the early 1740s.

33

While he was occupied with these problems. Chauncy's family concerns were multiplying. One of the major difficulties was money. His family increased, but his salary did not. By the summer of 1731 Elizabeth had conceived her second child. Both pastors were still beset by salary problems, although some parishioners tried to help. In August 1731 Deacon Jonathan Williams wanted to raise the weekly salaries to £6, but the money was not forthcoming, and the pastors had to settle for a couple of special collections instead.[31] After the birth on November 13, 1731 of Elizabeth, the Chauncys' first daughter,[32] the people took up another special collection specifically for the junior pastor, but they resisted efforts to raise the ministers' salaries to £6 per week.[33] The matter came up again in November 1733, a few weeks after the birth of Sarah, the Chauncys' third child, born September 22.[34] The problem was acute, not only because the salary was insufficient, but also because the church had been deficient "for Time past" in paying its ministers.[35] Again the proposal to raise salaries was rejected and another "occasional collection" was taken up, both to remedy past deficiencies and help with new family expenses.[36] This was to be the pattern until the 1740s: after failing to gain a salary increase that would bring them up to what most of the other Boston ministers were making, Foxcroft and Chauncy would divide "occasional collections" and hope that the church would be able to meet its payroll between occasions.

Three years after the birth of Sarah, on April 26, 1737, Chauncy and Thomas Prince, returning home from Cambridge after a Harvard Overseers meeting, stopped at the Chauncy home and found Elizabeth "dangerously ill."[37] Three weeks later, at the age of thirty-one, she died, leaving Charles, at thirty-two, a widower with three children: Charles, then eight; Elizabeth, five; and Sarah. Thomas Prince sadly records the event in his diary: "A most pretty, pleasant, virtuous, discreet, good Temp'd Gentlewoman. She was a Dear & Delightf. Friend to me."[38] Joseph Sewall, who had known her so well for many years, preached at the First Church on the Lord's Day after her death, taking as his text, "For if we believe that Jesus died and rose again, even so them also which sleep in Jesus will God bring with him."[39]

This was the latest in a series of blows that struck Chauncy in the spring of 1737. First Foxcroft suffered a stroke that nearly killed him. Then two of Chauncy's close friends, Deacon Jonathan Williams and President Benjamin Wadsworth of Harvard, died within days of each other. Now Elizabeth was dead. The words he had spoken in memory of Williams and Wadsworth seemed especially appropriate: "And considering our present circumstances, perhaps there is as much reason for the prayer *now* as there was in the days of *David*. How many holy good men, men of eminent piety and fidelity, both in *Church* and

State, have been remov'd out of the land by death, within the compass of a few years."[40]

With the illness of Foxcroft and the death of his wife, Chauncy had little chance to indulge his habit of digging into every New England library and dropping by the college to discuss his work with friends there. His time for the next year was almost completely taken up in parish and civic duties, preaching,[41] attending church meetings,[42] playing host to meetings of the Ministers' Association,[43] delivering the Thursday lecture,[44] "exchanging" with Prince, Sewall, and William Cooper,[45] and inspecting the public schools.[46]

Chauncy was able, however, to find time that year for courtship. A minister, especially a widower with young children, needed a wife. Apparently Charles found a prospect by the summer of 1738, for that June the First Church sent Robert Rand, David Collson, and Edward Gray as a committee "to view Mr Chauncey's House and see what Repairs are necessary and estimate the Expence."[47] Within a month the three men had a report ready for the church: "We find said House and Fences belonging thereto much impaired: and in Order to have the same put in proper and necessary Repairs, We have advised with Workmen, who have calculated the Charge thereof, and say, That the Materials that will be required therefor, with the Labour, will amount to forty and five pounds, and the Painting to Twenty pounds. . . ."[48] Would that modern committee reports could be so concise and to the point! The committee was instructed to contract for the work, and a meeting was scheduled to consider ways of raising money for this purpose. On July 25 the church, predictably, voted a "publick and special Contribution" to raise the money.[49] On January 8, 1739 Chauncy remarried.[50] His new wife was a parishioner and a widow, Elizabeth Phillips Townsend, who had been married to James Townsend of Boston. She brought to the Chauncy household a daughter, Rebecca, aged thirteen, and a son, William Blair Townsend, fifteen. She also brought an enormous estate. The junior pastor had probably haggled long enough over a two pounds-per-week salary increase.[51]

A month after Chauncy took his new Elizabeth and her children home, he reported to the church meeting "that his Wife out of her own Estate will lay out Five hundred Pounds in Repairs and Alterations of the Church's House in Summer Street Provided that She (in Case of her out-living Mr Chauncey) may be allowed to dwell in or have the Use of the said House for five Years."[52] Clearly, the sixty-five pounds put into repairs during the summer did not suit the new Mrs. Chauncy in the dead of winter. The First Church unhesitatingly accepted the proposal, with one rather blunt proviso: it agreed that "she shall have the Use of the said House accordingly, upon her laying out £500, *ut supra*."[53]

Chauncy was not able to spend much time enjoying the refurbished home with his family, however, for the circumstances of the next five years were to keep him either at his desk or on the muddy roads leading into the surrounding towns and villages. The first rumblings of the Great Awakening had already been heard in the towns outside Boston; they quickly reached a crescendo in every area and roared through Boston in 1740. Charles Chauncy had begun his ministry at the time of an earthquake, but no tremor of the ground ever shook New England as hard as did this new phenomenon of revivalism, this "religious commotion" that swept the colonies at the close of his first ten years at the Old Brick. Like almost all New Englanders he was deeply affected by the movement. His reaction to the revival and the way it developed was conditioned by all the years of training that had gone before, and especially by the events of those first ten years as a minister. At thirty-three he was no longer just a bright young Harvard gentleman with promise; he had reached maturity—a maturity tempered by the birth of children, the loss of a wife, and the passing of dear friends. Especially since Foxcroft's illness, Chauncy had gained power in managing the oldest, most firmly established Congregational Church in New England's most important town. And with the power came prominence: he was consulted and invited to express his opinions, both from the pulpit and in Boston's busy press. He had by this time carefully worked out the guiding principles of his life and had settled on the proper manner of Christian living: he had become convinced that the marks of faith were reverence, moral living, and rational action. After Davenport's conversion to Anglicanism, Chauncy had worked diligently to learn as much as anyone in the colonies about church organization and government.

Chauncy's experiences, his heritage, and his temperament had given him a strong sense of himself and the confidence to respond quite strongly when he found himself confronted by the great tide of excitement that swept into Boston from the countryside. As the movement advanced he began more and more to doubt that it was the work of God he had been praying for; as it reached its full extension, Chauncy's doubts crystallized into solid opposition. But this was not the case at the beginning. For years New England ministers, Chauncy among them, had stormed heaven with prayers for help, begging God to send His spirit among the people of New England and awaken them from their torpor. By 1738 it seemed certain to many that indeed the Lord had been listening.

CHAPTER FOUR

After the Surprising Conversions

The surprising conversions took place in Northampton during the mid-1730s.[1] The pastor there was young Jonathan Edwards, a man two years older than Chauncy and a graduate of Yale College. Edwards had followed his famous grandfather Solomon Stoddard (1643–1729) to the ministry of this northwestern town, and like his predecessor he was able to produce there a "harvest of souls." Within a few years after Edwards's settlement many people in Northampton began to take stock of their spiritual condition. Religious concern and activity quickened, especially among the younger men and women. Beginning in 1733 this awakening continued into the next year and spread throughout the town. Even the most wicked citizens seemed marvelously distressed about their sinfulness. Nearly everyone in town became a communicant.[2]

The good news of the visitation of the Spirit to Northampton spread swiftly. By 1735 there were signs of revival in many other towns.[3] News of the phenomenon reached Boston quickly enough, and early in 1735 Benjamin Colman, the venerable minister at Brattle Street, wrote a letter to young Edwards, asking for an account of the exciting events he had been hearing about.

Edwards replied in a letter to Colman dated May 30, 1735, with a brilliantly written, compelling "narrative" of the "work of God" in Northampton. After the letter was written, his wife's uncle, Joseph Hawley, committed suicide on June 1 by cutting his throat. On June 3 Edwards added an account of this catastrophe in a postscript:

Since I wrote the foregoing letter, there has happened a thing of a very awful nature in the town. My Uncle Hawley, the last Sabbath-day morning, laid violent hands on himself, and put an end to his life, by cutting his own throat. He had been for a considerable time greatly concerned about the condition of his soul; till, by the ordering of a sovereign providence he was suffered to fall into deep melancholy, a distemper that the family are very prone to; he was much overpowered by it; the devil took the advantage and drove him into despairing thoughts. He was kept very much awake anights, so that he had but very little sleep for two months, till he seemed not to have his faculties in his own power. He was in a great measure past a capacity of receiving advice, or being reasoned with. The coroner's inquest judged him delirious. Satan seems to be in a great rage, at this extraordinary breaking forth of the work of God. I hope it is because he knows that he has but a short time. Doubtless he had a great reach, in this violent attack of his against the whole affair. . . .[4]

Shortly afterwards the revival subsided: It appeared that God had abandoned the people to Satan. "God," said Edwards, "is pleased to let us see how entirely & immediately the great work lately wrought was his, by withdrawing, & letting us see how little we can do, and how little effect great things have without him. . . ."[5]

Although the revival in Northampton seemed to have diminished, interest in what had happened there continued to grow. At Colman's request Edwards wrote a longer, more detailed account. Excited by this extensive narrative, Colman circulated it among the Boston clergy and hastily printed an abridgement of it as an appendix to a volume of revivalist sermons he was then seeing through the Boston press. He sent the entire narrative to London, where his friends the Reverends John Guyse and Isaac Watts arranged for its publication in 1737 as *A Faithful Narrative of the Surprising Work of God in the Conversion of Many Hundred Souls in Northampton, and the Neighbouring Towns and Villages* . . . . The book sold well in London, and the events at Northampton soon became a topic of conversation on both sides of the Atlantic.[6] This, after all, was an awakening unlike the others New England had known. Without the prod of any calamity of nature, without an earthquake, the smallpox, or desolation, the people of many towns had abandoned licentiousness and indecency and apathy, revealing instead an ever-increasing concern about their souls and the souls of their neighbors. Had there been such an event, on such a scale, since apostolic times?

When in November 1738 an American edition of *A Faithful Narrative* was published in Boston, four of Chauncy's fellow ministers, Joseph Sewall, Thomas Prince, John Webb, and William Cooper, contributed a laudatory preface. In it they recall the awakening that followed the 1727 earthquake and the disappointing decline that set in shortly afterwards, and celebrate the recent "wonderful work at Northampton." There, they state, the Holy Spirit "was in a plentiful and extraordinary manner poured out on persons of every age and condition, without such remarkable providences going before to awaken them; as 'the dew falls in the night,' and yet the effects appeared as 'the light which goeth forth.' So that we might well admiring say, 'What has God wrought!'" They "earnestly recommend" Edwards's reports as "faithful" and skillfully done, "written with that judgment and skill in divine things, as declare him to be a scribe well instructed unto the kingdom of heaven." Finally they hope that the publication of the narrative will help to bring about a fresh awakening: "May it please God to revive his work throughout this land; and may all the ends of the earth see his salvation!"[7]

These men, so enthusiastic in their support of Edwards, were Chauncy's friends, and while *A Faithful Narrative* was in vogue he was frequently in their company. In his diary for 1736–38 Prince records many preaching "exchanges" between himself and Chauncy. He also mentions their joint visits to the home of Lieutenant Governor Dummer, their attendance at the Harvard Overseers' meeting, and their visit to the sickbed of Reverend John Adams. In addition Prince visited Chauncy's home for conferences and meetings of the ministers' association, and to mourn the death of Elizabeth Chauncy.[8] Joseph Sewall "exchanged" with Chauncy as well, visited his home,[9] helped him inspect the public schools,[10] and preached at the funeral of his wife.[11] Chauncy surely dissected the news of recent events in Northampton with these friends, even though he was also occupied with such unsettling events as Foxcroft's illness and Elizabeth's death. Moreover he was in frequent communication with his cousin Nathaniel Chauncy, pastor at Durham, Connecticut, whose parish Edwards singled out for praise in *A Faithful Narrative* and who could give him firsthand accounts of the surprising conversions there.[12] No evidence suggests that in 1738 he did not share the hope of his friends that the Northampton awakening would presage another remarkable visitation of the Spirit upon the land.

Chauncy had in fact anticipated Edwards in a sense, for his 1732 funeral sermon on Elisabeth Price was a case study of a converted soul that merits comparison with the two extensive case studies Edwards included in the final version of *A Faithful Narrative*—those of four-year-old Phebe Bartlet, the precocious child who shut herself in her closet until she was satisfied of her salvation, and Abigail Hutchinson, the young woman who underwent an intense and dramatic conversion during the Northampton awakening.[13] Because both Chauncy and Edwards use these cases as particular illustrations of their general theories about conversion, one can gain from these narratives a good sense of the relative positions of the men, in a few years to become public adversaries, on the threshold of the Great Awakening.

Chauncy believed firmly in early piety, and he believed that occasionally people were converted in early childhood: "A most distinguishing priviledge!—Thrice happy they that are the subjects of it!—The grace herein discovered, can never be enough magnify'd and admir'd!"[14] At the time of *A Faithful Narrative* he had three children of his own, all under seven, and one of them little Phebe Bartlet's age. Like many other New England parents who read Phebe's story, he must have been curious to see if similar signs of conversion appeared among his own children in the family home on Summer Street. It is most likely, however, that he recognized the striking similarities between Edwards's two stories and his own exemplar of early piety, Elisabeth Price, for she emerges in Chauncy's sketch as a precursor of both Phebe and Abigail, or perhaps as Phebe Bartlet-grown-up. At nearly every important point Elisabeth's childhood resembles Phebe's; and in her young womanhood and at her death she is very much like Abigail Hutchinson.

At age four Phebe Bartlet often retired for "secret prayer" and "grew more and more engaged in religion, and was more frequent in her closet; till at last she was wont to visit it five or six times a day: and was so engaged in it, that nothing would at any time divert her from her stated closet exercises."[15] In her childhood Elisabeth Price had precisely the same habit and was hardly less faithful in it. Chauncy says:

> From a child she was deeply impress'd with an awe and reverence of God. . . . She was observed to be constant, even from her most early days, in retirements *evening* and *morning*, to pour out her soul before God: except only when she now and then intermitted this duty; which she never did from a negligent careless frame of spirit, as is too commonly the case; but whenever she was blameable in this kind, it proceeded from perplexing fears and temptations, uncommon to one of her age; for which omissions she was heartily sorry, and would bitterly complain of her self.[16]

Phebe, Edwards says, "has been very strict upon the Sabbath; and seems to long for the Sabbath day before it comes. . . . And she seems to love God's house, is very eager to go thither. . . . When she is in the place of worship, she is very far from spending her time there as children at her age usually do, but appears with an attention that is very extraordinary for such a child."[17] She is also fond of remembering scriptural quotations.[18] Chauncy describes Elisabeth's regard for the Sabbath in almost the same terms: "She was a strict observer of the *Sabbath*; behaving her self as one that had an awakened sense of

40

the solemnity of the day: constantly went up to the *place of publick Worship*; where she appeared with a visible awe and reverence, and attended with such care and diligence, as that she was able to bring home, and *from her memory* repeat, more of the *preached word* than is common for persons grown to years; who yet are persons of good understanding."[19]

Edwards stresses Phebe's concern about sin. "She seems to have very much of the fear of God before her eyes, and an extraordinary dread of sin against him." As an example he cites her tearful reaction when she was told that she had sinned by taking a neighbor's plums without permission.[20] This was also a strong characteristic of Elisabeth Price, and Chauncy's description of her conscience would apply as well to Phebe. Like her more famous counterpart, Elisabeth was in her childhood "to a scruple fearful least in any thing she should offend God. . . . She was favoured with a peculiarly soft and tender conscience, which made her watchful against sin, careful to avoid even the appearances of it, and to maintain a close walk with God."[21]

Finally Phebe was also "wont many times affectionately to counsel the other children," especially urging her sisters to have concern for their souls and to pray.[22] Elisabeth also liked to counsel her "*brethren* and *sisters*," particularly when they were disobedient or unruly, and she was deeply grieved when they were disrespectful to their parents.[23]

Like Phebe, Elisabeth Price was converted as a small child, although her conversion was less dramatic than Phebe's. Chauncy did not believe that the time of conversion could always be established precisely; he never required such evidence as proof of regeneration. This was the case with Elisabeth:

> I don't remember she was able to fix upon the *particular time*, in which she tho't she might pass under a work of sanctifying grace. Nor is it at all to be wondered at: When it was never observed, that the principles of corruption were *habitually* predominant in her, in any part of her life. From the *first* appearances of reason, and *all along* till the time of her death, her *general* temper and behaviour were such as gave grounds to hope, that from *a child* she was savingly converted to God.[24]

But converted she was, nonetheless. Chauncy probably felt that the close parallel between the behavior of both girls reinforced his argument that one could be saved without a spectacular conversion experience.

If anyone ever had a spectacular and precisely documented conversion experience, it was Abigail Hutchinson. In telling her story Edwards tried to bring together all his general comments and theoretical statements about the revival in a particular and dramatic illustration. Using

41

the experience of Abigail Hutchinson as a fascinating case study, he follows the daily progress of her regeneration and then illustrates its effects by describing the manner of her death. In Elisabeth's case, however, early piety made such a remarkable awakening unnecessary; thus we have no narrative of dramatic conversion from Chauncy. But his story of Elisabeth's dying days offers some significant parallels with Edwards's description of Abigail's death.

Their situations are similar: both are dying young of a disease of the throat—probably the dread "throat distemper" that stalked New Englanders for centuries. The girls react similarly to their plight. Abigail, after her conversion, demonstrates extraordinary resignation to the will of God. "I am quite willing to live," she says, "and quite willing to die; quite willing to be sick, and quite willing to be well; and quite willing for anything that God will bring upon me!"[25] Elisabeth also stands as a model of patience and resignation: "Her bodily pains were great and of long continuance; which gave opportunity for the illustration of divine grace, in that uncommon degree of patience, meekness, contentedness and subjection to the father of spirits she she was an eminent pattern of; never complaining; never murmuring; but always acknowledging her own defects, and justifying God in all that he laid upon her."[26] Despite their own pains, both girls exhibit great concern for others. Consider, for example, Chauncy's description of Elisabeth's "final testimony."

'Tis to be hoped her *brethren* and *sister* will never forget her calling them to her bed-side; when with a holy freedom of soul she gave her dying testimony in behalf of religion, and took her farewell of them: with great earnestness beseeching and exhorting them, *to seek and serve God in their youthful days; to improve the present season of grace, and time of their youth to the purposes of a holy life.* And O! with what fervor of Soul did she repeat the words, O THAT WE MAY DIE IN PEACE! AND MEET TOGETHER IN GLORY AT THE DAY OF CHRIST![27]

In their last days Elisabeth and Abigail both experience assurance of salvation; neither fears death and both expect happiness after life. Elisabeth, "for many days before her death," has a "comfortable sense of her Interest in CHRIST; a good hope thro' his merits of future glory and immortality"; she is "freely willing to depart hence to be here no more."[28] Abigail, for her part, "a few days before her death," tells a solicitous friend who has asked about her fears that she has "not the least degree of fear of death. . . . there is . . . indeed a dark entry, that looks something dark, but on the other side there appears such a bright shining light, that I cannot be afraid!"[29] It is not surprising that they find peaceful deaths, Abigail continuing "in an admirable sweet composure of soul . . . to the last," and dying "as a person that went to sleep, without any struggling."[30] Elisabeth, "in a holy calm and blessed serenity of soul," quietly *fell asleep in Jesus.*"[31]

These case studies reveal Chauncy and Edwards operating in essentially the same way, seizing upon a particular subject to illustrate a general theory, observing their subjects (here, Phebe, Abigail, and Elisabeth) carefully, gathering and reporting the evidence, and drawing a lesson from the experience. Given similar subjects and parallel behavior, they reach the same conclusion: these girls had experienced the saving grace of the Holy Spirit. Moreover they seem in basic agreement about the manner in which the Holy Spirit operates. Both ministers accept the traditional Congregationalist view that conversion usually follows a more or less recognizable sequence—a series of psychological stages that the historian Edmund S. Morgan has called the "morphology of conversion."[32]

Conviction is the first step. The sinner, often as a result of hearing the preached Word of God, attains a deep distress over his sinfulness. This happened at Northampton. "In those whom awakenings seem to have a saving issue," Edwards wrote, "commonly the first thing that appears after their legal troubles[33] is a conviction of the justice of God in their condemnation, in a sense of their own exceeding sinfulness and the vileness of all their performances."[34] Once the sinners had undergone conviction, Edwards observed, they were moved to "earnest application to the means of salvation—reading, prayer, meditation, the ordinances of God's House, and private conference; their cry was 'What shall we do to be saved?' "[35] As the sequence proceeds, the sinner usually comes to recognize his absolute *dependence* on God's mercy, and places his *hope* entirely in Christ. Finally, after God accepts a sinner and grants him saving grace, he feels enormous relief, giving way to joy at his good fortune. Although Edwards insists that there may be variations within the scheme, those awakened at Northampton generally followed this pattern; Phebe and Abigail illustrate it graphically; it is essentially the same pattern that Edwards outlines in his *Personal Narrative*, a magnificent description of his own conversion experience.[36]

Chauncy has the same sequence in mind in his sermon on Elisabeth Price. Placing heavy stress on conviction and the joy of conversion, he tells the young people that they enjoy a great advantage, for "young persons may, at least ordinarily, be suppos'd to have least resisted the *Holy Ghost*, quench'd his motions, stifled convictions and oppos'd the methods of divine grace. . . . 'Tis in experience found true, the *holy Spirit* usually strives more with young persons than others: They are oftner bro't under convictions; filled with concern about their Souls; and made seriously inquisitive, *what they must do that they may inherit eternal life*? In this age, we are *most likely* to be wro't upon and prevail'd with: and therefore the holy Spirit does not lose this *best* opportunity; but improves it by *more abundant* strivings and motions in us."[37]

Edwards's account of the convictions of young people in 1735—even to the use of the same scriptural citation—reinforced for Chauncy what was "in experience found true" for him in 1732. And just as Edwards's town "never was so full of love, nor so full of joy,"[38] after the conversions, so Chauncy lists as the chief "*Spiritual* advantage" of conversion that "inward ease, peace and *religious* satisfaction, wherein consists the greatest happiness on this side heaven." Elizabeth Price attained it. It is, in the words of Scripture, "that *peace of God which passes all understanding.*"[39]

In this early sermon Chauncy also acknowledged the necessity of absolute dependence upon the mercy of God, and hope in Christ. "For of our selves we can never turn to God, or serve him to his acceptance. The assistances of divine grace are absolutely necessary hereto. . . ."[40] But there is a significant difference of emphasis at this point. Edwards's flock was convinced that it had no cause to expect such assistance; Chauncy, on the other hand, told his young parishioners that "in this time of life *these* [divine assistances] we do in some measure enjoy; and have the highest reason further to expect them, in degrees proportionable to our wants."[41] Chauncy believed in God's sovereignty and in the utter necessity of divine grace for salvation, but he emphasized the attribute of God's benevolence more than his justice. Herein lies an important difference between Chauncy and Edwards that colored their attitudes toward many problems throughout the eighteenth century. In general, however, Chauncy's view of the steps toward conversion is quite similar to that of Edwards.

Whatever other differences of emphasis Chauncy might have had with Edwards during the period after the surprising conversions, he shared with him, and with New England Congregationalists generally, a mythical view of history that provided a context for interpreting the spiritual and political events of the times. It is a view to which Chauncy gave stubborn allegiance all his life, even when he acted in ways that seem inconsistent with it. He and his compatriots believed that God had a special plan for New England and had given its people a sacred mission. They were to renew the church and provide a glittering example to the world. The Boston ministers had this sense of mission very much in mind when they introduced Edwards's *Faithful Narrative* in 1738: "Very remarkable was the work of God's Spirit stirring up our forefathers to leave a pleasant land, and transport themselves over a vast ocean into this then howling wilderness; that they might enjoy communion with Christ in the purity of his ordinances, and leave their children in the quiet possession of the blessings of his kingdom. And God was eminently present with them by his Word and Spirit."[42] When one generation of luminaries passed—and, as Chauncy repeatedly insisted, that passage was taking place before their eyes—continuity demanded that others advance to carry on the struggle of their fathers and grandfathers. The struggle, he was sure, changed its form but did not abate: as the first generation, in order to establish a reformed church, had battled the Anglican bishops, so their descendants, if they were to maintain the church of their fathers, had to turn back unremitting threats of Anglican incursion. As the early generations had struggled to establish a "city upon a hill," so their descendants were obliged to remain worthy to have "God eminently present with them by his Word and Spirit" and to show the world—as did the *Faithful Narrative*—that God works wonders in New England.

Meeting these obligations was perhaps more difficult in the present day than ever before. Not only did the Anglican threat persist, but the governing myth had lost much of its force. The zealous sense of mission that had energized earlier generations was flagging. The people had sunk into spiritual lethargy, heedless of their souls and heedless of the role history demanded of them. God had acted in several ways to rouse the people, sending the smallpox epidemic of 1721–22, the earthquake of 1727, and the outpouring of the Holy Spirit to the Connecticut Valley in 1734–35. But the people had responded only fitfully. Somehow, the ministers believed, the Holy Spirit would have to stir the young people, moving them by conviction, repentance, and justification to sainthood, not only because the churches were suffering as the older generation faded, but because God's design for New England demanded it, else the work of the fathers had been in vain. The only other possibility was the chilling one that God had abandoned his plan for New England—or that he would abandon it because the people had abandoned him. Within two years of the American publication of *A Faithful Narrative* the colonies were jolted awake by events suggesting that God was giving the place one last chance.

CHAPTER FIVE

The Outpouring of the Holy Ghost

Throughout 1739, while Chauncy's fellow ministers were helping the cause of *A Faithful Narrative*, the Boston papers carried frequent notices of the extraordinary success, in the southern and middle colonies of America, of another young revivalist preacher. His name was George Whitefield. An Oxford graduate, in 1739 he had been ordained a priest in the Church of England and had come to America to preach in Georgia. He was a rebel within the Anglican camp, charging his church with heretically abandoning the Calvinism on which it had been established. In 1740 Whitefield made his way to New England and brought with him the Great Awakening. His supporters claimed that he also brought the Holy Spirit.

The Great Awakening took place in America during the 1740s, and its effect was especially strong in New England from 1740 until about 1743. Religious excitement on a gigantic scale, it was stirred up primarily by a trio of the greatest preachers in American history, "The Grand Itinerants": Whitefield, Gilbert Tennent, and James Davenport. These men, and others who helped advance the awakening, emphasized direct, personal experience of God and the sinner's utter dependence on God's mercy. Powerful, fiery orators, masters of persuasion, they excited their audiences calculatedly by hammering at man's sinfulness and helplessness and at his crucial need to become convinced of his own depravity—for because of it he was doomed to everlasting agony. Although, as Edwards had explained in *A Faithful Narrative*, in theory this conviction of his own sin would lead a person to place his hope entirely in Christ, and this could possibly lead to conversion, the grand itinerants concentrated most strenuously on the first step: arousing anxiety about sin. As more and more New Englanders became convinced of their sins, and subsequently (at times simultaneously) convinced of their conversion, it began to appear that God, in his wisdom, had chosen this time and this place for an extraordinary outpouring of his Spirit. Many of this generation were to be numbered among the saved! The Holy Spirit was even now visiting multitudes! The revivalists quickly attracted enormous, excited crowds. Reports could be heard everywhere of thousands "struck" at one time with repentance and conversion, drowning out the voice of the preacher with their tears and groans of remorse. Church membership increased remarkably, and entire towns became preoccupied with religion.

There were also reports, however, that the Grand Itinerants had not only neglected their own parishes, but had infringed upon the prerogatives of local pastors. Many unordained, uneducated, and wild-eyed preachers, convinced of their own sudden conversion, had taken it upon themselves to travel about the countryside, addressing crowds and "exhorting." It was said that some preachers, lay and ordained, were expending less effort winning souls than in condemning local ministers as unrepentant, immoral, or worse. Traditional church organization seemed to have broken down in several towns, and people were seeking new ministers or establishing their own church groups. Finally, it was charged, preachers of all sorts, swept up in the excitement of the Awakening, were leading New England into doctrinal error. Some converts, awakened and overwhelmed by the Holy Spirit, had decided that their impulses were divine in origin and therefore worth acting upon. Others claimed that the converted were privileged to receive private revelations directly from God.

Everyone was involved in the Awakening. As one student of it has concluded, "There is . . . abundant evidence that this religious turmoil in New England was in fact 'great and general,' that it knew no boundaries, social or geographical, that it was both urban and rural, and that it reached both lower and upper classes."[1] Such intensity could hardly be maintained indefinitely. The Awakening in New England held its peak for about three years and then quickly diminished.

Chauncy had been preparing for a great awakening since the earthquake that struck Boston in the first week of his ministry. Yet when the event finally flared up and died he emerged as its foremost opponent, and probably the man who had done the most to hasten its death. What happened to make him turn against the major religious phenomenon of the century? What were his objections? Why did he make them? Even if he could not be an eager supporter of the movement, was it necessary for him to become its hostile opponent?

During the year that Whitefield came to Boston, Chauncy got involved in a nasty ecclesiastical fight, the "Osborn affair," that stirred hard feelings among the clergy and cost him some friends. Then Whitefield and his disciples encouraged a spirit of partisanship and rivalry among those who had been "awakened" and those who had not (yet) seen what came to be called the "new light." A victim of this censoriousness was Chauncy's friend Samuel Mather, who, in 1741, was removed from his position as assistant pastor at the Old North Church. When Chauncy came to his defense many of Boston's most influential religious leaders turned against him. Just as the Awakening was reaching its peak in 1741, he felt personally abused and alienated from many of the revivalists, but he had not yet rejected the movement in itself. It took Jonathan Edwards's theoretical defense of the Awakening and one more major personal affront to trigger Chauncy's campaign to bring the Awakening to a halt.

The Osborn affair brought to a climax a twenty-year spat between Samuel Osborn, pastor in Eastham, Massachusetts, and Nathaniel Stone, pastor in neighboring Brewster. Even before Osborn had settled in Eastham in 1718, the two men had quarreled. Over the years prominent men had supported Osborn in his squabbles with Stone, but as they died his position weakened.[2] In 1738 Stone saw his chance and attacked Osborn's most vulnerable point: his theology.

Osborn was "liberal." He slighted the traditonal doctrine of atonement. He did not insist, said his opponents, that Christ's sacrifice satisfied God's justice and that God imputed Christ's righteousness only to the elect. His teachings implied instead, they claimed, that Christ suffered merely to provide humans with an example of suffering and patient obedience to God's will. He also gave his congregation the distinct impression that they could control their own chances of salvation by their good conduct. That "which Christ did and suffered doth nothing abate or diminish our obligation to obey the law of God," he preached. Futhermore, said the ecclesiastical council investigating charges of heresy against him, he taught that "obedience is a considerable *cause* of a person's justification."[3] These sentiments smacked of Arminius's doctrine: "If we do what we can, and improve the natural abilities we have, and the means we do enjoy God will not deny to give us the grace supernatural we want."[4] Thus while some enthusiastic Awakeners faced charges of antinomianism for subordinating obedience to the law in favor of the experience of God's grace, liberals such as Osborn were said to subordinate grace to works and make salvation depend on mere behavior. New Englanders had been taught for generations to count both positions among the most serious of heresies.

Osborn refused to submit meekly to the dismissal recommended by the council. Expelled from his pulpit, he gathered those of his flock who remained loyal to him and began to preach in his home. At the same time he appealed the decision of the council, bringing his case to the eminent Benjamin Colman in Boston. Apparently Colman and his assistant, Thomas Prince, wanted little to do with such a touchy business, especially one involving a suspected Arminian, for they brought their influence to bear on many Boston ministers, advising them not to assist Osborn in his attempts at redress. Osborn went ahead anyway, visiting each clergyman on the council that had dismissed him. Finding no satisfaction, he pressed his case further, asking thirty-two churches by letter to send delegates to a new council. A group of these ministers met at Foxcroft's house and decided to dispatch an investigating team of six men to Eastham to discover if Osborn had sufficient cause for complaint. After visiting Eastham and inquiring into the matter there, the team advised calling another council. Osborn accordingly invited a council of thirty-two churches to convene at Eastham, but on the day appointed no one came. Osborn, "Abus'd and disappointed," then undertook a four hundred-mile journey, visiting each pastor invited to the council. He obtained their agreements, in writing, to come on another day—but when that day arrived, only Benjamin Prescott and Ebenezer Gay appeared. To add to his troubles, some of the townspeople took Osborn to court for holding services in his home. He appeared and stated that indeed he was preaching in his own house; the court found him guilty and fined him. Undaunted, he returned to Eastham and continued preaching anyway. The Osborn affair quickly became a cause célèbre in clerical circles, and Osborn himself indefatigably kept the issues alive for nearly five years.

Chauncy of course knew what was going on; in June 1740 he became personally involved. On May 27 Osborn had met with an advisory council convened in Boston. Apparently this council concurred in the charges advanced against him, and for some reason he signed their statement. Then, realizing that he had probably incriminated himself, he quickly sought to counteract the effect of this mistake by appealing to eleven other ministers, Chauncy among them, to give their opinions on the matter.[5] In Salem, on June 9, 1740, Chauncy signed a statement in support of Osborn, calling for Christian charity and denouncing the harsh treatment given the man. About this treatment, Chauncy and his fellow ministers said:

We can't but apprehend that said Mr. *Osborn* has had hard Measure, in the Treatment he has receiv'd from the major Part of said Church [First Church in Eastham], and from the Council they called in to advise them. And we can't but lament the Backwardness of the Churches, as to a seasonable convening upon his Case, agreeable to the Application by him made to them. By their Failure herein we think Mr. *Osborn* has been depriv'd of the proper Means of Redress under his difficult Circumstances. And his Brethren's Conduct, in not joining in with him, to forward another Hearing of his Cause, which he seasonably claim'd as his just Right, before they proceeded to dismiss him from his Pulpit and Office, to us appears unjustifiable.

As for the doctrinal errors charged against him, these ministers concluded:

> Having weigh'd them, together with what the Council above said, and the Parties, have wrote upon them, in the Papers exhibited; We can't find that said Articles necessarily couch or include in them any dangerous Errors. But that taking them with a christian, candid and charitable Construction, to us it appears, they well accord with the Truths laid down in the Gospel, and the Doctrine generally receiv'd by these Churches.[6]

Then they advanced a plea for charity, with the wry reminder that "For as without it some of Mr. *Osborn*'s Expressions might appear inaccurate and erroneous; so should any take the Expressions of the abovesaid Council's Result, and of the Brethren's Remonstrance, &c. and put a critical and severe Construction upon them, they would some of them appear, not only as inaccurate, but as couching in them dangerous Errors." The statement concludes with a weary "wish for the Time when Christians will be so wise, as not to abound in their own Sense, but instead of disputing with Heat, and censuring one another, upon Points meerly speculative, and which don't concern christian Practice, they would duly attend to the Apostle's Direction *Phil*. 3. 15, 16. and practice accordingly."[7]

Osborn was not reinstated, and his case, with its "Heat" and "censuring," court hearings and fines, name-calling and hard feelings, especially among the ministers, was precisely the kind of affair Chauncy had described only a few months before in an important sermon entitled *The Only Compulsion Proper to be Made Use of in the Affairs of Conscience and Religion*. Preached on a Communion day, it is in purport an exhortation to the people to participate in the communion service. But it also attacks a growing spirit of uncharitableness that Chauncy had noticed in Boston. The text is from Luke xiv. 23: "Compel them to come in." The only compulsion proper, Chauncy says, is not "*outward Violence*, but *internal Persuasion*; that which is effected, not by *Fines, Imprisonments, Racks* and *Tortures*, but by Application to the *Understandings* of Men. The *Compulsion*, our Saviour intends, is of that Kind, which the *Mind* of Man is capable of, and is sutable to it as *rational* and *intelligent*: And this is Compulsion by *sound Reasoning, good Argument*."[8]

For Chauncy the classic example of compulsion by "*outward Violence*" is the "*Church of Rome*, who interpret my Text as a *Divine*

Warrant to make use of *Force* and *Violence* in the Affairs of *Conscience* and *Salvation*."⁹ But, he continues, "Even *Protestants* themselves, of whom it could never have been expected, have too nearly resembled them in this *Antichristian* Practice."¹⁰ Then comes the dart:

Nor have any, among *Christians*, been more ready to practice themselves, and recommend to others, the Methods of *secular Discipline*, than many among the *Clergy*. They have not only been Enemies to a *Freedom of Inquiry*, and the *Right of private judgment*; they have not only been zealous to *make Creeds*, and *impose the Belief* of them on others; they have not only *delivered over to Satan* those, who were so unhappy as to differ from them, tho' in Points of more *Nicety*, than *Importance*; I say, they have not only come into such Methods as these, but have also stirred up the *civil Magistrates*, and got those *fin'd*, or *whipt*, or *hang'd*, or *burnt*, who could not bring their Consciences to a Compliance with their Decisions in Matters of Faith, And for the Proof of this, we may appeal to the whole Series of *Ecclesiastical History*, which contains little else but such Matters as these.

And after this salve:

'Tis worthy our thankful Notice, that the Principles of *Liberty* are every Day gaining Ground in our *Nation*, and that "*a censorious persecuting Bigot* is generally lookt upon with Contempt, and treated as a common Enemy to Mankind." It ought also to be mention'd to the Honour of the *Government* at *Home*, that "it is just and generous, invades no Man's Right of Conscience, nor threatens him with Punishment for the greatest Difference of Judgment, in Matters of Religion."¹¹

Clearly Chauncy's continuing study of church history had led him to fear the results of intolerance. There were also other reasons for his stand in favor of freedom of religious thought. His training at Harvard, for instance, had encouraged inquiry at the same time that strong factions were seeking to stifle it in the college. He had not forgotten Leverett so soon, and he still visited Edward Wigglesworth.¹² He wanted to keep a free tradition alive in Cambridge. He was also trying to be a scholar (believing that all ministers should be scholarly), and compulsion on "Points of more *Nicety* than *Importance*" does little to foster scholarship. It is also quite likely that he was thinking about such problems—especially the question of ministerial compulsion—because he was following the affairs of Samuel Osborn.

Chauncy's wish for a time when Christians would "attend the Apostle's Direction" was not to come true during the stormy 1740s. Osborn's battle continued, and the hard feelings became harder; during the next year Samuel Mather (one of the signers of the statement supporting Osborn) was embroiled in a similar controversy and was ousted from the Old North Church. With the tremendous growth of itinerant preaching and lay exhorting, "settled" clergymen everywhere

51

—including Chauncy—were brought under attack. As the spirit of censoriousness grew, Chauncy became more and more impatient with it. He finally chose it as the major target of his assault on the Great Awakening. The initial salvo in that attack was fired in 1739, before the Awakening was in full force, with the Osborn affair and *The Only Compulsion*.

A few weeks after Chauncy spoke in favor of Samuel Osborn the Great Awakening swept into Boston in style with the arrival of the grand itinerant George Whitefield. From this time until 1743 the town jumped with excitement about the Awakening. Chauncy published nothing either for or against it in the two years between September 1739 and September 1741. He did not immediately thunder out in sermon and pamphlet against the Awakening, and even when he spoke out in 1741 it was against certain flagrant abuses in the movement, but not against the movement itself. For a long time his attitude towards what was happening was one of concerned observation and deliberation.

And a great deal was happening. On September 15, 1740 Whitefield arrived in New England; on September 17 he left Newport, Rhode Island for Boston.[13] "Several gentlemen" met him on the road and conducted him to town. He preached the next day, first at Colman's meetinghouse, then at the South Church, "and Lord's Day in the afternoon having preach'd to a great Number of People at the Old Brick Church, the House not being large enough to hold those that crowded to hear him, when the Exercise was over, He went and preached in the Fields, to at least 8000 persons."[14] The Boston ministers vied with each other to have this remarkable man visit their pulpits. Foxcroft must have managed something of a coup by getting Whitefield not only to preach at the First Church on Sunday, but to come back Thursday for the regular weekly Lecture. During this first tumultuous week he also favored Webb, Checkley, Gee, Harvard College, and Governor Belcher, one of his greatest admirers—although he was forced to leave Checkley's meetinghouse on Summer Street because the crowd was so large (there were reports that five people had been killed in leaps from the gallery) and move to the Commons. (One wonders how the young pastor who lived in Summer Street's most recently remodeled house felt about the gigantic mob clogging the street that Monday afternoon.) After a week in Boston, Whitefield left for a tour of the countryside, but he was back the following week to preach at the Old South on October 9. He stayed until the following Sunday, October 12, and preached his final sermon to more than twenty thousand. It was a week unlike any Boston had experienced since 1727.

Thomas Prince describes what happened there after Whitefield left:

52

. . . great numbers in this town were so happily concerned about their souls, as we had never seen any thing like it before, except at the time of the general earthquake: and their desires excited to hear their ministers more than ever: so that our assemblies both on Lectures and Sabbaths were surprisingly increased, and now the people wanted to hear us oftener. In consideration of which, a public Lecture was proposed to be set up at Dr. Colman's church, near the midst of town, on every Tuesday evening. . . ."[15]

Chauncy held his peace and watched to see if the spirit of God were truly working to produce godly, faithful men. While Whitefield was still fresh in his memory—and on the minds of all Bostonians—another itinerant preacher was dispatched to the town. Whitefield sent his friend Gilbert Tennent from New Jersey to New England to "blow up the divine fire lately kindled there."[16] Tennent arrived in December and stayed through one of the worst winters in New England history. He finally left on March 2, 1741.[17]

Tennent had Whitefield's energy, but he was not so mellifluous an orator nor so polished a gentleman. He spoke extemporaneously and vigorously, and with more than enough heat to warm the chilly Boston meetinghouses. Like Whitefield he aimed at arousing the apathetic and hounding the secure, and he succeeded.[18] He also succeeded in reviving in the Boston clergy a taste for a lively way of preaching, calculated to keep the fire blown up when spring arrived and Tennent left.[19] The ministers found it effective in their churches; other preachers adopted not only the excited preaching style but also the practice of traveling around the countryside, stirring conviction and assisting the Spirit in conversion. In the summer and fall of 1741 such young men as Samuel Buell, Eleazar Wheelock, Daniel and Nathanael Rogers, Benjamin Pomeroy, Timothy Allen, and many others caused trembling and tears in crowded parish meetinghouses, in barns, in fields, and even in the streets.[20] It was fast becoming clear to many people who were "affected" during those hot, dusty, jam-packed revival meetings that you didn't need a minister properly "settled" in the local Church to unsettle your soul; all those years of attending dry-as-dust sermons in the meetinghouse had done nothing, while these young men—some fresh from school—were afire with the Spirit of God. You could *feel* the Spirit spark and flame from them to this person and that, from one neighbor to another, to you and your wife and friends, through the room or across the field until the whole crowd seemed about to roar up in a blaze of remorse and repentance and, gloriously, salvation.

If one converted person seemed capable of sparking conviction in others, why shouldn't anyone who had felt the finger of God—even a layman—go forth and teach? The Spirit did not seem to consider training and education as prerequisite to his visit: in fact, some of the most remarkable converts were plain, unlettered folk. A number of

53

these very people had already set out on journeys to spread the good news of the work of the Spirit, and they had succeeded in awakening many along the way. Could it be that the regular ministers had not produced similar harvests of converted souls because they were themselves unconverted? Some began to demand of the settled clergy that they give an account of their conversion experience that tallied closely with the sudden, overwhelming surge of faith they had themselves felt so recently. Without such an experience, how could one call himself saved? What did all that education signify if the ministers were not *new creatures*?

Tennent had been broadly suggesting the same thing all winter. When in the spring of 1741 Whitefield's just-published *Journal*[21] of his recent New England tour reached Boston, it was easy for some of the local pastors to guess where Tennent had learned such notions. There, in the journal of the man who had been the toast of Boston clergy a few months before, the ministers and the faculty of Harvard College read his reflections on the visit. What was his opinion of them? "Many, nay most that preach, I fear do not experimentally know Christ." And his judgment of the colleges? "As for the Universities, I believe it may be said, their Light has become Darkness, Darkness that may be felt, and is complained of by the most godly Ministers." After this, his rather left-handed compliment to New England seemed pale and insufficient: "In short, I like New-England exceedingly well; and when a Spirit of Reformation revives, it certainly will prevail more than in any other place, because they are simple in their Worship, less corrupt in their Principles, and consequently easier to be brought over to the Form of sound Words, into which so many of their pious Ancestors were delivered."[22] Those who supported Whitefield were embarrassed; those who had not been so impressed now had high-explosive ammunition at hand. One of Whitefield's failings, Benjamin Franklin remarks in the *Autobiography*, was his willingness to get into print: "His Writing and Printing from time to time gave great Advantage to his Enemies. Unguarded Expressions and even erroneous Opinions de[livere]d in Preaching might have been afterwards explain'd, or qualify'd by supposing others that might have accompany'd them; or they might have been deny'd; But *litera scripta manet*."[23] In this case the comment applies to his *Journal* as well.

As 1740 gave way to 1741 the innovations of the revival began to take some extreme forms. Among the most obvious was an insistence on "dramatic" conversion. People had begun to assume that the Holy Spirit operated only in spectacular ways, and the more spectacular the better: the greater the conviction, the better the chance for conversion; the greater the gift of faith, the more ecstatic the joy that follows it. For some, anyone who did not share this experience could not be counted among the converted, and was therefore confidently thought to be damned; anyone who suggested that the Holy Spirit might operate in a number of ways besides this—that he might not operate this way at all—or that the real proof of conversion was a change of character and increased good behavior, was suspect, and in some quarters was accused of being an enemy of the Holy Spirit. From enemy of the Spirit to agent of Satan is an easy jump, and some made it. This insistence upon a spectacular conversion experience—or at least one that strictly followed the pattern Edwards had set down in the *Faithful Narrative*—also caused great concern among sincere people who heard their neighbors claiming to be saved but who had themselves never felt the hand of God. Would they be passed over in this remarkable season of salvation while others became *new creatures*?

In June 1741, shortly after the arrival of Whitefield's *Journal* and the departure of Tennent, and as the good weather made it easier for itinerant preachers to travel, Chauncy decided to consider this question of "the new creature." It was a term on everyone's tongue, and he wanted to explain what it included—as well as what it excluded. On June 4 he delivered the Boston Thursday Lecture, which he aptly entitled *The New Creature Describ'd, and Consider'd as the Sure Characteristic of a Man's Being in Christ. Together With Some Seasonable Advice to Those Who Are New-Creatures.* The text, from Corinthians ii. 17, was familiar to revivalists: "Therefore, if any man be in Christ, he is a New Creature: old things are past away; behold all things become new." He had the sermon published later in the summer —his first publication since 1739.[24] In this lecture Chauncy described the true Christian, spelled out his ideas on the scheme of salvation, offered a practical set of rules to people concerned about their condition, and spoke directly to the abuses he had noticed during the past "awakened year."

He began, as he usually did, by defining his terms. The *new creature* is a metaphor for "that change which is wrought in men, when they are made true christians." This change is not physical, but "moral" and "religious," and it is drastic. New creatures undergo changes both in an inward and outward aspect. The inward change is "universal": "their whole inner man is altered; insomuch that they have neither the same apprehensions, nor resolutions, nor affections: they neither love, nor grieve, nor hope, nor fear, as they used to do." To take "apprehensions" as an example: "They had once a *notional* sight only of the being and perfections of GOD. His holiness, justice, goodness, and mercy, were matters rather of speculative opinion than real belief: But now they see these things in quite another manner. They are struck with a full conviction of their certain truth. . . . That is the inward sense and feeling of their mind, verily there is a GOD, who judgeth in the earth: And he is a being infinitely just and holy, and wise, and good."[25] As for the "Outward Course," Chauncy states that "the change in their *lives* is as great as the change in their *hearts*." Not only do they stop sinning, they also undergo a *positive* reformation and begin to do their duty to God, their neighbor, and themselves.[26] Clearly the New Creature is one with the Godly, Faithful Man of a few years before.

After this description Chauncy provided a rather sobering conclusion: "We have reason to fear from what has been offered, there are but few, who may be pronounced *new creatures*. . . . Here and there a man, a woman, a child, is *new formed*: but for the bulk of mankind, they remain as they were, unrenewed in their minds, unchanged in their lives. A melancholy truth this! It should deeply affect our hearts."[27] This was not what the people had been hearing from Whitefield and Tennent, who claimed great numbers of conversions in this wonderful time. Here was Chauncy repeating the old Puritan truism about the reservation of election for the privileged few. A most melancholy truth, indeed. But how does one apply this truth to his own life? What test, what rule, should a person use to judge the condition of his soul?

This is the age-old Puritan problem, and Chauncy had a handy but rigorous solution. One must ask, "how is it" with my "apprehensions?" What are my thoughts of Christ? How is it with my "Purposes?" With my "Affections?" With my life and manners? In other words, do I fit the description just given of the true Christian? This is the only "tryal": not whether one has experienced great "convulsions of soul," or whether he can specify the "time and circumstances" of his conversion, or whether he has attained "high rapture." The argument is worth quoting, because Chauncy states it so clearly and with more earnestness than a paraphrase can capture:

> In one plain, short word, The great thing you have to get satisfied about is, whether you are the subjects of *that change*, which will, in the estimation of the gospel, denominate you *new creatures*. All that are christians in reality and truth, agree in this, that they are *not conform'd to this world, but transform'd by the renewing of their minds*: But in what is previous, or preparatory to this, there is a latitude, and so great a one, that there are but few christians, whose experiences are just alike. If some have been speedily wro't upon, and fashion'd into a *workmanship of God*; others have had the same thing done for them in a more slow and leisurely way. If some have been exercis'd with great terrors of conscience, strong agonies and convulsions of soul; others have been recovered to GOD, in a more mild, and kind, and gentle manner. If some have been under a stated, perceptible and distinct course of operations from the SPIRIT OF GOD; others have been dealt with, in a more insensible and variously interrupted way. The

great thing necessary is, to experience a real and effectual *renovation* of *heart* and *life*; and as to the *way* and *manner*, how this, by the *divine* SPIR-IT, was bro't about, it's not of so great importance: Nor is it of any importance, whether the SPIRIT OF GOD has gone on, in just the same method with you, which he has taken with some others. Be rather concern'd about the thing, than the way in order to it. Get satisfied you have been thus wro't upon, and you need be at no further pains.[28]

He concludes with some words of advice to those fortunate creatures whose souls pass this trial: be thankful to God, for you have been saved only by his mercy; remember that you are in the infancy of the spiritual life, and "must expect *growth* and *ripeness* as the consequent of *time* and *diligence*"; beware of intellectual and spiritual pride; be judicious and charitable (and if you are not charitable, your condition is suspect); "see to it, that you know *your own station*, and act *within your own sphere*," for God commands order in all things (an admonition against lay exhorting); "see to it, that you *walk worthy of your character*." As a parting word he repeats in ringing tones the battle cry of New England Puritanism since the beginning:

Let this *Antinomian* principle, on the one hand, be forever rooted out of the minds of men, that what CHRIST has done makes our doing a thing needless; and let that *popish* principle, on the other hand, whoever are the maintainers of it, be as much laid aside, that by any thing we can do, we can merit any the least favour from GOD. Constantly adhere to the middle between these extreams. Take care to do the will of GOD; and yet, have no dependance on your own doing, but intirely confide in the *perfect obedience* of JESUS *your saviour*.[29]

The New Creature is a position paper. It had been an exciting nine months in Boston. The visits of Whitefield in the fall and Tennent during the winter had kept the townspeople skipping from one dramatic event to another. Now that Whitefield and Tennent had left, it was time to put the entire revival in perspective and guide its further development along truly Christian lines. As an acknowledged leader in the town, Chauncy took this role upon himself. He made his position quite clear. Obviously the uncharitableness he had experienced during the late 1730s was hardening into censoriousness after the visits of two of the grand itinerants. Clearly errors such as an insistence upon dramatic conversion were gaining currency. He wanted to correct them. But he did not call for a halt to the awakening or condemn the movement as a whole. Even if he had wanted to do so, he probably realized that there was no stopping it. Instead he tried to remind the people that by its very nature a religious movement must have a theological foundation, not merely an emotional surface. By pointing out clearly the nature of this foundation, he reminded New Englanders of

57

the traditional principles—the middle way between extremes—by which they might guide the awakening to Christian goals. He was doomed to disappointment. His guiding principles required charity, temperance, and self-control—qualities difficult to require of an excited people without stifling their excitement in the bargain, and difficult to impose with charity, temperance, and control.

Two weeks after Chauncy preached *The New Creature* he was called upon to sit in judgment over his friend and fellow minister Samuel Mather, assistant to Joshua Gee at the Second Church. The Mather case was a strange business; along with the Osborn affair it turned most of the old-guard Boston ministry against Chauncy even before he became an outspoken opponent of the Awakening. Samuel Mather was Cotton Mather's son. He had pursued an undistinguished career at the Second Church since 1732, when, despite considerable opposition, he had been chosen assistant pastor of his father's and grandfather's old church. Gee made no secret of his dislike for Mather, and in 1740 a number of parishioners began to agitate for his removal.[30] There were two major complaints: the "looseness" of his doctrines and the suspected impropriety of his conduct. In June Mather gave his opponents plenty of ammunition when he joined Chauncy in supporting Osborn. He remained, moreover, lukewarm to the task of arousing the emotional state of conviction, and later that year he courted trouble when he spoke strongly against Whitefield and the Awakening. In June 1741 the church decided to call an ecclesiastical council, inviting Foxcroft's First Church, Colman's Brattle Street Church, Sewall's Old South, Webb's New North, and Checkley's New South. The council met on June 19 and tried to smooth the matter over by drafting letters of advice to Mather and to the church, asking both parties to work for reconciliation and requiring Mather to sign a resolution that he would get his "mind further enlightened and settled in the important points mentioned by the council," preach more frequently and distinctly on those points, avoid anything in his "sermons or conversation which may tend to discourage the work of conviction among us," and henceforward "walk before [his] brethren with the humility required in the gospel, and with becoming circumspection."[31]

These humiliating resolutions, however noble, were short-lived. Within two weeks the church, deciding that Mather had insufficiently reformed, called the council back into session. Except for Chauncy and Benjamin Colman, all the ministers voted for dismissal. Chauncy thereby cut himself off from the influential Boston clergy, not only by voting against them, but by drawing up a rebuttal—a kind of minority opinion—for Mather to read to the congregation. As Ezra Stiles observed in later years, "This gave an irreconcileable Disgust to Messrs.

Gee, Foxcroft, &c., &c."[32] The atmosphere around the First Church must have been less than cordial during that long, hot summer.

The "Disgust" of the senior ministers in town, the exchange of bitter accusations in the Mather case (which dragged on from June until October), the excitement stirred up by the awakeners, the growing spirit of disrespect for the "opposers" of the Awakening, and frequent suggestions that such opposers were unregenerate and thereby unworthy of their positions—all these factors contributed to a deep anger building in Chauncy during the summer of 1741. Chauncy had the chance to release some of his emotion on September 10, when he presented the Boston Public Lecture. He did not waste the opportunity.

The title of his address indicates its subject: *An Unbridled Tongue a Sure Evidence, That our Religion is Hypocritical and Vain.*[33] In this sermon he strikes savagely at all the pettiness and backbiting that had characterized the past few months in Boston. Had there been profanity, blasphemy, deceit, flattery, falsehood, filthy talk? These are all evidences of tongues unbridled. But worse than these is defamation:

> No, the scripture is not more particular and express in cautioning against any sin, than this of *evil speaking.* . . . And the caution extends to *all the ways,* wherein men may hurt one another in their reputation: Whether it be by reproaches to their face, or behind their back; by open revilings, or secret whisperings; by direct slander, or oblique insinuation; upon express design, or heedlessly and inadvertently. In what way soever men blacken the character of their neighbour, they *speak evil* of him, in a less or greater degree, in the sense, in which the scripture so solemnly cautions against it: And in so doing, they *bridle not their tongue, but* give it a liberty, which cannot but be condemned; yea, which they themselves condemn, whenever it happens to be their own case.[34]

But there is even a more insidious evil afoot:

> Nay, what is still worse, are there not those, who, when there is nothing *visible,* upon which to ground a censure, will presume proudly to take to themselves the *sole prerogative* of the *omniscient GOD,* by looking into the *hearts* of their neighbours, and *judging* them *carnal, unregenerate* men? yea, PHARISEES, i.e., the most accursed of all *hypocrites.*
> How far good men, real christians, thro' weakness of judgment, rashness of temper, undue prejudice, faulty ignorance, or any other such like cause, may fall into this sin of *censoriousness,* I presume not to say; but this I must say, and I should with-hold from you an *important* part of the *counsel of GOD,* if I did not say it, that whoever the person be, whether preacher or hearer, man or woman, high or low, that *goes on in a course* of rashly and uncharitably judging his neighbour, and *allows himself* in it, that man has an *unbridled tongue;* His tongue is under no tolerable restraint, neither from *reason,* nor *religion.*[35]

To have an unbridled tongue indicates hypocrisy, and Chauncy's views on that sin had not changed. Chauncy used the imagery of hell fire infrequently, but this time he borrowed the rhetoric of the Awakeners themselves to insist that the worst torments in hell are reserved for hypocrites.

> They shall be sent away *to dwell with devouring fire*; yea, they shall dwell in the hottest place of that *lake, which burneth with fire* and *brimstone.*—Wo unto you hypocrites, for ye shall *receive the greatest damnation*! You are mark't out for it, by name, in the *revelations* of GOD!—O consider of this in time; and go not on mocking GOD, and deceiving the world, least he *cut you asunder, and appoint you your portion*, where *shall be weeping and gnashing of teeth.*—[36]

Dissension among the Boston clergy did not pass with the summer. In December 1741, when Chauncy delivered another Boston Public Lecture, factions among the ministers began to resemble war camps, and Chauncy found the traditions of the New England minister under attack from several sides. Preaching style, for instance, had become a stormy issue. The Puritan preacher had customarily cultivated a plain, calm manner of address designed primarily to enlighten the understanding of his audience. The awakeners were enjoying great success, however, by appealing to the emotions of the people with a flamboyant, excited manner that soon became the fashionable style. The new fashion in preaching contributed to a second problem, a weakening of church organization. New England Congregationalists held to a "settled" ministry and a covenanted church. Members of a particular church, having entered into covenant with each other, had a deep personal involvement in the organization. Now, however, those commitments often seemed shaky, for settled ministers found themselves competing with one another for audiences—and the main lure was an exciting preaching style. Finally, as traditional church structures were threatened, the problem of lay exhorters and untrained ministers became more acute. The New England Way had always provided for an educated ministry, but now some said such niceties were unnecessary. In his sermons Chauncy had tried unsuccessfully to retard the growth of these tendencies, but by now it was apparent that they had continued to increase and spread into the ranks of the ministers themselves.

Because of his actions during the summer and fall on behalf of Osborn and Samuel Mather, the accompanying charges of Arminianism, and his candid criticisms of the errors he had observed in the Awakening, Chauncy had felt the undisguised disgust of a good number of the Boston clergy. It was time to speak out about such squabbling. When Chauncy's turn to preach the public lecture arrived, he had a fine opportunity. The Boston ministers would be assembled there, a

60

captive audience, and since the Awakening one could count on a large gathering of the citizenry as well. By now there remained little opportunity for dispassionate argument. Those who were disgusted with him would have no patience with a sermon designed specifically to convince them of their mistakes. It must have been a temptation to return censoriousness in kind, if only for the sake of satisfaction. But Chauncy chose another course. Instead of a diatribe, he delivered a masterpiece of quiet, eminently charitable reasoning, entitled *The Gifts of the Spirit to Ministers Considered in Their Diversity*.[37] It is a brilliant example of rhetorical strategy, touching every sore spot, but astringently.

The device is classic: rather than descend to personal attack, grant the merit of everyone's argument, including your own—but stick to the abstract. This enables you to adopt the stance of the dispassionate man of good will, carefully considering a number of good proposals. Having established this rhetorical distance you can occasionally use irony, choosing illustrations carefully—without being tied to actual examples—and arrange your material with an eye towards its rhetorical effect. In the end you can establish your own case not as the only possible solution, but rather as simply the best of a number of good alternatives. Chauncy manages the device masterfully. He anticipates every objection, and so phrases his argument that to disagree would be to brand oneself a near-lunatic or a heretic. This is not to say that his rhetoric is empty, or that he falsifies his position. Not at all; his views are perfectly consistent with the principles he had enunciated time and again. Here, however, he employs his rhetorical skill to overcome a difficult situation.

Consider, for example, the way he handles the question of preaching style. If some ministers insist on hell-fire and damnation preaching to the exclusion of everything else, Chauncy does not try to counter by denying that style any merit and insisting that the calm, logical approach is the only effective method. Instead he distinguishes four gifts of the Spirit regarding style. The first is that of applying to the understanding of man. The preacher with this gift is able to set forth the truth in a clear light, and this kind of preaching is valuable because it makes men better and wiser. The chief scriptural example of such a man is St. Paul. The second gift is that of moving the passions. The preacher thus gifted has a good voice, good pronunciation and elocution, "becoming gesture," and a graceful air. This also has value, if it is used decorously, for it attracts men to the truth. Ezekiel the prophet serves as a good example. The third gift is that of touching the consciences of sinners. These ministers preach terror in order to rouse sinners from their security. John the Baptist preached this way, as did James the son of Zebedee and his brother John. This too has its value,

61

for ordinarily sinners are awakened by fear and thereupon try to "get into a state of safety." Tempered with hope, this can therefore be a valuable style. Finally, Chauncy describes the most useful gift: "Speaking comfortably to distrest sinners." The preacher talented in this way is mild, tender, and compassionate; he has a "dexterity in setting before the view of sinners the *loving-kindness of* GOD *in* JESUS CHRIST." The prime example of this style is Christ himself. Of course this situation is as it should be. God in his sovereignty reflects divine goodness by providing various ways to satisfy the diverse needs of his people. Thus God offers an occasion for both ministers and people to practice humility and charity towards one another.[38]

Chauncy's argument for recognizing the value of reason and compassion as well as excitement and terror is virtually unassailable: who would dare criticize the methods of Paul and Christ? But Chauncy finds a place for other styles as well; he makes it clear that to insist on a single method among ministers is to question the wisdom of God, who has provided for diversity. Few ministers would want to take that step either, especially since one of the key elements of Awakening preaching was insistence on people's utter dependence upon God's sovereign will.

Having established the theoretical foundation of his argument, Chauncy proceeds to the "application." Calling for charity, he cautions ministers against intellectual and spiritual pride and advises candidates for the ministry to improve the gifts of the Spirit by study and training. He warns the people against following ministers who decline to do so.[39] These words are aimed at specific innovations of the revival: intolerance, contention, an uneducated ministry, itinerant preaching, lay exhorting. He is especially hard on censoriousness and uncharitableness because these had hit closest to home. But Chauncy does not rant. He tries instead to soften his blows by deliberate understatement and restraint, offering his own attitude as an example of the spirit he wishes to revive in Boston. *"Brethren,"* he says, "I speak not these things with a design to offend any; but because they are a *word in season."* And, he continues,

> whoever is not sensible of this, must be unacquainted with the situation of affairs in this place. There has certainly been too much heat and strife about ministers; some contending for one, others for another: And, I believe, no one will pretend to justify those hard speeches, which have sometimes dropt from the lips of those, who, I would hope, are otherwise good christians. If you prefer some ministers to others, yet don't slight those, of whose gifts, you have not so high an opinion. If, in your apprehension, they be men of inferior gifts, they may not be so in the tho't of others; they may have a great esteem of their gifts; yea, and of their graces too: Don't do any thing to hinder their usefulness to those, who value them, tho' they shou'd not be so well fitted to be useful to you: Or, if their gifts are really small,

they are such as GOD has given them, and they ought not therefore to be despised: Besides, their gifts being small, their work is so much the harder: Dont make it still more burdensome, by heaping upon them the occasions of grief and discouragement.[40]

By December 1741—a year and a half after the advent of Whitefield—Chauncy had discussed nearly all the innovations in the New England Way resulting from the revival. Some of them, such as defamation of character, itineracy, and the acceptance of an uneducated ministry, he had forthrightly condemned. Others, such as an excessive emphasis on the preaching of terror, or the demand for a violent conversion experience, he had cautioned against. He was discouraged, for despite his warnings the situation seemed to be deteriorating, and the churches, instead of gaining strength through the operation of the Spirit, threatened to crumble under strife and dissension. And since the Awakening he had found himself more and more alienated from his friends—even from his senior at the First Church. As yet, however, he had not struck at the root question: whether or not the "situation of affairs in this place" was in fact a work of God. Despite growing excesses, matters apparently were not yet so far out of hand that they could be called the handiwork of Satan. Ironically the spur for Chauncy to seek the source of the Awakening came from Jonathan Edwards himself.

On September 10, 1741, the same day that Chauncy warned the citizens of Boston about the fatal dangers of an unbridled tongue, Edwards spoke at the Yale commencement. His topic: *The Distinguishing Marks of a Work of the Spirit of God, Applied to that uncommon Operation that has lately appeared on the minds of many of the People of this Land, With a particular Consideration of the extraordinary Circumstances with which this Work is Attended.*[41] His conclusion: despite the excesses, the "extraordinary influence that has lately appeared on the minds of the people abroad in this land, causing in them an uncommon concern and engagedness of mind about the things of religion, is undoubtedly, in the general, from the Spirit of God."[42] All the New England clergymen soon had a chance to read this sermon, which was printed in Boston with a preface by William Cooper. The issue had been brought out into the open.

The question bothered Chauncy during the winter of 1741–42. During that time a relatively recent and disturbing innovation became prevalent, and captured everyone's attention. Evangelistic preachers began to encourage extreme "bodily effects" in response to their sermons. "Visions and trances" had become common with the summer preaching of 1741. Prince tells us that these responses were unknown in Boston during the visits of Whitefield and Tennent,[43] but such traveling preachers as Wheelock, Buell, Bliss, and Pomeroy soon led

63

the people to expect groans and tears as signs of true remorse. From here it was an easy step to fainting and apparitions. In the spring of 1742 Chauncy tried again to point out that such conviction was only a step towards conversion and that bodily reactions were not a sure sign of conviction. The occasion was a day of prayer at the First Church "to ask GOD the effusion of his SPIRIT."

In an important sermon entitled *The Outpouring of the Holy Ghost*,[44] Chauncy restated the views on the conversion process which he had enunciated in *Prayer for Help* (1737) and *The New Creature* (1741). Once again he spelled out the manner in which the Holy Ghost usually works: 1) by convincing men of sin, which leads to conviction; 2) by producing in men "true gospel faith"; 3) by changing men to new creatures; 4) by assisting Christians in "the practice of their duty, to their *increasing in grace*, and *persevering therein unto the end*"; 5) by supporting them in suffering; 6) by granting "inward joy"; and 7) by satisfying men of their "*adoption* into GOD's *family*, and interest in the promises of the Gospel covenant."[45] Once again he cautioned his listeners that degrees of conviction differ vastly from person to person —"but in none, is this distress excited to so great a degree as to put them beside themselves, unless from their own weakness, or ignorance, or some faulty cause or other, which ought not to be ascribed to the SPIRIT of GOD."[46] He pointed out that conviction was not suffi- cient: "O take heed, you don't make a righteousness of your convic- tions, that you don't place them in the room of CHRIST, in the room of true Gospel repentance!"[47] He warned especially against mistaking momentary elation for the joy that attends the gift of the Spirit. True religious joy does not bypass the intellect: "The way to true *Joy* is a religious and impartial examination into the frame of our hearts, and the course of our actions, and if our Joy springs from a clear discern- ment of these as conform'd to the tenour of the Gospel covenant, we may hope it is the product of a divine influence; Whereas, if it is a sudden flash only, and arises we know not how, nor upon what it is bottom'd, 'tis much to be suspected. . . ."[48] There is one way to dis- cover if the Holy Spirit has been poured out to us: it is essentially the same "tryal" Chauncy had proposed a year earlier. Has there been a real and effectual change of heart and life?[49]

Although *The Outpouring of the Holy Ghost* essentially restates the position Chauncy had advanced in *The New Creature*, at the conclu- sion of *The Outpouring* he directly sets forth his judgment of the Awakening. Here, at the very height of the movement, he sums up his position as it had evolved over the past few years. One can see traces of all his previous thinking about the Awakening. All the points he had considered since the days before Whitefield's visit come to bear— from thanksgiving for conversions, to concern over the excesses that

64

have grown up so quickly, to hope for "the progress of real and substantial religion." It is as concise and accurate a statement of his attitude towards the Awakening as one is likely to find, and it represents him better than the snippets from *Seasonable Thoughts* that are usually advanced to illustrate his supposedly unfair and fanatical opposition to the entire movement.

Let us pray . . . for the *out-pouring* of the SPIRIT upon our land. There is room for prayer in this respect. A concern, I am sensible, has been generally awaken'd in the minds of people, in one place or another: And it has, I trust, been of spiritual advantage to many; who, it may be hoped, have been either *savingly converted* to GOD, or *enliven'd* and *quicken'd* in the work of religion, and their soul's everlasting salvation. There are I doubt not, a number in this land, upon whom GOD has graciously *shed* the influences of his blessed SPIRIT; and we ought to be thankful for what of the SPIRIT, we have reason to hope there is among us: But there is yet need of prayer; and the more so, as so many things have arisen among us, which are a dishonour to GOD, and may have a tendency greatly to obstruct the progress of real and substantial religion. Alas! what unchristian heats and animosities are there in many places, to the dividing and breaking in pieces of churches and towns? What a spirit of rash, censorious, uncharitable judging prevails too generally all over the land? What bitterness and wrath and clamour, what evil speaking, reviling and slandering, are become common; and among those too, who would be counted good christians? How alienated are many ministers from each other, and how instrumental of hurting rather than promoting one another's usefulness? What prejudices are there in the minds of too many people against the *standing ministry*, tho' perhaps as faithful a one as any part of the world is favour'd with? And how general is the disposition they discover to flock after every *weak* and *illiterate* EXHORTER, to the contempt of their *pastors*, who have spent, it may be, most of their days, in faithful services for their souls? How heated are the imaginations of a great many, and into what excesses do they betray them?

These and such like things, it is too evident to be disowned, are grown too common, not in a single place only, but in most places throughout the country. How they may appear to some others I know not; but to me, I confess, they afford no comfortable prospect.[50]

Two weeks after Chauncy took this stand on the Awakening, the general convention of the Massachusetts Congregational clergy was held in Boston. Here the battle lines were drawn, and Chauncy's home became the headquarters for those of his persuasion. Jacob Eliot of Connecticut was a visitor at the time and spent the evening of May 26, 1742 at Chauncy's house. He found the "conversation very profitable and edifying."[51] Such gatherings always offered a good opportunity to exchange news, and Eliot had a story or two about the Awakening to tell. He probably recounted an incident that he had recorded in his diary during the winter.

Noah Chappel & Mary Webster aet about 12 were at Night both in a kind of trance & so remained for near 2 Days 2 Nights sometimes. . . . . Screaming & Lamenting—calm and still, with their eyes open seeming as if they were writing or reading as they lay together on a bed they kept one spot between 'em peculiar to 'em; that if but a hair or mote was dropt there they would instantly take it away tho both blinded. They both pretended to be going to heaven . . . & . . . they had several conflicts with the Devil & that they had a vision of Christ & read in the book of Life in the Golden Capitals several names. Mr. Whitefield's first, then Mr. Wheelocks, Mr. Pomeroy's, Mr. Rogers, Mr. Warren.[52]

Whitefield in Golden Capitals in the Book of Life, indeed! Since Chauncy had been gathering such reports for some time, the story would not have come as a surprise. But Eliot must have also had fresh news of great excitement running through Connecticut as a result of the work of James Davenport. If Whitefield, Wheelock, Pomeroy, Rogers, and Warren had brought about visions and trances, Davenport had brought on hysteria and rioting. A disciple of Whitefield and Tennent, he had traveled with the grand itinerant on a preaching tour in 1740, and had conducted his own campaign throughout southern Connecticut in 1741.[53] With the coming of spring he had begun a new excursion there.

Davenport was the embodiment of everything Chauncy opposed. He was an itinerant in the wild style. He had been a colleague of Whitefield and Tennent. He had gathered about him in his travels a band of zealous lay exhorters. He preached extemporaneously, without notes, without preparation, without even a Scriptural text—but with much arm-waving and uncontrolled shouting. Convinced that he could predict the imminent end of the world, he deliberately sought to stir up terror, but beyond this he thought the Spirit came only through physical effects such as screaming, jerking, and fainting. He frequently concluded his meetings late at night by leading a madcap parade through town, singing lustily "with his Hands extended, his Head thrown back, and his Eyes staring up to Heaven."[54] To complete the picture, he was the epitome of censoriousness. If Whitefield had questioned the piety of the Boston clergy, and Tennent had preached on the danger of an unconverted ministry,[55] at least they had not presumed to burst into a man's study, demanding that he give immediate evidence of his salvation. But this was a favorite practice of Davenport's. He claimed infallible, intuitive knowledge of the elect and the damned. Those he considered saved, he addressed as "Brother"; others he called "Neighbor." (He addressed most ministers as "Neighbor.") Moreover he took it upon himself to denounce such ministers in public, sometimes calling them wolves in sheep's clothing, or blind men leading the people to hell, and urging congregations to abandon

66

their leaders if they valued their souls. He had already condemned Chauncy in public. During the same week in May that the convention met in Boston, Davenport was arrested in Ripton parish, Stratford, Connecticut, for violating the recently passed law against itineracy. His trial at Hartford occasioned a riot in the town; forty militiamen were summoned to restore order. The assembly there found him "under the influence of enthusiastical impressions and impulses" and therefore not in his right mind, and they deported him to his home parish of Southold.[56]

Everyone knew he was on his way to Boston. Advocates of the Awakening were as unhappy about this prospect as were the "opposers." He was certain to embarrass them, and yet how could they oppose him without appearing to oppose the entire revival? Davenport arrived in Charlestown on Friday, June 25, just as the Associated Pastors of Boston and Charlestown were gathering for their meeting.[57] On Sunday morning he worshipped in the Charlestown church, but he did not attend the afternoon service because he had decided that the minister was unconverted.[58] The next morning the Ministers' Association, "greatly alarmed," asked him to appear before them.[59] After questioning him the ministers decided that he was pious enough, but "enthusiastic" and imprudent, and they voted to deny him their pulpits. Undaunted, he went out to preach to thousands that day on Boston Common. On July 1, 1742 the association issued a declaration praising the revival but censuring Davenport.[60] To no one's surprise, but to the chagrin of the advocates of the revival, Davenport responded by publicly pronouncing the ministers unregenerate and unworthy of their posts.

Davenport—everyone was talking about him. Thousands were turning out to hear him in the fields. After the itinerant had been in the town a week, Chauncy entertained some friends at home. All agreed that, from what they had seen, the stories they had heard about this latest traveling preacher were true. The court at Hartford had judged correctly: he was "touched in his brain."[61] It did not take Davenport long to learn who was the chief opposer in town. One morning during his second week in Boston he appeared at the door of the handsome house in Summer Street. He was there, he announced, to inquire into the reason of the hope that was in the Reverend Dr. Chauncy.[62]

It had come to this. After years of study and preparation for the ministry, after fifteen years' labor at the First Church, after two harried years of struggling with the problems rising from the Awakening, it had all come to this: a man Chauncy firmly believed to be mad now stood as a judge at his door, challenging the state of his soul. A madman, perfectly willing to mount his perch in Boston Common that afternoon and shout to the world that Charles Chauncy of the Old

Brick was a carnal, unconverted wretch, merrily leading his flock to hell. Every error, every excess, that Chauncy had been pleading and scolding about now stood incarnate and insistent in his presence, boldly demanding: *Brother* or *Neighbor?*

Davenport was overmatched. He had hardly phrased his question before Chauncy turned the tables on him. What was to be a trial of Chauncy's soul rapidly became a scorching analysis of Davenport's character. The pastor of the First Church did not deign to discuss his spiritual life with his unexpected caller, but he was not shy about spelling out, in plain language, his views on young evangelists who come to town "under the influence of *impulses* and *impressions,* taking them for a *call* from GOD." Chauncy came to the point: "*Your own flock,*" he said, "is *your proper charge.*" Here in Boston, "instead of *good,* you will be the *occasion* of much *hurt,* to the interest of religion in these churches." By your wild actions you convince the irreligious that religion is "a wild, disorderly, imaginery business," By "going thro' the *town,* from one minister to another, to examine into their *religious experiences,*" you may prejudice the people against the ministry, but even more importantly, you place yourself in danger by violating "that solemn statute of heaven, JUDGE NOT." You are a sick man, and "I believe, if ever GOD gives you a *sound mind,* you will *cry to him from the deeps,* for this strange conduct you have unhappily fallen into." This is serious and dangerous business: "There is nothing, while in this state of mind, but you may be bro't to: And how far GOD may suffer you to be led aside, is known only to himself. . . . I beg, *Sir,* you would take warning! Whatever you may think of your self, you have certainly a *heated imagination.* 'Tis too evident to be denied, that you often take the *motions of your own mind,* for *divine communications.*"

Having stated his case, Chauncy brought the interview to a close by directing his remarks to the reason for Davenport's call. "And now," he said, "having spoken my mind so freely, if you deal with me as you have done with much better men, I may expect to be called a poor, carnal, unconverted wretch. But I assure you beforehand, I esteem it a *very small thing to be judged by your Judgment*; and the rather, because I *certainly know,* you are ignorant of my state towards GOD."

Chauncy ushered Davenport out. "But however you act towards me," he concluded, "I presume not to *judge you. To your own master you stand, or fall.* I have taken notice only of *that* in you, which is *visible* to the world; And tho' I have, and do condemn it, as what is opposite to the plain laws of GOD; yet, I pronounce no sentence respecting *your state.* GOD knows how far you may be under the power of a *disturbed imagination,* and will make all the favourable allowances your case will admit of: I desire to do so also, and would hope the best concerning you."

Davenport had little chance to consider the matter. As Chauncy put it afterwards, "my intention was, to deal plainly and faithfully with you: And I believe, you do not think, I was wanting upon that head. Whether you heard what I then said with *pity towards me*, or becoming *reflections on your self*, I know not: Time may discover which. But whatever the working of your mind was, I am abundantly confirm'd in it, that your *real* character was fairly laid open before you."[63]

To squelch Davenport's enthusiasm Chauncy set about writing and publishing a sermon on the subject. He also wrote a detailed account of their interview in an open letter to Davenport, and he included it as a preface to the sermon. The harsh irony of the salutation amply demonstrates his frame of mind:

> Your coming to BOSTON . . . was the occasion of my studying, and preaching, and afterwards giving way to the publication of the following Sermon: And, as I think, there is that in it, which may be a *word in season* to a gentleman of your cast of mind, I herewith make a present of it to you; and shall be glad, if it may be of service to you, as I hope it will to others, guarding them against the wilds of a heated imagination.[64]

Davenport was unappreciative. Chauncy's sermon with its accompanying letter, was one of the first items he pitched into the flames at the famous holocaust he staged a year later in New London.[65]

Enthusiasm Described and Caution'd Against: Chauncy preached this sermon on "the Lord's Day after the Commencement." After the bustle of Davenport's visit, the tale-swapping about him among the ministers at the commencement, and Chauncy's open letter, no one had to guess who was being described: "the *Enthusiast* is one, who has a conceit of himself as a person favoured with the extraordinary presence of the *Deity*. He mistakes the workings of his own passions for divine communications, and fancies himself immediately inspired by the SPIRIT of GOD, when all the while he is under no other influence than that of an over-heated imagination."[66] Such a person is mentally ill. To Chauncy, enthusiasm is "properly a disease, a sort of madness," and it especially affects "those, in whom *melancholy* is the prevailing ingredient in their constitution. In these it often reigns; and sometimes to so great a degree, that they are really beside themselves, acting as truly by the blind impetus of a wild fancy, as tho' they had neither reason nor understanding." It manifests itself in six ways: an altered countenance; a loosened tongue; convulsions; freakish behavior; imaginary intimacy with heaven; and most of all, "the disregard [Enthusiasts] express to the Dictates of *reason*. They are above the force of argument, beyond conviction from a calm and sober address to their understandings. . . . You had as good reason with the wind."[67] If enthusiasts such as Davenport were acknowledged as its leaders, then the Awakening had crossed the line separating excitement from madness.

Could Chauncy have been thinking of the *Faithful Narrative* as well as of Davenport? Could he have remembered the climax of the Surprising Conversions? In the Boston edition of 1738, Edwards described his uncle Hawley in these terms: "Towards the latter part of his time, he grew much discouraged, and melancholy grew amain upon him, till he was wholly overpowered by it, and was in great measure past a capacity of receiving advice, or being reasoned with to any purpose. . . . "[68] Whether or not Chauncy saw the parallel between Hawley and Davenport, the fact remains that with the rise of enthusiasm came the decline of the revivals. After Uncle Hawley, God withdrew from Northampton; after Davenport, Boston's "sweet season" began to wane.

CHAPTER SIX

Words in Season

[Ministers] are set for the *Defence of the Gospel*; 'tis one special Part of
the Work they are called to, *by sound Doctrine, to exhort and convince
Gain sayers*. And *now* is the Time when they should stand up for the *good
old Way*, and bear a faithful Testimony against every Thing that may cast a
Blemish on *true primitive Christianity*. And if they *now* hold their Peace,
they are too much under the Influence of that *Fear of Man, which bringeth
a Snare*; they are guilty of *Cowardice* which they can't give a good Account
of, either to GOD, or their own *Consciences*.

Charles Chauncy, 1744[1]

As Chauncy became convinced that the Awakening had deterio-
rated into something approaching mass hysteria, he began to consider
the movement dangerous and threatening. He saw himself threatened
personally by enthusiasts such as Davenport. He saw his religious beliefs strongly challenged, especially as Jonathan Edwards, a brilliant
adversary, began to publish formidable theoretical defenses of the
Awakening. He saw his very way of life as a minister threatened by
the divisive results of itineracy and censoriousness. And he saw his vision of a chosen people united in a sacred religious mission challenged
by the separatism and dissension ripping Congregationalism apart. He
had prayed for an Awakening that would fill his town with love and
joy, as the surprising conversions had done in Northampton; but in
1742 he saw around him nothing but bitterness and partisanship.
Surely, he believed, God had not sent his Spirit to thrust religious
people at each other's throats.

Chauncy was also a proud man with an extraordinary sense of vocation. He believed that as a minister he was especially accountable to God, honor bound to bear "a faithful Testimony against every Thing that may cast a Blemish on *true primitive Christianity*." He was proud of his ancestry, intelligence, abilities, scholarship, calling, and accomplishments; he was proud of his position and his own strength of will. If duty required a "word in season," he felt adequate to the task of speaking it.

For these reasons Chauncy established himself as the champion of the opposers. For three years, from 1742 to 1745, he conducted a campaign against the Awakening as it had taken shape from 1740 through 1742. These were not, of course, the only motives. Among the ministers of Boston, Chauncy was, after all, particularly well-suited, by position and experience, for the work. To begin with, the role was practically forced upon him by default. Samuel Mather and Mather Byles were the only other avowed "opposers."[2] In the summer of 1741 Samuel Mather had proved himself an unlikely leader. The job required someone with a secure position; Mather had been unable to hold his post at the Second Church, and his own, newly founded church was still struggling for a foothold in Boston as the Awakening reached its fullest force. Besides, Mather lacked the personality for the job. He was more interested in searching out recondite references and loading his sermons with scholarly paraphernalia than in gathering reports, sending letters, reading and correcting proof, and riding out into the countryside to see the operation of the Awakening for himself.[3]

Among the Boston Congregational clergy who did not support the revival, this left only Chauncy and the poet Mather Byles. The latter had the wit and literary talent to snip away at the excesses of the revival with pointed satire, but his deft strokes, cutting as they could be, were insufficient for the cause.[4] It required a heavier hand, and Chauncy was the likely candidate. His status at the First Church was secure. Disgusted as he may have been, Foxcroft was not the kind to work for his colleague's dismissal, which would have been hard to obtain anyway. Chauncy's pronouncements, while upsetting to many people because of their emphasis, could hardly be called scandalous, and unorthodoxy would have been difficult to prove. As for his personal behavior, it was beyond reproach. He had decently married a widow, and one of means at that, who had repaired church property from her own estate and who had taken charge of Chauncy's children. Moreover the First Church was still powerful and influential in New England. As Boston's oldest church, it had the honor of a respected heritage. A voice from its pulpit would be heard and heeded more readily than one from a new church, such as Mather's in Hanover

Street. Not only was Chauncy a strong force in the city, he was also a man to be reckoned with in theological circles, as the recent honorary degree from Scotland had so well demonstrated. Addington Davenport could testify to his scholarship and knowledge of church history, and the Hollis professor of divinity at Harvard could commend his intellect and "catholick spirit." He was the Reverend Doctor Chauncy, of the *First* Church in Boston.

Leadership of the Old-Lights required literary talent, for the printing press would be the greatest weapon in such a conflict. It also required staying power, honesty, and solid, firmly held principles. Victory in the tedious battle would come only to those with a strong belief in the cause. Chauncy, with his gifts for plain, orderly exposition and heavy irony, had the stylistic equipment, and his early studies and sermons were proof of his determination and conviction. Finally such a champion must be a living definition of the life-style he advocated. A friend once told Chauncy, "You live by rule." Nodding in agreement, Chauncy replied, "If I did not, I should not live at all."[5] In a battle for popular opinion, contrasts must be sharp and clear. What more striking contrast could one desire than "enthusiastick" James Davenport, singing through the streets, and disciplined Charles Chauncy, speaking a word in season?

The Old-Lights were hardly so well organized at this stage as to be called a "party," and Chauncy was not an official representative. But all those of his persuasion seem to have recognized him as the likely man. Especially after the shock of meeting Davenport, he was not reluctant to seek the role.

Chauncy was customarily thorough. During 1742 and 1743 he exchanged hundreds of letters about the Awakening with other ministers throughout the colonies.[6] In this way he collected a fat file of remarkables and extravagancies from the countryside—enough to convince him that flagrant errors were the order of the day. He also became the unofficial editor of every printed attack on the revival. "There was," he later wrote to Stiles, "scarce a piece against the times but was sent to me, and I had the labour sometimes of preparing it for the press, and always of correcting the press."[7] Letters and reports, however, were not enough for Chauncy, who wanted first-hand information as well. At New Haven, in *Distinguishing Marks*, Edwards had challenged his opponents to visit the outlying towns where conversions were taking place and see the revival for themselves.[8] This was an incentive to Chauncy, but it is likely that he would have made the trip without Edwards's invitation: Chauncy always insisted on judging for himself. Thus—probably in the summer and fall of 1742—he set out on a three-hundred mile circuit, riding through New England, New York, and

73

New Jersey. While visiting classmates and fellow Harvard graduates, or speaking with other ministers, he was always "narrowly observing."[9] It was an open secret that he was gathering material for a book.

The story that he was preparing a book, and—apparently—his practice of correcting errors on the spot, did not make him especially welcome to the New-Lights. Eleazar Wheelock, one of the most famous of the itinerant preachers, bitterly recalled Chauncy's visit: "I was upon that same road to N. Haven when that Dr. passed through this government (as I understand) to fill his crop with materials for that piece and I came several times within the scent of him (for he left a savour of what he fed upon when he lit). . . ."[10] This trip gave Chauncy personal experience of the Awakening outside Boston, but it also injured his health. The press of his work and the rigors of distant travel on bad roads combined to weaken him, and he was plagued with some sort of lingering digestive ailment.[11] In February 1746, at an especially low moment, he described it: "My disease is an inveterate *colick* which returns very often, and is obstinate with all the medicines I have been able as yet to use." In the eighteenth century the term *colick* referred to an aliment of the bowels; judging from a 1760 letter Chauncy suffered frequently from diarrhea and stomach pains.[12] He spent most of the winter of 1742–43 recuperating, tending to his ministerial duties, writing, corresponding, and editing.

At this time some of Chauncy's voluminous correspondence began to appear abroad. Late in 1742 *A Letter from a Gentleman in Boston, To Mr. George Wishart, One of the Ministers of Edinburgh, Concerning the State of Religion in New England* was published in Edinburgh. Chauncy's *New Creature* had recently been republished there, and the university had awarded him an honorary degree; he is almost certainly the "gentleman from Boston."[13] This letter is the first occasion on which Chauncy considers the current *State of Religion* as a whole. Significantly he decides that if one traces the disorders of the times back to their source, one can posit a single event that started it all: the arrival of George Whitefield. With Whitefield came itineracy, with itineracy came censoriousness and violence and discord; in short, when one considers the movement as it has evolved, one can determine the prime mover, and hence the chief villain: George Whitefield. Once Chauncy settled upon this explanation for the turmoil of the Awakening, he refused to budge from it, and it colored his opinion of subsequent events in 1743 and 1744.

Another explanation of the Awakening was on the way, however, which defended the phenomenon as a glorious work of God. Jonathan Edwards had been writing a new faithful narrative, this one entitled *Some Thoughts Concerning the Present Revival of Religion in New-England . . . In Five Parts.*[14] Chauncy knew of Edwards's project,

74

and some time during the winter of 1742 he obtained either the proofs or an advance copy. By March 16, 1743 he had read it through, even though it had not yet been placed on sale. On that day he wrote to his cousin in Durham: "Mr. Edwards' book of 378 pages upon the *good work* is at last come forth: And I believe will do much hurt; and I am the rather inclined to think so, because there are some good things in it. Error is much more likely to be propagated, when it is mixed with truth. This hides its deformity and makes it go down the more easily. I may again trouble myself and the world upon the appearance of this book. I am preparing an antidote, and if the world should see cause to encourage it, it may in time come to light."[15] The next day—a week before Edwards's treatise went on sale—Chauncy published an advertisement (the title page) of his "antidote." He planned to call it *Seasonable Thoughts on the State of Religion in New-England: A Treatise in Five-Parts.*[16] The title and the table of contents are obviously point-by-point parodies of Edwards's title; everyone could see this relationship in the next two issues of the *Boston Weekly News-Letter*, where Chauncy's advertisement appears directly below the announcements of the now-published *Some Thoughts.*[17] Chauncy had been planning a book for some time; now Edwards had given him a title, an outline, a good excuse to put into print the reports he had collected, and a cause which could rally support. He would spend much of his time for the next six months assembling the book that Perry Miller has called his "biggest bomb, a major work in American literature or in the century," *Seasonable Thoughts.*[18]

Part of this task was the gathering of "encouragement" for the book. Chauncy accomplished some of this work at the annual Massachusetts Bay ministers' convention in May. Chauncy sensed that the opinion of the clergy was beginning to turn his way. He wrote to Nathaniel Chauncy: "As I have spoken freely, and printed my sentiments as far as was proper upon the religious state of affairs among us, 'tis a satisfaction to me to think that I was so unanimously chosen by the body of the clergy in this *Province* to preach a convention sermon to them; which I should not have mentioned only, that by this you may argue the thoughts of the ministry of this government about the present work."[19] Chauncy should not have taken that much satisfaction from the honor, for opinion was not so unanimous as he thought. The convention proved to be the scene of one of the harshest battles of the Awakening. The New England minister Thomas Smith records in his *Journal*: "There was a sad division in the Convention of Ministers at Boston. Dr. Chauncey and others in opposition to the late work of God in the land. They obtained a vote against the disorders, &c, thereby expressly owning the work, which puts the ministers on the other side into a great ferment; the people throughout the country are also universally divided, and in the most unhappy temper. The opposition is exceeding virulent and mad."[20] The disunity among ministers which Chauncy had been predicting for three years had arrived, and he was a cause of it.

Leading the ministers on "the other side" was Chauncy's old Boston rival Joshua Gee, who had been instrumental in ousting Samuel Mather. Chauncy and Gee played politician throughout most of the convention, maneuvering forces to block opposition and finally descending to personal attack. It was not a pretty spectacle, and neither man acquitted himself with distinction. Chauncy delivered the keynote sermon. He then gathered forces and pushed through a "Testimony" against "Several Errors in Doctrine, and Disorders in Practice, Which have of late obtained in various Parts of the Land."[21] By now everyone acknowledged that there were disorders; but, as Smith's notation points out, the testimony did not acknowledge that there had likewise been good work done. This completely negative view was certainly not the majority opinion. Therefore Joseph Sewall insisted that a qualifying phrase "and where there is any special Revival of pure Religion in any Parts of our Land, at this Time, we would give unto God all the Glory." The provision passed by a small margin. It did not satisfy Joshua Gee, who objected that it was not an open aknowledgement of the "late remarkable Effects of a gracious Divine Influence in many of our Churches."[22]

After the testimony was published, Gee had further complaints. Beneath them all was the fear that the Awakening would be discredited in Europe: 1) since the convention was simply a gathering of ministers who happened to come to Boston for the annual election of counselors for the General Assembly, not an official synod, such a testimony, especially when presented as from the "Pastors of the Churches in the Province of Massachusetts-Bay in New England . . ." would be misleading to "distant observers," and would give the impression that it was authoritative; 2) only about a third of the Massachusetts Bay pastors were present at this meeting; 3) pastors from outside the province were allowed to vote.[23] Gee, however, was not permitted to voice his objections at the convention. Chauncy very neatly pinned him on the horns of a dilemma and silenced him. Apparently eight years earlier Gee, angry with the convention over its censure proceedings against Samuel Fiske of Salem,[24] had publicly withdrawn from the body and had not thereafter rejoined. When Gee rose at the 1743 convention to object to the *Testimony*, Chauncy raised a point of order with the moderator, Nathanael Eells, challenging Gee and requesting Eells to ask him if he desired to speak as a member. To do so, of course, Gee would have had to recant his earlier stand; without recanting he could not lodge his current objections. Gee was furious: one observer later chided him for "the Ruffle your Passions were unhappily put into" by "the Affront you so highly resented."[25]

Silenced at the convention, Gee took pen in hand and presented his objections in writing (and in print) to Eells. In the letter he openly sneered at Samuel Mather's character and assailed him for sending reports of the Awakening abroad. But he was especially angry with the title page of the *Testimony*. Chauncy had been asked by the convention to prepare the document for the press, and in doing so he had written its title. Gee demanded of Eells, "Whether the *Title-Page* affixed to the *printed Testimony*, is any Part of what was read and voted by that Assembly of Pastors?" And, Gee added, "If it was not, I shall leave the Rev. Doctor—to whom the Care of printing the Testimony was committed, to give the public some good Reasons, why he chose to publish it with such a pompous and delusive title."[26] Chauncy did not relish being called pompous; he particularly resented being termed deceitful. In a terse, dignified letter to the next day's *Boston Evening Post* he informed Gee that the title of the *Testimony* was indeed "Part of what was read and voted"; in fact, it was nearly a word-for-word transcription of the document's first paragraph. To prove his point Chauncy presented the title and the first paragraph in adjoining columns, so that "*you* and the *Public* may be able to come to a certain Determination upon the Matter." His honesty amply established, he demanded an apology, and signed himself "Your injur'd Friend and Servant."[27]

Within three weeks both Benjamin Prescott and John Hancock published open letters to Gee, defending the *Testimony* and reproaching him for his unbecoming loss of temper.[28] Gee wrote a brief, none-too-gracious apology to Chauncy,[29] but decided to answer the others with action. Easily angered but apparently not easily discouraged, he called for all the New England ministers to convene in Boston at the June Harvard commencement, "To consider whether they are not called to give an open conjunct Testimony to an Event so surprizing & gracious, as well as against those Errors in Doctrine and Disorders in Practice, which, thro' the permitted Agency of Satan, have attended it. . . ."[30] He was able to bring together about ninety men, and had solicited twenty absentee attestations from ministers unable to attend. The assembly—much larger than the original convention in May—approved a rival *Testimony* which affirmed that good as well as error was to be found in the revival.[31]

Aside from its testimony against the Awakening, the 1743 convention was confronted with another serious problem: the continuing struggle of Samuel Osborn. Osborn was still pleading his case, this time with a fresh complaint. During the autumn of 1742 he had been a candidate for a ministerial position at Brunswick. He now charged that Benjamin Colman, Thomas Prince, William Cooper, and Joshua Gee had deliberately sabotaged his candidacy by writing to the church in Brunswick, warning the people not to choose him because he was heretical. He lost the position as a result. Osborn was openly anti-itinerant, as well as outspoken in his criticism of the council at Eastham. He suspected that his stand on the Awakening had much to do with the backstage maneuvering of these four powerful, prorevival ministers. As he put it: "Gentlemen, Why would you prevent my Preaching? Is it because I don't yell, and roar, and endeavour to affright weak People? Is it because I don't cry to them to come to Christ, and threaten them with being double damned if they don't come to Christ?"[32] He calculatedly placed Colman in a difficult position by addressing his *Case and Complaint* to him in a letter "to be communicated by him to the Convention, for their Consideration." Unable to receive satisfaction at the meeting, and in order to offset attempts to silence the matter after the convention, he had the letter printed (probably with Chauncy's help) as a pamphlet the week before Gee's second convention convened, and in time for the Harvard commencement.[33] Osborn included in the pamphlet a copy of the 1740 opinion on his case signed by Chauncy, Samuel Mather, and nine other ministers, thus clearly and publicly setting Chauncy in opposition to Gee once again.

With these rival conventions and testimonies, the lines of the New-Light and Old-Light parties were established. Chauncy was the acknowledged Old-Light captain; Joshua Gee emerged during 1743 as his major opponent in Boston. Antagonisms that had been camouflaged for more than a year now became open and public. As the summer wore on, however, it became clear that despite the name-calling, the core of the conflict between the two squabbling parties was the question Jonathan Edwards had asked the year before in New Haven and had rephrased with the spring publication of *Some Thoughts*: Is the phenomenon currently affecting New England a work of God? This was the question underlying the turmoil at the May and July conventions; by September it was the question Chauncy was expected to answer in the magnum opus he was seeing through the press; and it was the central issue dividing Edwards and Chauncy in the Great Debate that signalled the climax of the Great Awakening.

Had their controversy been a formal debate, with the question posed as a resolution, with Edwards seated at the affirmative table, Chauncy speaking for the negative, and the rules of parliamentary procedure at hand, rendering an account of their views would have entailed little more than copying the public record. Edwards and Chauncy did not "debate" in this sense, however, and the account of the proceedings is not simple to produce.

In the first place, the adversaries were not always arguing the same points. Misunderstanding was thus basic to the disagreement, and it affected the arguments of both sides. Second, Chauncy and Edwards battled by exchanging a few tracts and sermons over a period of time. Only one of the tracts was directed specifically at the opponent.

In *Distinguishing Marks* (September 1741) Edwards had asked whether the Awakening was a work of God. In *Some Thoughts* he not only raised the issue, he threw down a challenge to any who opposed the "extraordinary work that has of late been going on in this land,"[34] asking if it were not "strange that in a Christian, orthodox country, and such a land of light as this is, there should be many at a loss whose work this is, whether the work of God or the work of the Devil? Is it not a shame to New England that such a work should be much doubted of here?"[35] Chauncy would not let such an invitation pass unanswered. Much of the controversy in the summer of 1743 was probably a direct result of Edwards's challenge. When Chauncy completed *Seasonable Thoughts* in September,[36] he faced Edwards directly for the first time. For much of the book he is more editor than author. He reiterates the position he had been formulating since 1741 and illustrates it copiously with accounts of disorders from throughout the country. But he recognizes the essential issue: censoriousness, itineracy, lay exhorting, emotional preaching, church quarrels are important, but the core of the dispute is the working of the Spirit of God. "Is it not the great Question of the Day," he asks, "how far, and in what Respects, the Work, going on in the Land, is the Work of GOD?"[37]

In his thoughtful treatises Edwards gives an analytical, affirmative answer, but with his customary precision he carefully qualifies his statement that the Great Awakening is a work of God. In *Distinguishing Marks*, when he says that the work "in general" is of divine origin, he means to distinguish its substance from its accidental effects. He also concedes that many excesses accompany the Awakening, and he discourages them. He emphasizes this point again in *Some Thoughts*. It is a mistake to dismiss the divine origin of the work simply because "the work is attended with a mixture of error, imprudences, darkness and sin; because some persons are carried away with impressions, and are indiscreet, and too censorious with their zeal; and because there are high transports of religious affection; and because of some effects on persons' bodies that we don't understand the reason of. . . ."[38] Edwards is convinced that these disorders do not damage his position. He devotes great effort, both in his New Haven sermon and in *Some Thoughts*, to explain how such irregularities can creep into genuine revival. Edwards summarizes his argument this way: "Thus I think the errors and irregularities that attend this work, may be accounted for, from the consideration of the infirmity and weakness and common corruption of mankind, together with the circumstances of the work, though we should suppose it to be the work of God."[39] By acknowledging and explaining the irregularities from the outset, Edwards steals his opponents' thunder. Merely discounting his adversaries' points, however, is not enough for him; it still remains to establish the "substance" of the movement, which is unaffected by accidental errors, and which is beyond contention.

A fair observer of the recent events in New England, Edwards contends, cannot fail to conclude that "there are some things wherein the main substance of this work consists, a certain effect that is produced, and alteration that is made in the apprehensions, affections, dispositions and behavior of men, in which there is a likeness and agreement everywhere."[40] In specifying what this effect is, Edwards follows the general lines he had set down three years earlier in *Distinguishing Marks*. At that time he had said that Scripture reveals five positive signs by which "we may safely proceed in judging of any operation we find in ourselves, or see in others."[41] If a work (1) convinces people of Christ and leads them to him; (2) works against the interests of Satan; (3) causes a greater regard for Holy Scripture; (4) leads persons to the truth; (5) "operates as a spirit of love to God and man," we can be sure that it is truly the work of the Spirit.[42]

This is what has been happening throughout New England. To take the first sign as an example, Edwards states that "multitudes in New England have lately been brought to a new and great conviction of the truth and certainty of the things of the Gospel; to a firm persuasion that Christ Jesus is the Son of God, and the great and only Saviour of the world; and that the great doctrines of the Gospel touching reconciliation by his blood, and acceptance in his righteousness, and eternal life and salvation through him, are matters of undoubted truth."[43] In *Some Thoughts* Edwards finds similar evidence for the presence of other signs. "From one end of the land to the other" men and women have been rejecting things of the world in favor of a "sober consideration of the things of the eternal world." Especially striking is the increase of "sensibleness and tenderness of conscience," which is reflected in the young (Edwards catalogues the sins they have given up: frolicking, keeping vain company, night walking, mirth and jollity, impure language, lewd songs) and the old (they have forsaken drinking, tavern haunting, profane speaking and extravagance in apparel). The "notoriously vicious," the wealthy, "great beaus and fine ladies," as well as Indians and Negroes—in fact, entire towns have been "transformed into another sort of people," full of respect for the Bible and the Sabbath, friendly to one another, concerned with the question, "What shall I do to be saved?"[44]

But Edwards says the substance of the work consists not only in changed behavior; it also consists in an alteration in man's "affections." On examination it is evident that the substance of the work consists essentially, not incidentally, in this alteration of affections. Traditionally the "fruits of the Spirit" are "the peace of God that passes all understanding," the joy of believing, the light of knowledge and the glory of God in the face of Christ, the love of God residing in the heart. These "affections" are at the heart of any work of true religion, Edwards says. He includes at this point a long and beautiful account of "a person" of his acquaintance, in whom these affections reached extraordinary heights, and whose behavior over a period of years under their influence became remarkably pure and exemplary.[45] He measures the new work favorably against this standard: "The great affections and high transports that others have lately been under, are in general of the same kind with those in the instance that has been given, though not to so high a degree, and many of them, not so pure and unmixed, and so well regulated."[46]

At the core of the Great Awakening is an alteration of affections, apprehensions, dispositions, and behavior of men. Under careful examination this effect fulfills the sure marks of the working of the Spirit, and its fruits as set forth in Scripture. "Those that don't think such things as these to be the fruits of the true Spirit," Edwards argues, "would do well to consider what kind of spirit they are waiting and praying for, and what sort of fruits they expect he should produce when he comes."[47] When all the evidence is considered, when false arguments are rejected, and a just view of the matter attained, Edwards finds only two alternatives possible: "Now this I say, is either a wonderful work of God, or a mighty work of the Devil; and so is either a most happy event, greatly to be admired and rejoiced in, or a most awful calamity. Therefore if what has been said before, be sufficient to determine it to be as to the main, the work of God, then it must be acknowledged to be a very wonderful and glorious work of God."[48]

In his answer to Edwards, Chauncy agrees that God is responsible for the work. But he does not believe that it is especially wonderful or glorious. He views New England as a "Scene of Disorder,"[49] and the disorder generally takes two forms: "enthusiasm" and doctrinal error. Edwards might pass the disorders off as "accidental" to the saving operation of the Spirit; Chauncy argues from the frequency and uniformity of their appearance that they are "natural" results of the operation, not "accidental" effects, and that to call such turmoil the fruit of the Spirit insults the Deity. Rather than a visitation of the Spirit of God, the events of the time re-enact the enthusiasm that threw New England into confusion shortly after the settlement of the colonies. Certainly *God* has visited the turmoil on the land; it is not for us to judge why, but "if he intended it as a *Punishment*," Chauncy comments, "'tis no more than we justly deserve." History shows us that such disorders have plagued sinful churches before. But if it *is* a punishment, Chauncy argues, it is capable "in the Wisdom of GOD, of being over-rul'd to great spiritual Advantage."[50] The Great Awakening for Chauncy finally comes to represent a great opportunity that has been wasted because of errors, enthusiasm, and disorder. Yet all is not lost. The ministers and people of New England can still gain spiritually by overcoming the errors and returning to a true religion:

> Hereby Occasion has been given for great Talk about Religion; and many, by this Means, may have been brought into an Acquaintance with it, who might otherwise never have made any Enquiries about it.—Hereby Occasion has been given for the setting forth some of the great Truths of the Gospel, in a clearer and stronger Light, than might have been expected, if it had not been for such Errors.—Hereby Occasion has been given for many to look more critically into the Ground of their Hope, than they might have done, if it had not been for that Spirit of *rash Judging*, which has been so generally prevalent.—Hereby Occasion has been given for an eminent Display of many Christian Graces, in those who have been reviled, and had all Manner of Evil falsely spoken against them, for Righteousness Sake; and by the frequent Opportunities they have had for the Exercise of these Graces, they may have been more firmly rooted and fixed in them. In a Word, hereby Occasion has been given for a more particular and faithful Application to Multitudes of Persons, by the Ministers of CHRIST, both in *public* and *private*, than otherwise there might have been Opportunity for; which may, in Time, appear in the Fruits of Righteousness.[51]

Chauncy posits two main sources for the errors: itineracy and a preaching style appealing solely to the emotions rather than to the intellect and encouraging "Bodily agitations" as signs of true conviction. The itinerants he treats with his customary disdain. As for the preaching, he devotes great effort to a painstaking analysis of its effects, offering a shrewd psychological description of the techniques and conditioning factors employed. Many of the preachers, he notes, conducted their meetings at night, and aimed their remarks particularly at women and children, deliberately setting in motion the powers of suggestion and imitation. The basic appeal was to fear, but frequently these preachers triggered a spurious kind of religious joy, manifested in "exstasies," laughing and kissing, and rising not from the true joy of knowing Christ, but from the force of what, in our terms, amounts to the power of suggestion. Such preaching encouraged censoriousness and also persuaded people that they were receiving visions, private revelations, and extraordinary missions. Since the Spirit no longer operates in this extraordinary manner, Chauncy states, ministers should encourage men to look for spiritual change within themselves, instead of visions from heaven. Such preaching leads to enthusiasm.[52]

82

As he had done in the past, Chauncy carefully points out in *Seasonable Thoughts* that he opposes neither the preaching of fear nor the work of conviction. "The *divine* SPIRIT often accompanies the *preached* Word," he said, so that sinners are awakened and filled with distress. But the Spirit must not "at Random, be made the Author of all those *Surprises*, operating in *strange Effects* upon the *Body*." These effects may be produced in other ways; in fact, "they have actually been produced, even by the *wild and extravagant Conduct* of some *over-heated* Preachers."[53] The preaching of terror "ought to be [done] in a Way that may enlighten the Mind, as well as alarm the Passions," for there is a difference in this "Business of Conviction" between "those *Fears* that are the *Effect* of *Truth duly imprest upon the Mind*, and those that arise from an *affrightned Imagination*."[54]

The itinerants and their preaching not only encouraged false emotional reactions in New England; they also propagated several doctrinal errors. Chauncy had discussed each one in turn as it appeared during the Awakening; here he had a chance to gather them together and consider them in detail. He concentrates on seven: 1) "that which supposes *Ministers*, if not *converted*, uncapable of being the *Instruments* of *Spiritual Good* to Men's Souls"; 2) Schism and faction as a result of the fear of "unconverted" ministers; 3) Presumptuous dependence on the Spirit, which is reflected in a disrespect for learning, disregard for prayer, distaste for spiritual reading and hearing the Word, and disrespect for Scripture itself; 4) making assurance essential to conversion; 5) "connecting a Knowledge of the *Time* of *Conversion* with the *Thing itself*"; 6) vilifying good works; 7) falling into the antinomian error that adherence to the moral law is unnecessary as evidence of one's conversion.[55]

Following his account of the errors and their causes, Chauncy concludes that, no matter what Edwards might think, the frequency and geographical extent of the "*bad Things* of the present Day" constitute sufficient evidence that they are the natural, not merely accidental, results of their causes.[56] The obligation of New Englanders is manifest: rid the land of the disorder within it.

Clearly Chauncy and Edwards agreed on some basic matters. Chauncy recognized from the start that "there are some good things" in Edwards's view of the Awakening. Both men knew of serious emotional and doctrinal disorders occurring in the colonies, and Edwards had no reason to dispute the essential points of Chauncy's definition of "That *Work of divine Grace*, which is sometimes, called the *New-Creation*; sometimes the *New-Birth*; sometimes the *Spirit's Renovation*; sometimes *Conversion*, or as 'tis otherwise express'd, a being *turned from Darkness to Light, and from the Power of Sin and Satan unto GOD*."[57] But they had quite different ideas of how the Holy

83

Spirit operated in people to bring about this work of divine grace. This key difference forced them into opposing judgments.

Chauncy stated his theory in several works. In *Seasonable Thoughts* he put it this way: "The plain Truth" is that "an *enlightened Mind*, and not *raised Affections*, ought always to be the Guide of those who call themselves Men; and this, in the Affairs of Religion, as well as other Things."[58] And again, "*Reasonable* Beings are not to be guided by *Passion* or *Affection*, though the Object of it should be GOD, and the Things of another World."[59] Chauncy believed that the universe is arranged in an orderly, unbroken, and ascending chain of being. The human system is organized in the same way. Its capacities ascend in rank from the lower bodily faculties (such as nutrition, growth, and reproduction) to the highest faculties of the soul (such as reasoning and willing).

To Chauncy the "faculties" are simply the various powers or abilities of humans—whether bodily powers or those of the soul; they are not separate organs or agents. Humans differ from the beasts and resemble the higher beings in that they perform intellectual activities; it follows that their intellectual activities are nobler than the others. (Yet this is not to say that the bodily powers are unimportant; borrowing from Locke, Chauncy asked, "How many of our ideas are we beholden to our *senses* for? They are indeed the *primary* inlets to the materials of knowledge, the true foundation of all *intellectual* happiness.") In religious experience, the "heart," with its passions, may influence the "head"—the "passions, when suitably mov'd, tend mightly to awaken the *reasonable powers*, and put them upon a lively and vigorous exercise"—or vice versa: humans could be moved to *love* God by *understanding* his beauty and amiability.[60] The danger lies in upsetting the balance either by relying solely on the heart or the head or by allowing the heart to rule the head. Should a conflict develop between the lower and higher powers, the higher powers must govern: the "*enlightened Mind*" guides the "*raised Affections*." For Chauncy a person guided solely by passions acts as less than a person not because the passions are evil per se, but because such a person fails to use the totality of his abilities.

During the time of his controversy with Chauncy, Edwards had not yet developed his ideas on the operation of the Spirit so completely or clearly as he was to do a few years later in *Religious Affections*. Nevertheless we can determine from *Distinguishing Marks* and portions of *Some Thoughts* that he believed the Spirit worked a change in the soul of man by moving the affections to "high acts of love; strong and vigorous exercises of benevolence and complacence; high, exalting, and admiring thoughts of God and his perfections; strong desires after God, etc."[61] Edwards continually insisted that true virtue is based on

84

holy affections. We have seen that he equated the "fruits of the Spirit" with the affections, and that this idea is at the heart of his statement that the Great Awakening substantially proceeds from God. He also used it as a weapon against those who pointed to such excesses as intemperance and zeal. Man's nature is inherently weak; if his emotions are suddenly stirred by God, it is not surprising that he is occasionally overcome. They can be divinely stirred because, Edwards insisted, both affections and inclinations spring from and depend upon sensation, which can be supplied only—and directly—by God.

How could Edwards place the source of the noblest human activity, religion, in a lower faculty, the affections? Because he denied that the affections *are* a lower faculty, for "the affections of the soul are not properly distinguished from the will, as though they were two faculties in the soul."[62] By identifying the affections with the will he raised them to the highest level of the soul's operation. To emphasize the role of affections in true religion is not to denigrate religious experience, but to honor it. His intention to do this is clear from an objection he offered to those who held the traditional view:

> In their philosophy, the affections of the soul are something diverse from the will, and not appertaining to the noblest part of the soul, but the meanest principles that it has, that belong to men as partaking of animal nature, and what he has in common with brute creation, rather than anything whereby he is conformed to angels and pure spirits. And though they acknowledge that there is a good use may be made of the affections in religion, yet they suppose that the substantial part of religion don't consist in them, but that they are rather to be looked upon as something adventitious and accidental in Christianity.[63]

That is the heart of the matter. For Edwards the argument that religious affections are suspect because they rise from a "mean principle" proceeds from a false premise. Also borrowing from Locke, Edwards constructed a counterargument that turns on the identity of the affections and the will.[64] Edwards agreed with Locke that what people know they know from experience. For Locke, "sensation"—our experience of particular sensible objects—and "reflection"—the "notice the mind takes of its own operations"—provide us with "all the *materials* of thinking." These operations furnish the mind with "simple ideas" (ideas such as yellow, white, heat, cold, soft, hard, bitter, sweet, and perception, thinking, doubting, believing, reasoning, knowing, willing). The mind also has the power to combine, compare, or abstract these materials, or simple ideas, thus forming either "complex ideas," "ideas of relations," or "general ideas." Hence we form such ideas as "beauty, gratitude, a man, an army, the universe."[65]

Edwards adapts Locke's concept of the simple idea to explain the kind of knowledge we gain in the spiritual order. The saint learns from experience. When he experiences grace, he has, in Edwards's words "an entirely new kind of perception or sensation"—a spiritual sensation— which could not be produced by "exalting, varying or compounding" the perceptions already existing in the mind, and which is "in its whole nature different from any former kinds of sensation of the mind, as tasting is diverse from any of the other senses." When the saint exercises this new idea in "spiritual and divine things," he perceives something "as entirely diverse from anything that is perceived in them, by natural men, as the sweet taste of honey is diverse from the ideas men get of honey by only looking on it, and feeling of it. So that the spiritual perceptions which a sanctified and spiritual person has, are not only diverse from all that natural men have, after the manner that the ideas and perceptions of the same sense may differ one from another, but rather as the ideas and sensations of different senses do differ."[66]

As the ordinary person needs light to perceive, so the saint needs light for his "spiritual perceptions." Thus the Holy Spirit, as the source of the spiritual idea, casts a "divine and supernatural light"[67] upon the mind of the saint. The Spirit does not provide merely a fleeting illumination; on the contrary, Edwards says, "The Spirit of God is given to the true saints to dwell in them, as his proper lasting abode; and to influence their hearts, as a principle of new nature, or as a divine supernatural spring of life and action."[68] The light shines constantly upon the souls of the saints. Moreover, as an active, indwelling principle, it causes them to shine forth as well. In *Religious Affections* Edwards clarifies this point by using his favorite image of emanation and re-emanation. The soul of the saint, he says,

> . . . receives light from the Sun of Righteousness, in such a manner, that its nature is changed, and it becomes properly a luminous thing: not only does the sun shine in the saints, but they also become little suns, partaking of the nature of the fountain of their light. In this respect, the manner of their derivation of light, is like that of the lamps in the tabernacle, rather than that of a reflecting glass; which though they were lit up by fire from heaven, yet thereby became, themselves burning shining things. The saints don't only drink of the water of life, that flows from the original fountain; but this water becomes a fountain of water in them, springing up there, and flowing out of them; cf. John 4:14 and ch. 7:38-39. Grace is compared to a seed implanted, that not only is in the ground, but has hold of it, has root there, and grows there, and is an abiding principle of life and nature there.[69]

Here Edwards uses three traditional metaphors for the operation of the Spirit—the shining of light, the flowing of water, and the implanting and growth of a seed—to indicate analogically an epistemological point. This new spiritual sense is "not a new faculty of understanding, but it is a new foundation laid in the nature of the soul, for a new kind of exercises of the same faculty of understanding." It enables the saint to exercise his powers in a new way. "So that new holy disposition of heart that attends this new sense, is not a new faculty of will, but a foundation laid in the nature of the soul, for a new kind of exercises of the same faculty of will."[70]

It follows from Edwards's argument, then, that only those affections (those "vigorous and sensible exercises of the inclination and will of the soul") arising from the new simple idea of grace are "holy" or "spiritual." Affections arising from impressions on the imagination, bodily sensations, merely human teaching, or any other source are vain. The chief holy affection, and the "fountain" of all the others, is love of God. From a "vigorous, affectionate, and fervent love to God," Edwards insists, "will necessarily arise other religious affections: hence will arise an intense hatred and abhorrence of sin, fear of sin, and a dread of God's displeasure, gratitude to God for his goodness, complacence and joy in God when God is graciously and sensibly present, and grief when he is absent, and a joyful hope when a future enjoyment of God is expected, and fervent zeal for the glory of God. And in like manner, from a fervent love to men, will arise all other virtuous affections towards men."[71]

To sum up, if the Spirit casts the divine and supernatural light upon a person, providing the new spiritual perception and abiding as a new principle of activity, then spiritual and gracious affections, based upon love for God, will attend this new idea. Edwards can hereby conclude that true religion consists not merely in good behavior, in pious practices, or even in intellectual assent to doctrine, but instead in "holy affections." One might understand divine truths passively as a matter of mere speculation. But true religion requires more. The emotions, or affections, of the truly converted person must come into play: he *loves* truths and *desires* God; in short, unless he "relishes and feels" his experience is counterfeit. True religion, properly understood, is a religion of the heart.

Edwards set up a clear-cut challenge to Chauncy's philosophy in *Some Thoughts*. How did Chauncy react to it? He knew that Edwards was proposing a different philosophy, and the challenge was not lost on him. But when he came to discuss Edwards's analysis of the affections, he skipped over the theory with this interesting comment: Edwards "himself, under this very Head, made use of more *Philosophy* (and in a Manner not altogether exceptionable, as we may see afterwards, if I can find Room), than anyone that I know of, who has wrote upon the Times."[72] Apparently he ran out of room, except for this parting shot at the end of the book: "There is the Religion of the *Understanding* and *Judgment*, and *Will*, as well as of the *Affections*; and if little Account is made of the *former*, while great Stress is laid upon the *latter*, it can't be but People should run into Disorders."[73]

87

Disorder, not Jonathan Edwards or Edwards's psychology, was the main target of Chauncy's criticism of the Great Awakening.[74] He would probably have taken more satisfaction in squelching James Davenport and Joshua Gee than in distinguishing the will from the affections. To do so would have necessitated rethinking his own psychology in light of Edwards's proposals; with the printer calling for copy and the Awakening in need of an antidote, it is disappointing but not surprising that Chauncy decided to steer away from a theoretical puzzle until he found room to handle it.

In November 1743, when *Seasonable Thoughts* had become a best seller, Chauncy wrote to Nathaniel Chauncy: "Some, I understand, are for burning not only the book I lately put out, but me also, had they the power in their hands. But this, I am thankful, they have not; and hope the time will never come when it shall be dangerous for men freely to write their thots upon the affairs of religion."[75] Chauncy's understatement does not conceal his delight with the book's reception. The thick volume that had cost him so much was an enormous success. Not everyone liked it, but everyone, friend and antagonist alike, was reading it. Even the famous Isaac Watts of London wrote him "a very long answer."[76] Such minor rivals as Joshua Gee were merely pesky now; the Chauncy-Edwards controversy had been a joust of giants. By the end of the year the issue was no longer in doubt. "Edwards," Perry Miller observes, "was beaten, an awesome but discredited figure. . . . Chauncy was the great man. . . . To judge by appearances, Edwards had been overwhelmed by a barrage of highly *Seasonable Thoughts*."[77]

Chauncy, however, was not satisfied that New England's ills were cured. Just as the Awakening seemed to wane, word arrived that Whitefield was returning from England for another visit. For over a year Chauncy had been convinced that the Grand Itinerant was the prime cause of New England's disorders; he had said so explicitly in *Seasonable Thoughts*. Now, with the antidote beginning to take effect, Whitefield was to return bearing more poison. Chauncy was not sure the patient would survive. "I can't but think the Churches in this land are in a very dangerous state," he told his cousin Nathaniel, "and if God dont mercifully interpose they will many of them be broke to pieces. I dread the thot of Whitefield's coming again. If he should, every man's hand would be not only against his brother, but his minister, and I'm ready to think it would give the finishing stroke to our religious constitution.—But I hope God means better things for us."[78]

During the ensuing year Chauncy tried on the one hand to discourage churches from accepting Whitefield, and on the other to reestablish solid church government in New England. At the time of *Seasonable Thoughts* he believed that to stop the itinerants' emphasis on terror would stop the disorders; if order reigned, peace would follow.

88

But the Great Awakening in New England, as C. C. Goen observes, "brought not peace but a sword. . . . Out of the complex of issues that led to open rupture came almost one hundred separatist churches, marking a permanent shattering of the Congregational establishment in New England."[79] Chauncy could not prevent Whitefield's visit, but the "ecclesiastical fragmentation"[80] would have taken place even if he had stayed away; New-Lights withdrew for many more reasons than could be traced to itineracy or censoriousness. After the turmoil of the Awakening, the New England Way could never be the same again.

By the autumn of 1744 Chauncy admitted this sad fact. "We have had a long and sore tryal," he wrote to his cousin, "and it's like to be continued whether Mr. Whitfield comes or stays. There is scarce a week passes but some or other of our churches are sent for to sit in Council; and so deep rooted are the alienation of many people and ministers, that I fear they will not get rid of them till the next generation."[81] Known to history as the theological liberal of the century, Chauncy faced ecclesiological issues as a staunch conservative in the tradition of Cotton Mather.

By the end of 1743 some of the "disorders" did appear to be diminishing, at least among the people if not among the ministers. In November Chauncy observed that "the Spirit of crying out &c seems to be subsiding."[82] He must have also felt a certain satisfaction—and hope—when Davenport, following the bonfire at New London, seemed to come to his senses and published a humble *Confession and Retractions*, admitting his "misguided zeal."[83] Near the end of May 1744 Chauncy believed the worst had passed. His own stock was rising; he had been asked again to preach the convention sermon. In this address he was confident enough to call the Awakening the "late Day of Trial," and the "late Times in this Land."[84] He felt that it was important at this point to restore equilibrium among the clergy, with the hope of avoiding future turmoil; therefore his two major efforts of 1744, *Ministers Cautioned* (the convention sermon) and *Ministers Exhorted* (an installation sermon in November),[85] were devoted to a discussion of the nature and role of the ministry.

Chauncy's text at the convention was a clause in the epistle to Titus: "Let no man despise thee."[86] Arguing that there has always been a disposition in people to despise Christ's ministers, and that sometimes ministers themselves are prone to this attitude, Chauncy asserts that, although everyone should try to overcome this disposition, ministers are obliged never to *deserve* such contempt; and that therefore they must be exemplary in learning, holiness, charity, and the performance of their duties. The criteria he had outlined three years before in *The Gifts of the Spirit* remain valid, but he now offers a new suggestion for itinerants:

And are there not vast Numbers, in the neighbouring Governments of VIRGINIA and NORTH-CAROLINA (not to say any Thing of the Natives) who live almost in heathenish Darkness? And would it not discover as much Love to Souls, and as disinterested Zeal to serve the Redeemer's Kingdom, for Ministers to travel up and down, preaching the Gospel to these People, as to go about from Place to Place, where the Gospel is preached every Sabbath-Day, and by Persons call'd to the Work, qualified for it, and fixed in it? *There* is Room for *itinerating*: And the more abundant any are in it, the greater will be their Glory: Nor will any one be dispos'd to withhold from them the Praise that is their just Due.[87]

The Grand Itinerant, however, headed straight for New England. True to the rumors, Whitefield arrived at York on October 26, 1744, seriously ill after a difficult and taxing voyage. Chauncy did little to speed his recovery. Two weeks after Whitefield's arrival the Old Brick pastor traveled to Plymouth for the installation of Thomas Frink as pastor of the Third Church there. In the course of his sermon he delivered a truly savage attack on Whitefield, sternly warning New England to beware lest the late disorders begin again. The installation was an apt opportunity for a "word in season," and Chauncy seized the occasion. The Third Church owed its existence to the recent New-Light/Old-Light clash. It had been organized in May 1744 by citizens who had broken from the First Church because they disliked the evangelistic practices there. Pastor of the First Church was Nathaniel Leonard (A.B., Harvard, 1719), whom Chauncy had known at college and who employed the emotional technique. During the early days of the revival Leonard had entertained Whitefield and such disciples as Tennent and the volatile Andrew Croswell. In Frink the new Third Church had chosen another of Chauncy's Harvard friends (class of 1722). The new pastor had had a checkered career as minister in Rutland and was known for his high seriousness and high temper. Frink had left Rutland because his people there wanted a more impassioned preacher; he had come to Plymouth to counter a man whom some considered patently too passionate.[88] By choosing Frink as pastor and inviting Chauncy to preach the installation sermon, the organizers left no doubt about their position on the Awakening.

Chauncy spoke strongly about Whitefield, reiterating his charges that the troubles of recent days had their source in his work and admonishing the people to forbid him their pulpits should he come their way again. This tirade comes in the "application," at the end of the sermon.[89] Though seasonable, it is only casually related to the main thrust of the address, which restates Chauncy's ideas of the ministry and examines the doctrinal points which the Awakening had caused him to consider. The people especially remembered the strictures against Whitefield, however, and when the sermon appeared in print

90

all New England could see that Doctor Chauncy was busy fortifying the defenses he had erected in *Seasonable Thoughts.*

In January Whitefield came to Boston. As luck would have it, he met Chauncy in the street. William Sumner's nineteenth-century account of this encounter is one of those anecdotes that make history and legend seem indistinguishable:

> Soon after Whitefield landed in Boston, on his second visit to this country, he and Dr. Chauncy met in the street, and, touching their hats with courteous dignity, bowed each to the other. "So you have returned, Dr. Whitefield, have you?" He replied, "Yes, Reverend Sir, in the service of the Lord." "I am sorry to hear it," said Chauncy. "So is the Devil!" was the answer given, as the two divines, stepping aside at a distance from each other, touched their hats and passed on.[90]

In print, however, the two were less laconic. Whitefield read *Seasonable Thoughts* and was displeased. Naturally he disliked the section labeling him the "*Occasion* of those unhappy *alienations, Contentions, and Confusions,* which have been so hurtful to Religion."[91] He had not been in Boston for very long before he replied to the charges in a pamphlet addressed to Chauncy.[92] Chauncy responded in kind with a letter "vindicating certain Passages" Whitefield "has excepted against," and "shewing that he has neither sufficiently *defended himself,* nor retracted his *past Misconduct.*"[93]

Chauncy's opening shot indicates very well the tone and intent of his pamphlet, which relentlessly refutes each point of Whitefield's defense:

> You must have been sensible, *Sir,* upon the most cursory reading of my *Book,* that I considered you as the *true Source* of several of the *Disorders* I complain of as generally prevalent in the Land. A heavy Charge this! I am sure, it very nearly touch'd your Character. And yet, how little have you said to remove away the Grounds of it? I could wish, from the Bottom of my Heart, you had been more thorough in *vindicating,* or *censuring* your self. 'Tis a thousand Pities, as you so earnestly desire 'the *Prosperity* of the *Ministers* and *Churches* of *New England,*' you did not more effectually *qualify* your self to be an Instrument in promoting it, either by making it evident to *them,* and all the World, that you have not been, in a *faulty* Sense, the *Occasion* of those unhappy *Alienations, Contentions* and *Confusions,* which have been so hurtful to Religion; or otherwise, by *frankly confessing your Faults,* and *taking all the Blame to your Self.*[94]

Chauncy actually expected Whitefield to follow Davenport's lead: "And it may be, you will, sooner or later, see your Mistake, after the example of Mr. *Davenport,* a Gentleman highly celebrated in one of your *Journals.*"[95] It is clear from this letter that Chauncy formed his attitude toward Whitefield more by reading the *Journals* and other writings, and by observing his followers, than from the evangelist's brief stay in Boston four years earlier. Chauncy must have read with some care everything Whitefield wrote "on the times," for he delighted in citing numerous contradictory texts as evidence of Whitefield's confusion. The letter is a tongue-lashing in print, at times plain, at times savagely ironic, always angry.

The discrepancy between Chauncy's avowed stand in favor of charity and his animosity toward Whitefield was not lost on the other Boston ministers. On January 30, 1745 Thomas Prince, once Chauncy's close friend, sent this note to Chauncy's house:

Rev. Sr

I desire to know [?] you judge there is any need of my asking your consent to my inviting a minister to preach my Lecture at the O. B. [Old Brick] In answering which you will oblige.

Jan. 30. 1744-5

Your humb. Servt.
T.P.

It is hard to believe that Prince actually expected Chauncy to acquiesce to such a request; at any rate, he could not have picked a less likely moment to ask the favor. The note arrived as Chauncy was busy writing his reply to Whitefield condemning his itineracy; he was not at all receptive to inviting Whitefield to his church. He dashed off a note to Prince in reply:

To the Rev. Mr. Thomas Prince.
Rev. Sir.

In answer to your question, I would ask you another, viz, whether you would express a suitable regard to me, and some others who statedly attend the *Thursday-lecture*, and are united with you in carrying it on, to ask a gentleman to preach it, whose conduct has been such (in our apprehentions) that, if he preaches, you know we cannot be present, but must be obliged to tarry at home?

Prince sent the messenger back to Summer Street with this tart—and quite incisive—rejoiner:

Rev. Sr

I perceive the purport of your letter is, that if I got Mr. Wh. [Whitefield] to preach, that you and some others are of such a separating spirit that you will not attend the public Lecture: which I am sorry to see. In such a season as this should you not rather set a contrary example while you are publickly condemning such a spirit in others? Mr. Wh. will hear you, but you will not hear him. Pray who appears most for separation or union? Methinks you should be glad of an occasion to show as good a spirit as he.[96]

The two clergymen continued to trade insults until Whitefield left Boston in March without having given Chauncy satisfaction by retracting his past misconduct.[97]

92

These were only minor skirmishes, however. By 1745 the Awakening was feeble and New Englanders were turning their attention in another direction. In March 1744 King George's War had been declared.[98] Before 1745 was out, Boston began preparing for an expedition against the French fortress at Louisbourg—an audacious expedition undertaken by the colonies themselves under the direction of Governor Shirley. Volunteers were being enlisted in New England; one of them, just prior to sailing, went to hear Chauncy preach at the Old Brick.[99] Like all New Englanders Chauncy was excited about the prospect of a provincial army's attempting such a feat, and like all New England ministers he considered it something of a holy war, directed against the ominous threat of Catholicism to the north. But he had another, more personal reason for directing his thoughts to Louisbourg in 1745: Shirley had chosen to command the expedition General William Pepperrell, who was Chauncy's brother-in-law.[100]

CHAPTER SEVEN

After the Great Awakening

Between 1745 and 1760 Chauncy's life and ideas changed significantly, although not so dramatically and suddenly as in the earlier years of his ministry. He was forty years old in 1745; his children were growing up; his community was expanding and developing rapidly; the colonies were being called upon to participate in a series of wars. Ten years later he was a grandfather and something of a senior statesman among New England clergy. By then he was also a heretic in doctrine, while he remained a Puritan in temperament.

During the last years of the 1740s Chauncy was preoccupied with regaining his health and with following the course of King George's War. In both endeavors he acted like a military commander who characteristically considers his experiences in terms of problems to be solved. His health had been poor since his inspection tour of the Great Awakening. Because medicines did not seem to help, he decided to regain his health by a program of travel and "resolute severity as to regimen."[1] During the next several years, therefore, he undertook a "great number of journeys of seven, eight, nine and ten hundred miles,"[2] visiting such friends as Edward Holyoke in Lexington,[3] John Taylor in Milton,[4] and Ebenezer Bridge in Chelmsford.[5] He was even found "reading" in "the churches of North Carolina."[6] This seems rather an arduous way to recuperate, but Chauncy believed that his program worked: because of it, he said, "I so far recovered my health as to be able to pursue my studies again; though never since with that constancy and long attention I could do before."[7]

94

It may be that his program of journeys helped him regain his strength, but one suspects that his "resolute severity as to regimen" had at least as much to do with it. Although he believed unshakably that Providence would assist him if he acted aright, he also felt obliged to contribute the full measure of his own capacities to any task he attempted. Trust in the wise governance of God was the cornerstone of Chauncy's piety—in times of deep trouble he consoled himself with the phrase, *God reigns*[8]—but he keenly understood the dangers of presumption. Duty obliged him to use his talents fully and wisely; knowing human weaknesses, Chauncy decided that the only way he could fulfill his duty was by cultivating will power and rigorous discipline.

Central to his program of discipline were "improvement of time" and self-denial. When, in 1768, he called Cotton Mather "the greatest redeemer of time I ever knew," and said that Mather "lost as little of it as anyone could do in his situation,"[9] he was offering high praise indeed; for, Chauncy continued, had Mather only possessed powers of judging and reasoning to equal this ability, he would have ranked among the three greatest men in the history of New England. These were also qualities he particularly esteemed in President Chauncy.[10] Joshua Gee, on the other hand, his Boston adversary during the Awakening, he recalled as a man of great powers, but his "foible was a strange indolence of temper. He preferred talking with his friends to everything else."[11] Now no one liked chatting with friends better than Chauncy. An old friend, Bezaleel Howard, remembered his conversation as "pleasant, social and very instructive."[12] His lively good spirits once delighted John Adams at a dinner party.[13] And the diaries of his acquaintances are dotted with references to sociable evenings spent with Dr. Chauncy. But he believed that there was a proper time for such business, and he simply could not fathom why a man might prefer it to "everything else." He planned his own time methodically. "At twelve o'clock," Howard once recalled, "he took one pinch of snuff, and only one in twenty-four hours. At one o'clock, he dined on one dish of plain wholesome food, and after dinner took one glass of wine, and one pipe of tobacco, and only one in twenty-four hours." Chauncy told Adams that he never read or studied after eight o'clock. He was "equally methodical," said Howard, "in his exercise, which consisted chiefly or wholly in walking." He believed that "if he had not lived as regularly as the sun moves in the Heavens, he should long ago have mouldered to dust, so as not to be distinguished from common Earth."[14]

Such methodical temperance reflects Chauncy's concern for developing self-control. He once remarked that he knew from experience that a man, by the sheer force of his will, could withstand the grinding pain of a toothache, headache, rheumatism, or gout for an entire night without whimpering.[15] He believed that these qualities must be developed by practice, and took inconvenience as an opportunity to exercise his will. The neurotic potential here is of course enormous, especially since Chauncy lacked Benjamin Franklin's talent for smiling at his own efforts to bring absolute order to his life, but Chauncy's efforts at self-discipline seem not to have interfered overmuch with his ability to function productively.

He probably wished he had been a general. His pride in New England made him chauvinistic to a fault. He had enjoyed mapping out his campaigns against Addington Davenport and his opponents during the Awakening. Chauncy was certainly never bashful about telling town militiamen and colonial generals how to run their business.[16] During his brother-in-law's command of the 1745 expedition against Louisbourg and Cape Breton Island he had a wonderful opportunity to play unofficial counselor.

He anxiously followed the news of the battle. On June 4, 1745, while Pepperrell was busy mounting a siege on Louisbourg, Chauncy decided to obtain some first-hand information and wrote to his brother-in-law. After a word of encouragement comparing Pepperrell to Joshua, Chauncy asked for a report: "Your time and thots I am sensible are much employed about greater things, but if you could spare a few moments to write me how affairs stand with you, it would be agreable to me."[17] A month later, when word came that the Americans had captured the town, Chauncy—along with all Boston—was positively ecstatic. He dashed off exuberant congratulations to Pepperrell. Of course, the credit must go to God, but the general also deserved gratitude: "As God has made you an instrument of so much service to your country, at the hazard of your life, and the expense of great labor and fatigue, your name is deservedly and universally spoken of with respect, and I doubt not will be handed down with honor to the latest posterity." Everyone joined the celebration. "We had last night the finest illumination I ever beheld with my eyes, I believe there was not a house in the town, in no bye lane or ally, but joy might be seen through its windows."[18]

Chauncy preached the Thanksgiving sermon a few days later, on July 18. Entitled *Marvellous Things done by the right Hand and holy Arm of God,*[19] it is a paean to Providence and a hearty vote of thanks to Pepperrell and the other leaders. Modern scholars, while praising the acumen of Pepperrell and others, attribute much of the expedition's success to "American luck."[20] Chauncy also recognized this "Concurrence of favourable Circumstances" but assigned the credit to a "truly wonderful . . . Train of Providences." In fact, he said, "I scarce know of a Conquest, since the Days of *Joshua* and the *Judges*, wherein the Finger of God is more visible."[21] Not that God interposed miraculously, as at Jericho; but even in "the *ordinary* Course of Providence," God sometimes does "*marvelous Things*," "either, by a secret and invisible Influence, disposing and ranging second Causes in such a Manner as to operate beyond all humane Expectation; or by interposing such a Coincidence of Events, as could not have been foreseen; and when bro't to pass, draw the Attention of wise Observers, and force from them an Acknowledgement, that God's Throne is in the Heavens, and his Kingdom ruleth over all."[22] Louisbourg was the perfect example, and Chauncy, who knew the entire operation thoroughly, discussed in turn each providential event from the initial conception of the project to the conquest.[23]

He speedily had *Marvellous Things* printed, and dispatched it to Pepperrell, along with a letter, on July 27.[24] The letter is less enthusiastic than the sermon. Since the initial flush of victory Bostonians had heard rumors that Commodore Warren, having assisted Pepperrell with three British ships, was claiming credit for the conquest.[25] This would never do, Chauncy sternly informed the general:

> It is indeed *highly resented by every New-England man in Boston, that Mr. Warren should pretend to assume the government at Louisbourg*, and he has lost a great deal of credit by his conduct in this affair. And some things are said to your disadvantage for not exerting yourself for the honor of New-England upon this occasion. How far you did exert yourself we do not indeed know; but your best friends wish you had insisted upon the pre-eminence due to you and the troops under your command, so as even to have given up the capitulation if it had not been conceded to. *If the High-Admiral of England had been there he would not have had the least right to command any where but in his own ships.*[26]

Finally Chauncy advised, if you are not installed as commander, "quit the place and come home."[27]

The rumors were ill-founded. As Byron Fairchild explains:

> The situation was aggravated by a certain amount of confusion attending the surrender of the city. Being not too well versed in the minutiae of military procedure, William [Pepperrell] demanded the keys to the city and proposed to march in before the capitulation was fully and properly ratified. Warren, to whom the French governor protested, pointed out to William the irregularity of such a course and mentioned his fear that William's haste arose from "a kind of jealousy." The imputation was, however, merely a cat's-paw rippling over Warren's mind; his chief concern was to have the proprieties of the occasion observed religiously. However, back in New England there were a number of no doubt well-intentioned busy bodies . . . who kept advising William not to let himself be pushed into the background by Warren. Their fears, founded partly on such reports as Captain Waldron's, magnified the surrender incident many times.[28]

Chauncy must be numbered among these "well-intentioned busy

97

bodies," even if he would not have considered himself one. Although chauvinistic, as a relative he did have a personal interest in Pepperrell's success and reputation. Naturally, then, he was delighted when King George "commissioned William Pepperrell colonel in command of a regiment in the regular army and conferred upon him a baronetcy."[29] Apparently New England and its general were not to be slighted in England after all.

Chauncy now addressed his letters with a flourish to "Sir William Pepperrell, Baronet, Lieutenant General of the New-England Forces at Cape Breton,"[30] but he tempered his congratulations on these new honors with this pastorlike admonition: "I hope you will make it your endeavour to do all the service you can and are furnisht with ability and advantage to do by your superiour station in life. God will expect more of you in proportion to what he gives you, and I hope you will wisely and faithfully improve every talent he puts into your hands."[31]

In January Chauncy still insisted that the government "at home" did not appreciate the "vast importance of the acquisition that has been made to the British dominion" and the "bravery of our New-England men in obtaining it."[32] Otherwise, he asked Pepperrell in a letter,[33] why did they send over so many British officers to staff the new regiments? "'Tis a most scandalous contempt of our brave officers," especially when one considers that the British officers are "but boyes, raw young persons scarce fit to be taken from school." There was however another reason besides pride in New England for Chauncy's discontent: "This management from home fills me with fear, as to the repayment of the charge we have been set."[34] Chauncy was to strike this note frequently in future years, especially during the episcopacy controversy and the Revolution. When he said that he was filled with fear at the prospect of "management from home," he spoke his mind accurately.

During the winter of 1745–46 Shirley urged a further expedition to conquer Canada. Pepperrell was in poor health; as plans unfolded, his new unit, the Fifty-first Regiment of Foot, was ordered to remain at Louisbourg as the garrison force.[35] This regiment was gathering few recruits—New Englanders were reluctant to join a royal regiment, and Shirley was also recruiting—but there was no problem finding candidates for commissions. In fact a scramble for various posts of preferment ensued, and Pepperrell was swamped with requests for positions for sons, sons-in-law, nephews, and other relatives of prominent New Englanders. On two occasions Chauncy entered into these negotiations, once appealing to Pepperrell the wealthy merchant, the other time to Pepperrell the commander of a newly formed regiment.

In August 1745 he wrote on behalf of Mr. Shute Shrimpton, the husband of his sister-in-law Bethiah Willoughby. "I have heard he intends to settle at Louisbourg, if he can meet with encouragement,"

Chauncy told Pepperrell, and "I am the rather inclined to be sollici-
tous in beseeching your favourable regards to him as he has a growing
family and is under difficulties (as you may have heard) by means of
disappointments and losses in his business."[36] In October 1745
Chauncy was called again to solicit Pepperrell's generosity, this time
on behalf of Governor Belcher's son-in-law, Byfield Lyde. Lyde was
the grandson of that dear friend of Chauncy's youth, Judge Nathanael
Byfield, and Chauncy had known Lyde at college. He thought little of
the man; he told Pepperrell, "What it is in particular he desires I dont
know; but I suppose any office that will bring in the cash will be agreable to him." Chauncy apologized for writing: "I told him if you had
any places to dispose of those who ventured their lives in the expedition and were upon the spot were most likely to be preferred. But he
insisted upon my writing to you, which I have accordingly done, and
should be glad if he might, consistent with justice to other persons,
be gratified in his desires."[37] In February 1746 Chauncy wrote again
on Lyde's behalf, giving Pepperrell an "out": Governor Shirley had
promised Lyde the first captain's vacancy in his regiment if Pepperrell would do the same.[38] Reading between the lines, one can see that
Chauncy was asking Pepperrell for a pro forma nod in Lyde's direction so that his candidacy with Shirley might be advanced.

Without playing any further important role in King George's War,
Chauncy kept his eye on the military situation until hostilities finally ceased. Like many Americans he was probably insulted and angry
when Louisbourg was returned to the French in accordance with the
peace treaty—especially since he had been trying all along to convince
Great Britain of its worth. Perhaps he suspected that getting it back
the next time would not be so easy.

During the war Chauncy's son, Charles, was a student at Harvard.
The young man had been brought up in the strict old way. Chauncy's
nephew, William Sumner, who as a boy frequently visited the Chauncy
family, provides a rare glimpse into the Doctor's child-rearing methods.
In phrases similar to those Benjamin Franklin used about his father,
Sumner remarks that Chauncy "never lost a moment in imparting instruction, but took every occasion to convey some useful lesson to
those about him, especially children." On one occasion William and
the other children visited him in his study:

> The doctor took some raisins in his hand, and showing them to the children,
> said, "Now, children, I am going to teach you a lesson of *self-denial*; I will
> throw these raisins upon the floor, and you must not touch them until I
> give you leave." He then scattered them upon the floor, and we all stood
> around looking wistfully at the forbidden fruit and sorely tempted to taste,
> until the doctor, having made us wait sufficiently long to test the truth of
> his lesson, told us to "*scrabble for them*," which we did with earnestness.[39]

99

Stern as this description seems, the incident was not merely capricious teasing. Whatever the event might tell us about his subconscious, Chauncy was—again—following a program that he believed was based on scriptural and philosophical grounds. In his 1745 sermon on the death of Cornelius Thayer, a deacon of the First Church, he set forth his ideas on family government. The guiding principles should be those of Joshua—"As for me and my House, we will serve the Lord"—and the Biblical Cornelius—"a devout Man, and one that feared God with all his house." *Family-Religion*, therefore, must be maintained, "especially that the *Children*" be "well-instructed and governed." Chauncy continued:

> Their *good* or *evil* Behaviour, when they are grown up, and gone forth into the world, will very much depend upon the Care that has been taken of them, while *Children* in the Family. If they have been early taught the Principles of Virtue; if their Minds have been betimes impressed with the Fear of GOD; if, from their first coming to a Capacity of *moral* Conduct, they have been kept under Restraints from Sin; if they have, all along as they grew up, had a good Example set before them, there will be a happy Prospect of their rising up a Generation to seek and Serve the Lord. These are the Children that are the Hopes of a Country, and of whom it may be expected that they will be Blessings in the World.[40]

This stern program did not turn the Chauncy children into lock-stepping automatons. Not long after the doctor preached his sermon, his son, Charles Jr., was demoted six places in the Harvard class "for keeping a dozen false Keys and persisting in lying about Them." During his Harvard days young Charles also drew fines for "riotously breaking into a study in the night," and for "hollowing" in a "contemptuous Manner." One might guess that occasionally he failed to imitate his father's temperance. As his father had done before him, however, Charles survived the demotion; upon presenting a "humble Confession" he was reinstated just prior to graduation.[41] The extent of Dr. Chauncy's influence in obtaining this apology remains unknown.

Young Charles graduated in 1748, the year the war ended. Although he was "strongly inclined" toward the ministry, his health was too weak; hence Chauncy took advantage of Pepperrell's return and sent Charles to Maine to take up a mercantile career with his uncle.[42] The next year Sir William sailed to England for an extended visit, leaving the business in the care of Andrew Pepperrell, his son, under whose tutelage the junior Chauncy worked until Andrew's sudden death in March 1751. Young Charles then assumed most of the responsibility for the Pepperrell shipping concern.[43] If he could not follow his father into the ministry, importing proved an excellent second choice. He had the Chauncy industry and intelligence, and he soon set up a successful company of his own.

The merchant's had always been an honorable station in New England (especially if one were a country squire, like Pepperrell), but at mid-century it became increasingly attractive. Boston had "forty wharves, more than a dozen shipyards and six ropewalks";[44] with the religious excitement of the Awakening substantially abated and the war over, New England began to prosper in a growing economy. The man of commerce in the late 1740s thus found himself able to live more comfortably than ever before. The man of the cloth, however, faced two serious social problems during this time: first, to maintain his own standard of living; second, to combat the widespread secular materialism and religious laxity accompanying the booming prosperity.

Chauncy and Foxcroft had struggled with the first problem for many years, haggling for small salary increases and making do with whatever the congregation could provide. But by 1747 Foxcroft had a dozen children, and Chauncy—despite assistance from Elizabeth's estate—also found it hard to keep pace with rising costs. Most ministers felt the pinch; some even took their plight to the press. The ministers of the Old Brick, although more discreet, finally grew just as impatient as the others. On February 2, 1747 they addressed a joint letter to the First Church, stating in blunt terms that some drastic measures to alleviate their situation were required.[45]

A good part of the problem was the uncertain state of the currency. Since businessmen found it hard to get money because the colonies had no banks, and hence no effective machinery for currency clearance and control of credit, government notes were issued. These did not prove successful. As two recent students of colonial economy observe, "New England merchants thought of paper money as an anathema. . . . They had seen their government time after time clutter the market with promises which soon became as worthless as the paper on which they were printed. As money depreciated, prices fluctuated wildly and solid property values melted as snow under a warm spring sun." Financial difficulties multiplied, of course, during wartime. During King George's War, for instance, "provincial paper was exchanged for sterling at discounts of ten or eleven to one."[46]

For some time Massachusetts ministers had used the annual election sermons to prick the government about the hardships connected with an unstable currency.[47] But until May 27, 1747, when Chauncy accepted the coveted invitation to deliver the annual election sermon, no one had spoken so openly and sternly to the governor and legislators about the problem. *Civil Magistrates Must be Just, Ruling in the Fear of God*,[48] thundered Chauncy's title, and if the assembled civil magistrates wanted to fulfill their obligations to justice, they had better "pitch upon some *certain standard*, to which the *current medium* may be so related, as that it's true value, at different times, may be

101

nearly ascertained: And if this was established as the rule in all *public payments*, as well as *private contracts* and bargains, it would be no other than what is right."[49] Current conditions penalize people who must rely on a fixed income. "And will you," Chauncy scolded, "our honored rulers, by any positive acts, or faulty neglects, suffer yourselves to be instrumental in the continuance of such a state of things? God forbid!" Peering down at the elite of the province, he declared:

> You are, my fathers, accountable to that God, whose throne is in the heavens, in common with other men. And his eyes behold your conduct in your publick capacity; and he sees and observes it, not merely as a spectator, but an almighty and righteous judge; one who enters all upon record, in order to a reckoning day. And a day is coming, it lingers not, when you shall all stand upon a level with the meanest subjects, before the tremendous bar of the righteous judge of all the earth, and be called upon to render an account, not only of your private life, but of your whole management, as intrusted with the concerns of this people.[50]

According to custom the election sermon was always printed at government expense, but when a motion was introduced in the general court to send Chauncy a letter of thanks and request a copy of the sermon for the press, several angry members put the matter up for debate. When one of Chauncy's friends rushed to tell him about the court's hesitation, he snapped in Johnsonian fashion, "It shall be printed, whether the General Court print it or not. And do you, sir, say from me, that, if I wanted to initiate and instruct a person into all kinds of iniquity and double dealing, I would send him to our General Court."[51] The court printed the sermon.

The election sermon undoubtedly won Chauncy friends among the metallic-standard advocates, but the controversy continued for three more years until Parliament reimbursed New England £183,650 for the expense of the Cape Breton expedition.[52] Massachusetts received the largest portion and used it to redeem its promissory notes. The government then passed laws making all contracts payable in silver and declaring all notes of the other New England colonies illegal in Massachusetts.[53] Crowds jammed Boston on the day the notes were redeemed. That afternoon Dr. Chauncy entertained several visitors at dinner. Among them were Judge Stephen Sewall, William Cooke of Wayland, Oliver Peabody of Roxbury, and Ebenezer Parkman of Westborough.[54] The topic of conversation was surely the triumph of the advocates of the metallic standard. The new sound-money policy bolstered the economy and brought further prosperity to the rising merchant class. No one expected it to solve all the ministers' problems, but everyone thought it would ease some of the pressures on their small, fairly stable incomes. Despite the improvement, few pastors—especially those from the countryside—ever planned to live a life of luxury. Most were fortunate if they could live comfortably; few lived as well as did most of their merchant parishioners.

They were better off, however, than the Boston poor. In 1752, seeking to help those unfortunates (as well as themselves), some enterprising Bostonians founded the Society for Encouraging Industry and Employing the Poor. They asked Chauncy to address one of their early fund-raising meetings.[55] The industry they encouraged was the manufacture of linen, and they sought to employ the poor in their mills. Chauncy enthusiastically supported the project. He was not against philanthropy and public charity, but he saw this scheme as a way to provide jobs for those who wanted to work. Christians, he held, were obliged by the great "Law of Love" to assist the poor. Only those who refused to work because of sloth should be denied the "Bread of Charity." Those unable to work because of "Sickness, or Lameness, or the Decays of an infirm old Age," must be given charity, as must those who are willing to work but unable to find jobs. But it was better, he believed, for the able poor to work than to subsist on charity. He hoped that the linen industry would offer the poor—even women and children—a chance to improve their lot.[56]

Chauncy's sermon is a classic restatement of the early New England doctrine of industry. It is not surprising to hear so industrious a man insist that everyone, including the rich, must be busy. "If Persons possess ever so great an Abundance, this gives them no Licence to be lazy."[57] The necessity of work is inescapable: it is a law of nature. Our "Bodies are so made as constantly to require Food and Raiment: Nor can these Necessaries be supplied but by Labour. . . . The *Birds of the Air sow not*; neither do the *Lilies of the Field toil or spin*: But we are obliged to do both." Besides, lack of industry leads to physical and moral debility.[58] Labor is also a positive law of God. "*In the Sweat of thy Face thou shalt eat Bread, 'till thou return to the Ground.*"[59] Men are not excused from this law even to devote all their time to "the Spiritual Concerns of their Souls and another World," for the Christian religion "requires its Professors, not only to mind the Things of another World, but the Affairs of this also."[60] The Christian law of "Industrious Labour" is the path both to public and private good. There cannot be a "flourishing People" without it. "It is by Improvement in Arts and Trade, that they must grow in Wealth, and Power, and become possessed of the various Emoluments tending to the Benefit and Pleasure of Life; and these Arts take their Rise from, and are carried on by, the Industry of particular Persons."[61] Moreover it is the way to wealth for individual men: "those, who have their Fortunes to make, must certainly take Pains." In the style of Poor Richard, Chauncy concludes: "They may as well expect to be learned without Study, as to be rich without Diligence."[62]

103

Diligence. More than a century earlier John Cotton, the first minister of the First Church, said: "There is another combination of virtues strangely mixed in every lively, holy Christian: and that is, diligence in worldly businesses, and yet deadness to the world. Such a mystery as none can read but they that know it."[63] Discussing this statement of what Max Weber has called "the Protestant Ethic," Perry Miller observes: "Actually, it is a logical consequence of Puritan theology: man is put into this world, not to spend his life in profitless singing of hymns or in unfruitful monastic contemplation, but to do what the world requires, according to its terms. . . . It was a razor's edge, and the true Puritan was required to walk it."[64] The mid-eighteenth-century Bostonian, however, was more likely to mix his diligence with a lively interest in the world. This was the second social problem for Chauncy and his colleagues. An extraordinary surge of materialism and religious laxity swept Boston in the 1750s; but was the minister, having for so many decades exalted wealth and "making a fortune" as private and public goods, now to condemn his parishioners for their materialism? No—not for materialism, but for a lack of balance between concern for this world and the next and for vices that accompany prosperity. Although Chauncy argued for such a balance, it was delicate and hard to appreciate at best; booming business left little time for tightrope acts.

Yet the clergy felt that they were not working alone. During this period God sent natural warnings that could be interpreted only as calls for reform. Drought struck New England in May 1748. A historian of New England describes the results: "The harvest was greatly shortened, which added to the scarcity then prevailing on account of the war. Grain of all kinds was scarce. Indian corn rose to thirty-two shillings a bushel, rye to forty-six, and wheat to three pounds in old tenor bills." Thus the expectation was heightened the following season. The farmers planted as usual in 1749, and were at "a great expense for seed." Despite their expectations and several days of fast and repentance, however, the drought was worse in 1749, and it was accompanied by infestations of grasshoppers and worms. Until rain fell at last on July 6, 1749, Fast Day jeremiads provided New England's only thunder.[65] Nor was drought the worst judgment. Smallpox struck the city in the summer of 1752.[66] And in 1754 the uneasy truce of Aix-la-Chapelle, which was to have ended King George's War, began to crumble. Serious skirmishing broke out that year; by 1755 the Seven Years' War was well underway in North America. By the summer of 1755 everyone could see that the French held the upper hand. New Englanders, Chauncy believed, should have recognized the warnings. Instead they inclined even more toward secularism. Attendance at Sabbath services dropped sharply. One could expect this, perhaps, of sailors and other strangers, but even the ladies and gentlemen of Boston were paying more attention to the latest fashions and entertainment than to spiritual duties.

On November 18, 1755 their security was shattered by a powerful, damaging earthquake, the worst since 1727. Mary Fleet of Boston decided that day to start a diary, and wrote:

> At a quarter after four in the morning of the 18th day there was a terrible earthquake which shattered the whole Town very much and threw down a great many chimneys and parts of many houses. Another small shock took place about six the same morning. Dr. Sewall preached at 11 o'clock in the forenoon to a very crowded audience from the words in Mark, Chap. 13, verse 36. Lest coming suddenly he find you sleeping.[67]

Throughout their history New Englanders had considered the earthquake one of God's sternest reproofs. The clergy—as the example of Sewall's text indicates—agreed with Chauncy, who entitled his sermon on the occasion, *Earthquakes A Token of the Righteous Anger of God*.[68] The causes of God's anger were easy to discover: uncleanness, Sabbath-breaking, pride, unrighteousness, and drunkenness.[69] By God's mercy the country had escaped devastation this time, but unless the people gave up such sins and returned to undefiled religion, there was little likelihood that God's anger would be abated. Even John Winthrop's demonstration that earthquakes had natural causes (an argument that Chauncy accepted) did not weaken God's power to arrange such causes as he wished, so as to reprimand his people.[70] Besides earthquakes and other natural calamities, Chauncy contended, Providence might soon punish New England by unleashing the force of the French. At the time of the earthquake the war was growing and the enemy was winning.

Once again Chauncy had occasion to pay close attention to the progress of the war. Thoroughly convinced that the British cause was just, he prayed that Providence would assure its triumph despite the unfaithfulness of the people. Meanwhile the conduct of the war displeased him. Although Colonel Monckton, with a body of militia and a small force of regulars, captured two French forts in Nova Scotia in June 1755, a month later the French and Indians trounced the British regulars under General Braddock near Fort Duquesne on the Monongahela River.[71] The defeat angered Chauncy. He knew why Braddock had failed: the British general had "no Idea of the *manner of fighting* in use here, and therefore wholly neglected the only effectual expedients to guard against the fatal consequences that arose from it." Chauncy said as much in his first political tract, which he published anonymously as a *Letter to a Friend*.[72] After reviewing the details of the battle and pinpointing the blame, he clearly stated his solution to the problem: the army needed colonial command and experienced local soldiers. "The plain truth is, *Regular troops*, in this *Wilderness-country*, are just the same that *irregular ones* would be in *Flanders*."[73] Regulars are fine for laying siege to a fortress, Chauncy declared, but while they are marching through the woods to the fortress the sharp-shooting Canadians and Indians pick them apart. Native officers and soldiers know the forests and how to fight in them. If the disaster at Fort Duquesne convinces the government of this fact, and, moreover, if the threat of French conquest alarms the lethargic southern colonies, then all is not lost. Perhaps, Chauncy concluded, the defeat was really "one of the grand links in that chain of causes, by which Heaven may intend to chastise the *French*" and "curb their insolence."[74]

In early September, when New England troops under William Johnson defeated a French force at Lake George (in one of the most confused battles in American military history),[75] Chauncy felt his analysis of the situation had been vindicated, and jumped at the chance to restate his views. He dashed off *A Second Letter to a Friend; Giving a more particular Narrative of the Defeat of the French Army at Lake-George, By the New-England Troops, than has yet been published.*[76] Hailing the victory as "the *greatest Action*, in its kind, that ever happened in *North-America*"[77] and claiming that "hereby the disgrace that was reflected on the *British* arms, on the banks of the *Monongahela*, is wholly wiped away,"[78] Chauncy awarded most of the credit to the fact that New Englanders commanded and conducted the operation. Of Johnson he said, "Perhaps, the best bred *regular* could not have disposed matters, under like circumstances, with greater wisdom."[79] But he was angry with New York and the southern colonies for not contributing their share of men and money. He also insisted that "the burden laid upon the *New-England* colonies is, in point of *charge*, far beyond what they are able to bear, if *Great-Britain* does not interpose for our help."[80]

Chauncy's ardor cooled quickly, however, when Johnson failed to push on towards Crown-Point. The commander—now "knighted, made a baronet, and confirmed by the Crown in his position as superintendent of Indian affairs"—soon resigned his military commission on the grounds that he needed to "devote himself to administrative duties with the Indians."[81] His force was reduced to garrison strength, and the French continued to hold Crown-Point unmolested. They even began construction of Fort Ticonderoga, ten miles to the south.[82] Chauncy was furious. Why was the expedition abandoned, especially when—as he had heard—"the *private soldiers* would gladly have pursued, but were restrained?"[83] What had New England gained by the expedition, except "a burden of charge very grievous to bear; and the more so, as we are in far worse circumstances, with respect to the

106

taking of this place, than before we were involved in this heavy charge, which now lies upon us as a *dead weight* we groan to be delivered from."[84] The French were clearly ascendant, and New England was suffering. Chauncy saw the hand of God in this and warned the people: how far God "may make use of our *French* neighbours, and the *Indian-natives* in their interest, to impoverish, weaken, and gradually depopulate us, is more than we can any of us say at present. The face of our affairs, in military respects, looks dark."[85]

For the next two years affairs grew worse, not better, as the French avenged Lake George by demolishing Fort William Henry, took firm control of the Ohio Valley, and applied greater pressure to New York. The British regained the initiative only after William Pitt set colonial affairs in order (Chauncy's demands were largely met) and after bloody Ticonderoga. Another, and much more costly, expedition to Louisbourg, however, and engagements at Frontenac, Duquesne, Niagara, St. Francis, and Quebec were necessary before New England could relax once again in the smile of Providence.[86]

In addition to the parching and trembling of the earth, the terror of disease, and the rumble of battle that unsettled all New Englanders, Chauncy suffered a series of personal shocks in the 1750s. The greatest of these came in the spring of 1757. On April 11, almost exactly twenty years after the death of Chauncy's first wife, Elizabeth Townsend Chauncy died.[87] In the eighteen years of their marriage, she had helped her husband battle the Awakening and had raised his children along with her own. By the time of her death all but Sarah were grown and gone from the house on Summer Street. Charles Jr., newly married, conducted his merchant's affairs in Kittery;[88] William Blair Townsend, the son of Elizabeth's first marriage, was married and a respected importer of English and West Indies merchandise in Boston, with headquarters at the "sign of the Three Doves" in Marlborough Street.[89] Rebecca Townsend, Elizabeth's daughter, was dead. She had borne four sons since her marriage in 1746 to Professor John Winthrop, and she had died in August 1753 at the age of twenty-seven.[90] Elizabeth Chauncy had recently married Benjamin Greenleaf of Harvard's class of 1751. Sarah (called Sally by her friends) did not wed until 1771, when she married Amos Adams, an energetic preacher who had settled in Roxbury after his graduation from Harvard in 1752.[91]

With the death of Elizabeth, Chauncy was nearly alone. Of course, occasionally he visited his seven grandchildren,[92] but in Boston, except for Sarah and his two black servants,[93] he was left to his study and the empty house. His grief increased in 1758 when his son Charles lost his young wife and baby in childbirth.[94] Doctor Chauncy put up with his loneliness for a decent interval, then courted and won a Boston lady named Mary Stoddard. Forty-five, the eldest daughter of

107

David and Elizabeth Stoddard,[95] a woman of "exalted purity and devotion, the most extensive benevolence, unaffected humility, forebearance, and condescension,"[96] she married the doctor at the church in Brattle Street on June 15, 1760, and they moved into the parsonage.[97]

The minister "welcomed himself into his new wife's family" with a letter to her nephew, Shute Shrimpton Yeamans. As Clifford Shipton observes, the letter demonstrates "the typical eighteenth-century mixture of sentiment and practicality." It is also a mixture typical of Doctor Chauncy:

> You have heard of my Marriage to her whose Name was Mary Stoddard, and I rejoice in this near relation I sustain to a person so well fitted and disposed to make life happy to me. Her alliance to you as an Aunt puts me upon making the tender of the most affectionate respect towards you: And should it lay in my power, in any way what ever, to serve you, it would be with pleasure I should do it. . . . I have drawn on you for my Wife's Annuity of Ten pounds Sterling.[98]

Mary Stoddard Chauncy occupied the minister's pew in the Old Brick for the next twenty-three years.

CHAPTER EIGHT

A Body of Divinity

When Chauncy rode out for his health or to visit friends, he improved his time on horseback or in his carriage by meditating upon the nature of God and humans. His habit of deep thought gained him a reputation for absent-mindedness, but he was not woolgathering. He had set himself the task, after the Great Awakening, of working out a grand plan, a new "Body of Divinity" that squared with his own ideas of reason, with revelation, and with his own experience.[1]

His temperament and principles werè essentially Puritan. With his emphasis on the Bible as authoritative for faith, on the necessity of the atonement, on justification by faith, on the operation of Providence, on the congregational form of church government, and on Puritan practices such as Bible-reading, rigorous keeping of the Sabbath, self-examination, discipline, industry, and moral living, he was a true son of the seventeenth century. Chauncy did not reject his Puritan heritage when he reconsidered his theology. Norman Brantley Gibbs argues persuasively, in fact, that he stands in the great Puritan tradition of Richard Baxter, and that Baxter more than anyone else profoundly influenced his thinking. This seems to be true; yet, as Gibbs also indicates, Chauncy was open to the lessons of the eighteenth century as well.[2]

Despite his stubbornness on so many points, Chauncy was always curious, and he tried hard to be honest. "I was at first brought into this train of thought," he said of his revolutionary theory of universal salvation, "by being willing, in opposition to previous sentiments and strong biases, to follow the light wherever it should lead me."[3] And of his theory of original sin he once said, "It will not, I believe, comport with what is called orthodoxy, but I am verily persuaded it contains the real truth."[4] Between 1745 and 1761 Chauncy thought out and wrote down theories of the nature of God, the creation and destiny of humans, original sin, salvation, ethics, eschatology, and ecclesiology. In sum, he attempted to reconstruct New England theology by applying to his basic Puritan principles the lessons he had learned from the Awakening. He tried to meet the challenges set him by the changing patterns of life in New England and by new developments in the European Enlightenment.

The Great Awakening convinced Chauncy that New England needed such a reconstruction. The events of those New-Light years persuaded him that when a theology insisted so strenuously on God's severity toward universal human depravity, and hammered home the probability of damnation, it lent itself by its very nature to abuse. To retain it was simply to beg for another reign of terror when a fresh generation arose and a new Whitefield zealously set about exploiting the irrationality which Chauncy felt was at the heart of the New-Light theology. What value would such turmoil have? Certainly not enough to override the inevitable cost in bitterness and fragmentation. All along Chauncy had considered it blasphemous to attribute violent disharmony among Christians to the Holy Spirit; he had also suspected the authenticity of many dramatic conversions. All around him, as the Awakening subsided, he saw people who supposedly had become *new creatures* return with ease to their old ways. If orthodox theological tenets inevitably gave rise to "awakenings," and if these awakenings brought merely a rash of disorders and false conversions, then perhaps the tenets themselves were at fault.

But no one, least of all a New England Puritan, easily discards his religious tenets when he has devoted his life to them. Doubt was insufficient for Chauncy; he had to discover the truth. And to discover the truth about religious doctrines, he insisted, one had to test them against the ultimate standard: Scripture. Moreover, to be honest in such an examination, one must be thorough and fair. If it turns out that orthodoxy comports with the Word of God, then orthodoxy it shall be; if not, then one is obliged to continue, and try to learn, as well as his talents permit, what doctrines Scripture *does* proclaim. To conduct such an investigation was Chauncy's great project during the 1750s.

He proceeded with characteristic intensity. In 1768, recalling those days, he wrote to Stiles that once he had decided that his health was strong enough to permit serious study again, he had gone to work:

My next study was the *Bible*, more particularly the Epistles, more particularly still those of the Apostle Paul. I spent seven years in this study, in which time I read every thing that I could hear of in any of the libraries

110

here or at Cambridge, that had an aspect upon illustrating the scriptures, and sent to England for a considerable number of writers recommended by Doct. Doddridge, which I suppose are no where in the country but in my study, unless they have been sent for by the Cambridge college since the fire [1764], as I desired some of them to take care that they might be.[5]

Apparently he began with Paul. Judging from the frequent references to the Apostle that dot his sermons from the outset of his career and increase from 1744 onward, Paul's writings were on his mind for some time before he was ready to begin his systematic study. He appears to have started this project early in 1752, for on April 14, 1754 he wrote to Nathaniel Chauncy: "I have made the Scriptures my sole study for about two years; and I think I have attained to a clearer understanding of them than I ever had before. . . . I wish I could have an opportunity to converse with you, or to let you see what I have written upon Paul's Epistles. I think I could let you into an entirely new set of thoughts, which it is surprising has escaped the notice of so many as have written on the Apostle's Epistles. The commonly received opinions are quite remote from the truth."[6]

During the seven years Chauncy spent on this project he produced, besides his work on the epistles, "a large parcel of materials fitted to answer several designs."[7] In 1768, nine years after completing his investigations, he described the contents of the parcel to Stiles and asked for advice about publishing them. Since this part of Chauncy's letter is the chief source of information about his work in the 1750s, it merits extended quotation:

The materials for one design I have put together, and they have lain by in a finished quarto volume for some years. This is written with too much freedom to admit of a publication in this country. Some of my friends who have seen it, have desired I would send it home for publication, and to have it printed without a name. I question whether it will ever see the light till after my death, and I am not yet determined whether to permit its being then printed, or to order its being committed to the flames. It is a work that cost me much thought and a great deal of hard labour. It is upon a most interesting subject.

I have the materials for an octavo volume upon another subject, and they are mostly put together; but the work is as yet unfinished. It will contain the three following dissertations; "On the one man Adam in his innocent state." "On the one man Adam in his lapsed state." "On the posterity of the one man Adam as deriving existence from him, not in his innocent but lapsed state." The whole is written from the scripture account of these matters, and not from any human scheme. It will not, I believe, comport with what is called orthodoxy, but I am verily persuaded it contains the real truth. I do not know but I shall venture it into the world with my name to it, leaving the event in regard of its affecting my character with the all-wise Governor of all things.

111

I have moreover materials for another work, and a very useful and important one, but they lie as yet in a disjoined heap. It is what may be called a key to the New Testament, more especially the Apostles' writings. The design of this is to prepare the mind for reading and understanding the New Testament writings; and, as I imagine, it would happily tend to guard one against mistakes, and lead into a true understanding of the inspired writings. I have still another piece, which, when I have leisure, I will publish with all freedom. It wants little more than transcribing to finish it. It is upon *the benevolence of* GOD, its nature, illustration, and consistency with evil both natural and moral. This was written many years ago. It will make a moderate octavo volume.

I have been, you see, very free with you; and I desire you would use the same freedom with me. Let me have your sedate thoughts and most mature advice relative to these things.[8]

It is safe to conclude, from Chauncy's own testimony, that his body of divinity—the ideas in *The Benevolence of the Deity* (1784), *Five Dissertations on the Scripture Account of the Fall* (1785), and *The Mystery hid from Ages and Generations, made manifest by the Gospel Revelation: or, the Salvation of All Men* (1784)—were substantially worked out before 1760.[9]

It is appropriate here to present the body of divinity only in its skeletal form. If one is to grasp the outline of Chauncy's system, *The Benevolence of the Deity* is the best starting point. Although one cannot know precisely when Chauncy wrote this long dissertation—he may have finished it even before he began his scriptural study[10]—it is a pivotal document. Its main ideas are central to an understanding of the other treatises, for once Chauncy insisted on the paramount position of benevolence among God's attributes, he had to face the doctrinal consequences.

As he had done in earlier controversies, Chauncy wrote this work in response to challenge. The attribute of divine benevolence, he claimed, "has been objected to by some, and abused by others." Further, "it may be, more objections have been levelled against, and greater reproaches cast upon, this attribute of the Divine Nature, than any of the other." Just as he wrote *Seasonable Thoughts* as an antidote to Edwards's treatise, he offered this book as an "attempt . . . to remove away these *objections*, wipe off these aspersions, and set forth the *benevolence* of the *Deity*, in its *true glory*." He could easily dismiss the peevish complaints of persons dissatisfied with their lot, or the mistakes of those who misunderstood the nature of benevolence. Other objections were more serious: they positively misrepresented the doctrine:

A more shocking idea can scarce be given of the *Deity*, than that which represents him as *arbitrarily dooming the greater part of the race of men to*

112

eternal misery. Was he wholly destitute of goodness, yea, positively *malevolent* in his nature, a worse representation could not be well made of him. And yet, this is the true import of the doctrine of *absolute and unconditional reprobation*, as it has been taught, even by those who profess faith in *God* as a *benevolent*, yea, an *infinitely benevolent Being*: But they could not have taught this doctrine, it would have been impossible, if they had not first entertained *intirely wrong* conceptions of benevolence, as attributed to the *Deity*. 'Tis indeed strange that any, who feel within themselves the working of kind affection, should give in to an opinion so reproachful to the Father of mercies. To be sure their ideas of goodness in *God*, if they have any, must be totally different from all the ideas we have of goodness, as we apply the term to *ourselves*, or any created intelligent agent whatsoever. And if their ideas are thus different, and may consequently signify the same thing with what we call *cruelty* in men, or any other creatures endowed with moral agency, they can really mean nothing when they say, that God is good: And it is of no importance, of not the least significancy, whether they call him good, or not.[11]

The title page provides a brief outline of the book. Chauncy arranged his argument in three parts. The first "explains the sense, in which we are to understand Benevolence, as applicable to GOD." The second "asserts, and proves, that this perfection, in the sense explained, is one of his essential attributes." And the third "endeavours to answer objections." Chauncy further explains:

Under one or other of these heads, occasion will be taken to view man as an *intelligent moral agent*; having within himself an *ability* and *freedom* to WILL, as well as to *do*, in opposition to NECESSITY from any extraneous cause whatever:—To point out the ORIGIN OF EVIL, both *natural* and *moral*:—And to offer what may be thought sufficient to shew, that there is no *inconsistency* between *infinite benevolence* in the Diety, which is always guided by *infinite wisdom*, and any *appearances of* evil in the creation.[12]

At about the same time that Chauncy was working on *The Benevolence of the Deity*, Jonathan Edwards was denying the freedom of the will in his famous treatise *A Careful and Strict Enquiry into the Modern Prevailing Notions, of that Freedom of Will, Which is supposed to be essential to Moral Agency, Vertue and Vice, Reward and Punishment, Praise and Blame*, which he published in Boston in 1754.[13] Clearly Chauncy's views did not accord with what passed for orthodoxy in some quarters.

True to his plan, at the outset Chauncy carefully defined divine benevolence as a natural state of mind in God, inclining him to the communication of good, "analogous to *kind affection* in us men, only as kind affection *in us* is attended with frailty, *in him* it is absolutely perfect, both as to *mode* of existence, and *manner* of exercise." That is, as he exists a *free agent*, in the highest and most glorious sense, he is not *mechanically*, or *necessarily*, urged on, from this *natural disposition*, to the communication of good; but acts herein *voluntarily*, and of *choice*: And, in fine, that, as he is an infinitely *wise* and *intelligent*, as well as free, *agent*, his exertions, in order to the production of good, are never *unfit*, never unreasonable, but always *fit*, *reasonable*, and *absolutely* and *perfectly* so. So that, in one word, *benevolence* in the *Deity* signifies precisely the same thing with "a disposition freely to communicate all the good that is consistent with *wise* and *fit* conduct." For, supremely perfect benevolence of nature, being, in him, conjoined with an all-comprehending understanding, and unerring wisdom, he must know all the ways of producing happiness, and the *greatest* sum of it that can be wisely produced: And this therefore is the happiness that may reasonably be expected should be produced by him; that is to say, all the happiness to the *whole*, and every part of the creation, than can be, not in respect of *omnipotence*, considered as *natural* power, but in the way of *fit* and *reasonable* conduct.[14]

Chauncy relied chiefly on two arguments to demonstrate that benevolence is a divine attribute. First he repeated the traditional metaphysical theory that God, having always existed without limitation, must be the subject of all perfections. As we attribute omnipotence to him, so may we justly attribute benevolence. The second argument is inductive. We can conclude that God is benevolent by observing the effects of his goodness "we every where see in our world, and in all parts of the universe."[15]

Chauncy saw the universe in a traditional way: as part of the great chain of being, that immense series of links arranged in a hierarchical scale from the lowest grade of existence up to the highest. Underlying this scheme, as Chauncy conceived it, were the principles of plenitude, gradation, and continuity. A. O. Lovejoy, the principal historian of this idea, uses *plenitude* to describe two basic concepts: "not only the thesis that the universe is a *plenum formarum* in which the range of conceivable diversity of *kinds* of living things is exhaustively exemplified, but also any other deductions from the assumption that no genuine potentiality of being can remain unfulfilled, that the extent and abundance of the creation must be as great as the possibility of existence and commensurate with the productive capacity of a 'perfect' and inexhaustible Source, and that the world is the better, the more things it contains."[16] At various times Chauncy uses the term in both these senses. *Gradation* refers to the hierarchical structure, subordinating inferior to superior beings. The term *continuity* refers to the principle that the ascending grades of being shade off one into the other without gaps in the scale; there are no "missing links."[17]

Chauncy outlined such a realm of being, from inanimate to divine, in the second part of *The Benevolence of the Diety*. He embraced it,

114

however, not only because it appealed to his sense of order, but also because it seemed to confirm his own experience and that of other thoughtful men. As Lovejoy observes, in the eighteenth century the conception of the great chain gained its "widest diffusion and acceptance."[18] Among those who granted the stamp of approval were such influential philosophers as Locke, Addison, and Edmund Law.[19] When Chauncy, therefore, presented an extensive statement of this theory, and applied it thoroughly, and quite subtly, to the question of divine benevolence, he argued from widely accepted premises. Some might quarrel with his understanding of the concept, or with his conclusions, but few would object to the scheme itself.

Chauncy knew that the two key problems in the scheme—especially if he were to use it to demonstrate benevolence—were the place of humans and the question of evil. Humans, Chauncy saw, occupy a position between the animal and spiritual gradations; they are a compound, "partly *animal*, and partly *rational*, being allied both to the *highest*, and the *lowest* orders of beings in the universe."[20] These powers relate so intimately to each other that a human constitutes "one person" or "living agent." His capacities, naturally, accord with his place in the scheme and with God's plan:

And the giving us *this constitution* is an illustrious instance of the Divine goodness, and naturally leads us to conceive of the *Deity* as *absolutely* and *perfectly* benevolent. . . . For it is by means of this *compound* make, that *inanimate nature* is not only *enjoyed* but *perceived* to have *beauty* and *order*, and to be a contrivance worthy of the Supreme Creator. The *inferior kinds* are variously capable of a *lower* sort of happiness, from their relation to, and situation in, this material world: But this is all. Being destitute of *reason*, at least in any considerable measure, *sensitive enjoyment* is the *highest* they can attain to. It is the union of *reason* and *sense*, in such a *superior* degree, that enables us *men*, at the same time that we enjoy *sensitive* good, in common with the *inferior* creatures, to discern the wisdom, and power, and benevolence, of the *Deity*, herein displayed. And it is from hence also, that we become capable of that *more noble* happiness, which is the result of the exercise of *reason* upon the *order* of the *material* world, and the adjustment of bodily organs thereto, so as to occasion so much *sensitive* pleasure. . . . I say, if there had not been some such order of creatures, this *material* world must have been *comparatively lost*.[21]

The questions of the way reason and sense operate, and how a person exercises his reason, led Chauncy to discuss human psychology. Here again the principles of order, continuity, and gradation apply. As he had argued in *Seasonable Thoughts*, the faculties of the mind are arranged from lower to higher, from the powers of sensation to the understanding. These faculties, it must be remembered, are not discrete, but interdependent. With Locke, Chauncy believed that the

115

mind begins as a tabula rasa, that knowledge depends upon the senses, and that the understanding and will in turn depend upon knowledge and upon each other.[22]

But beyond our intellectual capacities, Chauncy contended, there are superior, *moral* powers, "fitting us for *moral* happiness, the highest any being can be made capable of."[23] These powers provide us with "a new sort of knowledge, superior in its nature to that which results from *sensible* ideas."[24] This new knowledge is nonmaterial; it permits us to transcend the material world and examine what Chauncy calls the "moral world," the moral order between God and man. The moral abilities are the *moral sense, self-determination*, and *conscience*.[25] The moral sense is a kind of Shaftesburyian, internal, a priori principle, implanted by God in humans, by which we are "enabled at once, without the labor of a long train of reasoning, to distinguish between moral good, and moral evil, in all instances that are of primary importance, and essentially connected with the good of the moral world."[26] Just as by "the intervention of our bodily organs, we directly perceive the difference between white and black, sweet and bitter, and know that the one is not, and cannot be, the other," so, by this power, "we perceive, in the like direct and immediate way, these and those qualities of temper and conduct, and are at once satisfied that they are either morally good, not evil; or morally evil, not good." This is furthermore a power common to all humans.[27]

The second moral ability is *self-determination*. In addition to a power that will enable us to know right and wrong, man must possess a faculty that "will subject his volitions to his command, and constitute him the efficient of those effects that are consequent upon them." Otherwise there is no such thing as moral obligation. We are free agents, and we know it: "To go about to prove this, by a long train of reasoning, would be very like holding a candle to the sun, in its meridian lustre, for light that we might be able to see. It is a first, and fundamental principle in morals, and to be evidenced, not by arguing, but by an appeal to common sense, or, in other words, the perceptions of mankind universally. We all feel the existence, and operation of this power every day we live.[28] This is as it should be in the divine scheme. God, free "both to will, and to do,"[29] made humankind in his image; thus humans, by their status as free agents, reflect "that perfection of [God's] nature which is his greatest glory," and are also "capable percipients, in a degree, of that happiness which is his highest."[30]

Working with the moral sense and free will in the moral order is the third power, *conscience*. Its "office," Chauncy explained, "is that of a witness, not of a law-giver. The work appropriated to it is, not to point out to us the virtues we ought to practice, or the vices we ought to avoid, which would be to invade the province of some other of our

116

powers," but instead to be "in our breasts a testifier for, or against us, as we have done that which we knew to be right, or wrong."[31]

If, however, God is benevolent—if he is disposed to communicate good—why is there evil at all? This is the second major problem. Chauncy recognized that he had to account for three kinds of evil: the "*imperfect powers* of so many of the creatures who are capable of happiness," *moral disorder*, and *natural evil*.[32] Before explaining the existence of these evils in the system, he issued a caveat: "No appearance in nature, capable of being alledged, ought to be looked upon as conclusively arguing an *inconsistency* with goodness, MEERLY or ONLY because we may not be able particularly and fully to point out their consistency with each other: I say, meerly or only for this reason, because there is an evident difference between our not particularly discerning wherein the *consistency* of two things lies, and clearly perceiving that there is a *real inconsistency* between them. . . . No eye but God's can take in the *whole scheme* of creation and providence."[33] Like most thinkers who tried to explain these difficulties in the great chain, Chauncy relied heavily upon the principles of plenitude, gradation, and continuity.[34] His argument generally follows William King's *De origine mali* (1702) as it was translated by Edmund Law.[35]

Without the first difficulty, limitation, there could not have been any creation at all. "Absolute perfection," claimed Chauncy, "is an incommunicable glory of the only true God," and to suppose a perfect creature would be to suppose it equal with its creator. Besides, mere imperfection is really no evil: nothing has been taken away from us, since we started from nothing.[36] To answer the related objection that a benevolent Deity would not have created "so many creatures so imperfect, as to be capable of happiness in such low degrees only," Chauncy appealed to the principle of gradation in the great chain. "If the whole result of communicated good was nothing more than the production of such imperfect beings," his opponents would have a case. This, however, is not so: If "there are other beings gradually rising, in the scale of existence, to an inconceivable height in their capacities for the enjoyment of happiness, and of the most superior kind too, why should it be thought strange, that there should be imperfect ones also, in the like gradually descending scale? Especially if they are all considered as parts of some GREAT WHOLE, severally concurring to make one universal, gloriously connected system, capable of yielding as much good, as the infinitely benevolent Being, guided in his exertions by unerring wisdom, has thought fit to communicate."[37] From here Chauncy buttressed his argument by applying the principles of plenitude and continuity:

. . . the capacity for happiness, in the universe, is enlarged by means of the diversity of beings that have existence in it. And if the capacity is enlarged,

117

it is, from hence, demonstrably certain, that the *quantum* of good *may* be *greater* than it could have been, if, instead of this *diversity*, fewer orders of beings, or a single one only, had been made.

It is, indeed, from this diversity of beings, duly subordinated to each other, that the *plenitude* of nature arises. A few orders of beings only would not have served to this purpose. The creation is *filled up*, by that admirably nice and curious variety in the classes of creatures, whereby they are fitted to be proper links in the chain of existence; all concurring, as so many well adjusted parts, to constitute *one whole* without *void* or *chasm*.[38]

Chauncy's conclusion on this point is a classic statement of the eighteenth-century position on limitation: "The short of the case is, the creation of God, by means of this diversity of beings, gradually and regularly rising in perfection, even to the highest possible degree, becomes a *most perfect and contiguous whole*, demonstrating the riches and glory of the Creator's goodness, far beyond what it could have done, if the *continuity* had been broken, by the *non-existence* of any of the ranks of creatures, which now make it an *absolutely full and well-connected universe*."[39]

Moral evil is harder to understand. It is, "perhaps, a difficulty that cannot be perfectly removed, in the present state of human faculties. But this is no proof that it cannot be done."[40] We are a low order of creatures; another, higher order may be sufficiently gifted to understand the reason for moral evil in the world. Nevertheless, within our limitations, we can show that the two facts, moral evil and infinite benevolence, are not inconsistent. Chauncy's argument is lengthy and detailed; the main conclusions are these. Moral evil has two aspects, "*irregularity* in the beings charged with it," and a "consequent *unhappiness* as the *fruit* thereof, either by the *constitution of nature*, or *positive infliction* from the *Deity*." In his wisdom, and in order to communicate "the highest good in kind" (if men had not been made, "This kind of good would have been wanting in creation"), God created humans free agents, thus capable of erring. To prevent such creatures as these from erring would require divine interposition. But such interposition would destroy free agency (and thereby morality); it would thus be inconsistent with wise and fit conduct. From such premises it follows that "the *actual defection* of free agents is not to be imputed to any *deficiency* of goodness in the *Deity*; and therefore that there can be no *real* inconsistency between the existence of this *moral depravity* and *infinite benevolence*, whatever there may be in appearance."[41]

Furthermore, if we suffer as a result of our faults, we have no complaint. In fact unhappiness consequent upon moral irregularity indicates benevolence towards men: it is God's way "to reduce them to a right conduct, if they have been faulty, and to preserve them inviolable

118

in their attachment to virtue, if they have been innocent."[42] As for the *"sufferings* of the virtuous, by the wickedness of the vicious," these, "upon supposition of *another* state (which cannot be proved to be *unreasonable*; much less an *impossible* one) may be, in the end, for their *advantage*; as they are capable of being improved so as that the fruit, upon the whole, shall be *more* happiness, than if these sufferings had not been endured." The conclusion is therefore inescapable: "And if they may possibly be a *means* to produce *greater* good, they cannot prove a deficiency in the benevolence of the *Deity*, but are rather an argument in proof that he is endowed with this attribute."[43]

The common complaint about *natural* evil is that God not only permits it, he appoints it, since it results from "that constitution of things, which he contrived, and established, and has all along upheld."[44] However, Chauncy cautions, it should be remembered that many so-called natural evils result from our moral disorders; for example, "had it not been for the lusts of men, we should never have heard of many tormenting diseases, which multitudes now lie groaning under."[45] One must also realize that, in the long run, natural evils are "the effects of established laws, the design and tendency of which are greatly beneficial."[46] In fact it may have been necessary that "we should live in a world of *discipline*, a world that would, in the natural course of things, be the occasion of difficulties, inconveniences, and trials," for in this way we "might be formed to a meetness for another world, in which we should be totally freed from them."[47] The extent to which Chauncy's eighteenth-century optimism is tempered by a harder, Puritan view of life is revealed in this comment: "An uninterrupted state of ease and pleasure, would, morally speaking, be the ruin of mankind."[48] As will become clear shortly, this attitude also has significance in Chauncy's view of salvation.

Admitting the imperfection of this world, Chauncy asks nonetheless "whether the making such a world as this, is not a proof of more benevolence, than a chasm would be in that part of the creation, which it now occupies. If so, imperfect as it is, comparatively speaking, it is better it should be, than not be."[49] In a sense he agreed with the famous proposition of his time that "whatever is, is right." "And," he continues, "for such an imperfect world as this ought to be, in an indefinitely variegated creation, in order to its being a proper part in the chain of existence, no alteration, it may be, notwithstanding all the complaints that have been made of deficiencies, redundancies, deformities, and evils, could be made without damage to the system."[50]

These statements would seem to place Chauncy in the camp of the eighteenth-century optimists, whose "common thesis" was that this is the best of all possible worlds.[51] Yet his position differs significantly from Lovejoy's description of the optimist's creed: "To assert that this

is the best of possible world implies nothing as to the absolute goodness of this world; it implies only that any other world which is metaphysically capable of existence would be worse."[52] Chauncy claimed
that a *chasm* would be worse, but he did not believe that "any other
world which is metaphysically capable of existence would be worse."
Quite the contrary. He reasoned that "a better world than this, more
perfect, and more powerfully adapted to make happy, might be created
by the Deity; but then it ought to be remembered, such a better world
may be already one of the links in the diversified chain of existence."[53]
Not only might there be a better world; perhaps humans—sufficiently
perfected—could occupy it. His natural theology suggests this startling
possibility; revelation, the final arbiter, seems to confirm the suggestion. In a fascinating aside to his discourse on moral evil, Chauncy
adds this speculation, anticipating, in a sense, later and more explicit
philosophers of creative evolution:

> I shall only subjoin, upon the whole, that we know not but those beings,
> who are the percipients of happiness, in the lowest and most imperfect de-
> grees, may be designed for a much higher state of existence. This may be
> possible to the power and wisdom of the infinitely benevolent Creator; and
> that he has not actually made provision for it, in the *plan* upon which he
> intends to operate for the *general good*, is more than any one can pretend
> to determine. It is highly probable from *reason* only, and certainly from
> *revelation*, that *man*, though, at present, one of the lowest *intellectual moral*
> beings, is yet designed for exalted perfection and happiness. He is now in an
> *infant* state, compared with what this may be introductory to. And, for all
> that can be proved to the contrary, he may go on in *intellectual* and *moral*
> attainments, till he had reached as great perfection, and is possessed of as
> great happiness, as, at present, comes to the share of any of the ranks of
> created beings: Though they also may be supposed to be gradually rising in
> perfection and happiness, in proportion to their *greater* original capacities;
> so that the distance will still be preserved among the various orders of crea-
> tures, and go on to be so, forever.[54]

The Benevolence of the Deity is basically an essay in "natural religion," relying for its arguments chiefly on reason unaided by Scripture. But natural religion, although valuable, Chauncy believed, is in-
complete in itself. True religion requires the intermeshing of natural
and scriptural principles, and during the 1750s he was deeply involved
in the study of both. The problem of human destiny, so vital to *The
Benevolence of the Deity*, remained at the forefront of Chauncy's
thinking during his investigation of the scriptures. It came also to the
forefront of the major theological dispute of the mid-century: the debate over original sin. In this debate the question of moral evil was
naturally crucial. H. Shelton Smith, who has thoroughly studied the
changes in this doctrine in American theology, describes the general

nature of the controversy: "Prior to 1750 New England Puritans maintained their doctrine of original sin with practical unanimity. Within the next decade, however, dissenting notions began to attract attention; and by the end of the century the original doctrine had been considerably modified by some of the more liberal thinkers."[55]

Some of the more radical secular thinkers, of course, had already concluded that one could readily account for the world without having to posit a fall. Science, not Scripture, had revealed the true nature of the universe as a smoothly functioning, marvelously balanced mechanism governed by mathematically demonstrable and unchanging laws; it did not seem to behave like a fallen world laboring under a curse. Theologians working within the Protestant tradition, however, no matter how liberal, were loth to go that far; for his part, Chauncy reinterpreted the doctrine of original sin but refused to abandon it.

Puritans believed that when Adam violated his covenant obligations to God by disobedience, he fell from a condition of righteousness to sin. Losing his original righteousness, he incurred guilt and suffered the total corruption of his nature. This position was challenged in the 1750s; also coming under attack in the 1750s, moreover, were the traditional doctrines that Adam's descendants exist in this sinful state as well, for they sinned in him; that is, they participated directly in his transgression; and, additionally, that they are in this predicament because Adam, as their *representative*, failed his obligations under the covenant.[56]

The work of Daniel Whitby (1638–1726) and especially that of John Taylor (1694–1761) directed the attention of New England theologians to these problems.[57] Taylor argued that Adam and Eve had begun their lives not in a state of righteousness, but on a primitive moral level; that therefore the fall was a falling *short* of righteousness, not a falling *from* it; and that their guilt is not transferable, since guilt can only be personal. Instead of the traditional theory he argued that humans are born neither righteous nor sinful, but capable of being either, as they improve or neglect "the Goodness of God."[58] Taylor's bold views struck close to the heart of traditional Puritan belief, and they prompted quick rebuttals. The most effective was that of Jonathan Edwards, whose treatise *The Great Christian Doctrine of Original Sin Defended* (1758)[59] "was a potent force in keeping the controversy alive for many decades."[60]

Taylor based much of his challenging theory upon his reading of St. Paul. Because Chauncy concentrated on the Pauline epistles, he studied Taylor carefully, respected his work, and disagreed with him. "I am without all doubt," he wrote to Nathaniel Chauncy, "that Mr. Taylor for whom I have a great value, and to whom I am much beholden, is very much mistaken in his doctrine of original sin, and in his performance on the *Epistle of Romans*. Nay, I am entirely satisfied that he has not so much as entered into the main design of the Apostle Paul's writing."[61] From this remark one might judge that Chauncy still defended the traditional doctrine of original sin that figured promi≠ nently in his work in the 1730s and even into the 1740s. In fact he now advanced a fresh theory, neither covenant theology nor Taylorism, which bears his own stamp and which he touched upon in his sermons at the time of the earthquake and set forth in his *Five Dissertations*. He did not publish these dissertations until 1785, but we know from his remarks to Stiles that they were nearly finished in 1768. His letter to Nathaniel Chauncy indicates that he had worked out his new theory of original sin as early as 1754.

In 1758, having been pulled into a debate between Samuel Webster and Peter Clark, Chauncy revealed that he had rejected the traditional covenant doctrine. In 1757 Webster had written a pro-Taylor tract entitled *A Winter Evening's Conversation Upon the Doctrine of Original Sin*.[62] Clark replied from the orthodox standpoint with *The Scripture Doctrine of Original Sin, stated and defended. In A Summer Morning's Conversation, between a Minister and a Neighbor*.[63] He claimed to present the Calvinist doctrine of imputation, but actually modified it drastically by excluding infants from damnation.[64] Joseph Sewall, Thomas Foxcroft, Thomas Prince, and Ebenezer Pemberton endorsed Clark's "Conversation," thus lending him a certain prestige.[65] Clark and Webster traded pamphlets during the year, and the exchange stirred up tempers and hard feelings among the New England clergy. In the heat of the controversy, Clark asked Chauncy several times to give his opinion of the *Summer Morning's Conversation*. Finally Chauncy astonished Clark by publishing an anonymous, scathing attack on Clark himself.[66] Chauncy demonstrated that Clark, while claiming strict Calvinism, actually had departed significantly from traditional doctrine. Not that Chauncy agreed with the harsh Calvinist viewpoint on the damnation of infants; he simply wanted to make clear that such theologians as Calvin himself and Michael Wigglesworth affirmed infant damnation, and that one could hardly be a Calvinist without doing the same. If Clark did not believe in infant damnation, then he agreed fundamentally with Webster, who did not believe in it either. If this was the case, then Clark should not have abused his opponent by calling him Pelagian and other heretical names.[67]

By scolding Clark, Chauncy showed that he had "given up" the traditional position. Since he rejected Taylor as well, what were his own new ideas on this central question? How, he asked himself, can one "reconcile the *unavoidable sufferings* of the race of men, as occasioned by, and taking rise from, the *lapse* of their common father *Adam*, with the perfections of God, particularly his infinitely perfect and un-

122

bounded benevolence?"[68] Several of the answers he gives to this problem grow out of and develop ideas found in *The Benevolence of the Deity*; his central argument is anchored in scripture.

In its essentials the argument proceeds in this order. Adam was created in the image of God, but he was not given moral perfection. He possessed, in a fully developed state, all the powers of the soul, but he did not have knowledge—the mind starts as a blank tablet—and he was not morally mature. He was, rather, a moral infant, equipped with "nothing more than those capacities which are proper to a being of that order in which he was created." Not having created him morally perfect, God could not require Adam to enter a covenant of perfect obedience. As if in recognition of his undeveloped moral state, God gave him special help, such as pointing out the specific tree that was forbidden him.[69]

Although God had set for him only such requirements as were appropriate to his condition of moral infancy, Adam disobeyed. His disobedience unleashed two kinds of evil, natural and judicial. The first included fear, shame, and guilt. The second was God's curse upon the land, changing it from paradise to a place of labor, suffering, and death, "with its forerunners, and appendages, in all their frightful and tormenting forms."[70]

As for Adam's descendants, we do not sin in his sin. The conventional doctrine of imputation is a misinterpretation of Romans 5: 12–19. One person cannot sin for another. Neither are we created wholly corrupt. Moral corruption, because it is the consequence of personal choice, cannot be passed on from parent to child. Thus far Chauncy agrees with Taylor. But Taylor is wrong in holding that our human nature remains unimpaired. On the contrary, it is impaired; we do suffer as a result of Adam's fall. In the first place, we are subject to death. We derive our existence from fallen Adam, and since the first father was made mortal in his lapsed state, he could beget only mortal offspring. We in our turn bear the burden of mortality. In the second place, our nature is impaired because we are incapable of obeying our Maker as well as Adam could have obeyed him in Paradise. St. Paul, Chauncy claims, makes this clear by stating that when men "are capable of moral action, they will so far transgress the rule, as to be incapable of claiming justification upon the foot of naked law."[71] In short, what Paul is saying in Romans 5:12 ("Wherefore, as by one man sin entered into the world, and death by sin; and so death passed upon all men, for that all have sinned") and throughout the rest of Romans 5, is that the fall caused two kinds of evil, involuntary (death) and voluntary (sin), and that sin is a *consequence* of death. (Chauncy takes the word "that" in the phrase "for that" to refer to "death," and the word "for" to mean "upon which," or "in consequence of

123

which," basing his reading upon his translation of the Greek version.)[72] Death, then, because of such "appendages" as labor, pain, fear, sorrow, and anxiety, unfailingly presents us with many serious temptations; weakened, we yield to such temptations; therefore death is an "occasional cause" of sin.[73]

This theory of the relationship between natural and moral evil leads straight back to the dilemma Chauncy faced in *The Benevolence of the Deity*. An infinitely benevolent God afflicts us with the punishment of death, which causes sin, as a consequence of an offense we did not commit and of which we are not guilty. If God gives us death, and we sin because of it, and face condemnation for our sins, how then can we call God benevolent? Chauncy had a startling answer, which he found in Paul. The source is Romans 8: 19–24, a passage Chauncy considered a companion piece to Romans 5:

> For the earnest expectation of the creature waiteth for the manifestation of the sons of God.
> For the creature was made subject to vanity, not willingly, but by reason of him who hath subjected the same in hope,
> Because the creature itself also shall be delivered from the bondage of corruption into the glorious liberty of the children of God.
> For we know that the whole creation groaneth and travaileth in pain together until now.
> And not only they, but ourselves also, which have the first fruits of the Spirit, even we ourselves groan within ourselves, waiting for the adoption, to wit, the redemption of our body.
> For we are saved by hope: but hope that is seen is not hope: for what a man seeth, why doth he yet hope for?[74]

Chauncy, after long and careful exegesis, reads these passages to mean that God does not subject us to this suffering condition as a final condemnation, but as a disciplinary measure. "The sum of the matter is," he says, "the apostle, comparing his discourse *here*, with his discourse in the fifth chapter, from the 12th verse, is evidently speaking of the *whole human race*. And what he says of them is, that they are subjected to a *suffering* state; that they were subjected to it, not on the account of *any sin*, or *sins*, they had been guilty of *previous* to this subjection, but by the *will of God*, taking rise from, and grounded on, the *sin* of the *one man Adam*; and that he subjected them to this *suffering* condition, not as a *final condemnation*, but upon having *first* given them reason to *hope*, not only that they should be delivered from their *sufferings*, but with ABOUNDING ADVANTAGE, by being *finally* made meet for, and then crowned with, *immortality* and *glory* as the sons of God." In his goodness and wise governance, God has arranged a means of deliverance—the sacrifice of Christ—to atone for the sin of Adam and of humans, and to save all humankind.[75]

Chauncy never committed himself completely to the Grotian doc-

124

trine that Christ's function was primarily to serve as a perfect example of obedience to God's law and veneration for his wisdom. He considered Christ's role as example (and as revealer of God to humans) a vital aspect of the atonement, but he stressed more emphatically the idea of Christ's "sacrifice of himself, which, in the fullness of time, he was to offer up to God to put away sin,"[76] and by which alone sinners are justified. He rejects as irreconcilable with God's mercy and benevolence the doctrine that Christ's righteousness is imputed only to the elect. To be sure, only those who "become believers in Jesus Christ"—who enjoy saving faith—obtain this mercy, but one must not place restrictions upon the scheme of an all-powerful God. Christ's mediatorial function continues beyond the time-span of this life; even beyond history. Eventually all will receive this essential faith. Since he created us free moral agents, God's scheme to accomplish this end must accord with our moral nature. We must therefore be prepared for heaven in a moral way. Those who fail to attain moral perfection in this life must undergo a period of purgation after death. The very wicked will go to hell for a long time; but hell is a "purging fire,"[77] and Christ, the new Adam, the Savior, the Mediator, will devote himself unswervingly to winning these souls away from their enmity towards God. He shall succeed: one cannot suppose that Satan "should *finally* get the better of him, by effecting the *everlasting damnation* of the *greater part* of those whom he came from heaven on purpose to *save*."[78] When Christ rescues a sinner, that happy soul passes into heaven. The process continues until all people finally reach heaven, at which time the Son, having perfectly discharged his obligations as mediator, will "give up his *mediatory kingdom to the Father*, who will, from this time, *reign IMMEDIATELY himself*; making the most glorious manifestations of his being a God, and Father, and Friend to all, in all things, without end."[79]

Not only this—the Scriptures also reveal that "heaven" will in truth be the earth itself, "bro't back to its *paradisaick* state, or one that is better; and that the *very world we now live in*, thus changed and made new, is the place, where good men, after the resurrection, and judgment, shall live and reign with Christ forever and ever."[80]

The doctrine of universal salvation follows naturally from the premise of universal atonement, accords nicely with the doctrine of benevolence, confirms Chauncy's suspicions about a better, more perfect human race and a better world to come, and explains unavoidable suffering. It seemed to Chauncy to dissolve his dilemma. "It is this thought only, so far as I am able to judge, that can reconcile the *unavoidable sufferings* of the race of men, as occasioned by, and taking rise from, the *lapse* of their common father *Adam*, with the perfections of God, particularly his infinitely perfect and unbounded benevolence. And this, as I imagine, will effectually do it."[81]

CHAPTER NINE

Liberty, Civil and Religious

Chauncy may have kept his ideas to himself because of timidity, but he was not ordinarily timid. He may have doubted his conclusions and set his manuscripts aside until he could be sure he was correct; but as early as 1754 the letters he wrote about his investigations were confident and assured, and in subsequent correspondence, before the publication of *The Mystery hid from Ages*, he firmly reiterated his position. There is a further possibility: he may have feared a reaction so violent that it would seriously damage New England Congregationalism, already shaky from the disruptive effects of the Awakening and the disputes over original sin and the Sacrament that added fresh antagonisms in the 1750s. It would surely cause great unhappiness close to home, at the First Church. He could hardly rail at the New-Lights for shattering the ecclesiastical pattern of New England and then himself do what they did. True, he had entered the controversy over original sin, but reluctantly. To conduct a campaign for such strikingly radical theories as universal salvation would be to invite further factionalism and misunderstanding. Neither the church system nor the people were ready for it.

Had Jonathan Edwards lived into the 1760s he might have prompted Chauncy to abandon caution and bring his ideas to light, for Edwards could never be ignored. This is not to say that the New-Lights flickered out upon Edwards's death in 1758. His disciples, using Edwardsean Calvinism as the basis of their theology, emerged during the 1760s as a strong group in their own right. Edwards's close friend Samuel Hopkins was their leader. They were called "New Divinity" men, or

126

"Hopkinsians," and Chauncy feared them. "I had much rather be an episcopalian, or that others should, than that I or they should be Hopkintonians," he once wrote.[1] Chauncy distrusted them because they were heirs of the Awakening. They disrupted the established churches, either by causing separations or driving the people into the Church of England. As for the "New Divinity," with its emphasis on damnation for the glory of God, on total depravity and the inefficacy of means, and on God's "vindictive justice," "Tis as bad," said Chauncy, "if not worse than paganism."[2] The Hopkinsians were troublesome, but neither Hopkins nor his compatriot Joseph Bellamy was an intellectual giant of Edwards's stature. During the 1760s and 1770s they did not attract overwhelming numbers of adherents. Although Chauncy took issue with them in this period on the questions of free will and justification, they did not give him occasion to reveal his theory of universal salvation.

One could, however, discuss these speculations among sympathetic colleagues; Chauncy privately distributed his manuscripts to those men he thought would find them congenial. He also scouted for converts to his point of view,[3] but he broached the matter discreetly—so discreetly, in fact, that those "in the know" about Chauncy's writing spoke of it only in code: they called it *the pudding*.[4] Whenever groups of ministers gathered, those who had read Chauncy enjoyed a small pleasure by hinting mysteriously about having tasted the pudding, or bringing it to boil. Before long the cluster of initiates took on the earmarks of a small-scale, secret fraternity. Chauncy's own references to the subject were always circumspect, and sometimes merely coy.[5]

He had to set the pudding aside in the 1760s because at that time the Congregationalists faced a new threat that terrified them and drove home the need for unity. For the first time in years serious plans went forward in England to establish Anglican bishops in America. This prospect had served as one of the great American bugaboos for more than a century; rather than foment dissension in a crucial hour, Congregationalists needed to close ranks against a legendary enemy. "Let all mankind know," Cotton Mather had written in 1702, "that we came into the *Wilderness*, because we would worship God without that *Episcopacy*, that *Common Prayer*, and those unwarrantable *Ceremonies*, with which the *Land* of our *Fore Fathers' Sepulchres* has been defiled; we came hither because we would have our Posterity settled under the pure and full *Dispensations* of the Gospel; defended by *Rulers, that should be of our selves*."[6] Mather's successors reaffirmed his sentiments; his position had already become a staple of American history, preserved and passed on from one generation to another. Any proposal to establish episcopacy in America revived the memory of Charles I and Archbishop Laud and was cause for alarm.

127

This was of course true of no one more than Chauncy, who from his youth had nurtured the tale of his great-grandfather's sufferings at the hands of Archbishop Laud, and who had made a hobby of studying his famous ancestor's career. One can see from Chauncy's 1768 biographical sketch of the "Life of the Rev. President Chauncy" how strongly Chauncy's long-standing antagonism toward anything smacking of Archbishop Laud and ecclesiastical courts governed his thinking in the 1760s. Reviewing the story of his ancestor's escape from Laud and eventual rise to eminence in America, Chauncy portrayed his great-grandfather as a hero whose life was a classic type of the Puritan errand into the wilderness.

An essential part of the legend, however, was the hero's one failure of nerve, an error his descendant determined to avoid. Recalling the time in 1635 when his great-grandfather, having tangled with the court over his refusal to erect a communion rail in his parish church, recanted rather than go to prison, Chauncy was severe in his judgment: "His making an open recantation in court, and in the form that had been prescribed, and in order to a release from an adjudged penalty, was greatly dishonourable, though the effect of a great temptation." However, Chauncy added, "he never forgave himself this weakness and folly. The resentment of a rebuking conscience for such unworthy conduct made him often uneasy to his dying day." And of course that uneasiness carried through generations of Chauncys because of the president's will, which admonished his posterity never to dishonor the family in such a fashion. One way to keep faith with family honor was to resist any attempts to establish Church of England bishops in the colonies.[7]

In the eighteenth century such attempts had increased around the time of the Awakening, then subsided while Britain busied herself with waging war.[8] Chief proponent of the plan in Chauncy's time was Thomas Secker, bishop of Oxford. As early as 1741 Secker encouraged the missionary Society for the Propagation of the Gospel in Foreign Parts (popularly known as the S.P.G.) to request bishops in the colonies. Bishops were needed, ran the standard argument, to ordain native ministers, govern and discipline the Anglican churches, and perform ecclesiastical functions reserved in the Church of England to a bishop. As matters stood, candidates for orders sailed to England for ordination, and affairs of church government were entrusted to commissaries —"officers whom bishops of the Church of England are accustomed to appoint to exercise ecclesiastical jurisdiction in particular parts of their dioceses, where, owing to distance or to other causes, they cannot attend in person."[9] The commissary arrangement satisfied some Anglicans, but for many it was a source of hardship and confusion. Traditionally the archbishop of Canterbury presided over the S.P.G.

128

Secker gained that post in 1758 and planned an episcopate for the colonies. Many believed he would make it part of the settlements following the Seven Years' War.[10]

Young Jonathan Mayhew (1720–66), minister of Boston's West Church, led the colonial opposition to episcopacy.[11] In order to appreciate Chauncy's part in the episcopacy controversy, it is necessary to understand Mayhew's position, for they were coworkers in this cause. The son of the famous Experience Mayhew, Jonathan was born in Indian country at Martha's Vineyard. He graduated from Harvard in 1744. The wealthy West Church called him in 1747 to succeed its popular minister, William Hooper, who had surprisingly gone over to the Church of England.[12] Having rejected traditional Puritan doctrine while at Harvard, Mayhew was a rationalist and a moralist. He leaned toward Arminianism. Moreover he opposed the orthodox theories of original sin and the Trinity. Many Boston clergymen objected to Mayhew's ordination: he had already demonstrated a tendency to broadcast his unorthodox learnings. Some suspected that Chauncy arranged Mayhew's candidacy, for their opposition to the New-Lights and their emphasis on rationality made the two men allies. Despite the difference in their ages, they soon became fast friends. For his first fifteen years in Boston Mayhew's views earned him the displeasure of New-Lights and Anglicans alike; although Arminianism traditionally signified Anglicanism to the New England mind, Mayhew went out of his way to antagonize the Church of England.

In 1750, the year after his series of *Seven Sermons* prompted some Scottish friends of John Taylor to secure Mayhew the degree of Doctor of Divinity from the University of Aberdeen, he preached his most famous sermon, *A Discourse Concerning Unlimited Submission and Non-Resistance to the Higher Powers.*[13] The sermon powerfully affirms the natural right not only to disobey rulers who seriously abuse authority, but also to overthrow them. These sentiments would themselves have been enough to arouse controversy, but Mayhew's use of the revolution against Charles I as the classic example of a just revolt infuriated Anglicans all over the world. The Church of England, he said, might celebrate January 30, the anniversary of Charles's death, but he was a tyrant and deserved his downfall. Furthermore the best defense against the renewal of such tyranny was to steer clear of bishops and like clergymen.[14] Clearly his parishioners could rest assured that Mayhew would not follow his predecessor to the Church of England. The *Discourse* won Mayhew fame and indicated his strong opposition to the Anglicans. It proved later to be a "catechism of revolution" and a classic of revolutionary literature.[15]

In 1763, having been scorned as a heretic by many Boston ministers for more than a decade, Mayhew suddenly emerged as the figure around

129

whom Congregationalists could rally to meet the threat of episcopacy. Theological differences seemed less important in view of this more immediate, practical problem, symbolized for many by the erection of a handsome Anglican church in Cambridge, nearly within the shadows of Harvard Yard. Mayhew opposed episcopacy on theoretical grounds, to be sure—he believed that "their order itself is unscriptural"[16]—but, like Chauncy, he also brought a deep prejudice to the arena. "I own, that early in life, I imbibed strong *prepossessions* against diocesan bishops," he acknowledged, adding that he believed bishops "have generally been a pernicious set of men, both to church and state."[17] To his prejudice he joined personal antagonism towards Governor Bernard. He wanted, moreover, to dissociate his brand of Arminianism from Anglicanism, for he feared that his own congregation might fall to the "temptations of Anglican high society in Boston."[18] As a result he had no trouble believing the S.P.G.'s missionary work among the Indians actually masked a plot—aided by the Governor—to "dissolve and root out all our New-England churches; or . . . to reduce them all to the episcopal form."[19]

Mayhew believed his suspicions confirmed in 1762 when the S.P.G. helped block the establishment of a rival, the Congregationalist "Society for Propagating Christian Knowledge among the Indians of North America," which Mayhew helped organize. He made his charges public and argued the case with such able opponents as Henry Caner and Secker himself in a series of lengthy pamphlets published between 1763 and 1765: *Observations on the Charter and Conduct of the Society for the Propagation of the Gospel in Foreign Parts; A Defence of the Observations* . . .; and *Remarks on an Anonymous Tract*.[20] During the controversy the lines of argument shifted from charges against the S.P.G. to disputes over Secker's plan to install colonial bishops, for the archbishop admitted that he had such a plan. He outlined its provisions in his *Answer to Dr. Mayhew's Observations on the Charter and Conduct of the Society for the Propagation of the Gospel in Foreign Parts* (1764). Secker printed his *Answer* anonymously, however, and his authorship was discovered only later.[21]

The archbishop proposed that bishops would operate in America under strict limitations. They would have power to regulate only Anglican clergy, not laity; they would not share in civil government or interfere with the authority of the governor or other officials in such matters as probates and marriage licenses; and the colonies would not bear the expense of their maintenance.[22] Mayhew remained unconvinced. There was no assurance that the proposal of an anonymous writer was official; even if it were, he could not bring himself to believe that such limitations were meant seriously. Finally, despite protestations, nothing could shake Mayhew's convictions that once bishops arrived the door would be open for future tyranny. "Bishops being once fixed in America," he said, "pretexts might easily be found, both for encreasing their number, and enlarging their powers."[23] Who could tell? The next step could well be the suppression of Dissenters, or, at the least, heavy taxation for the support of the hierarchy. No amount of arguing could convince Mayhew that the Archbishop's plan was innocent. When, at the age of forty-five, Mayhew died of a stroke on July 9, 1766, Bostonians honored him as "a friend to liberty both civil and religious."[24]

Chauncy preached Mayhew's eulogy[25] and, in an uncommon gesture, prayed over his body at the funeral.[26] Although Mayhew was fifteen years Chauncy's junior, they were "intimate companions";[27] after Mayhew's death, Chauncy took up his cause. Their opinions on the question coincided at almost every point.

The older man had not watched idly while the struggle raged. For the first few years he worked behind the scenes, arranging for publications, pulling political strings, organizing the opposition forces. He felt he knew the theological arguments for and against episcopacy as well as any man, since he had devoted four hard years of study to them and had collected a deskfull of extracts and evidence. Referring to his *Compleat View of Episcopacy*, he said, "If I am qualified for any thing, 'tis for a work of this nature."[28] In 1762, having been invited to deliver the annual Dudleian Lecture at Harvard, he publicly identified himself as a theoretician of the anti-episcopacy movement by choosing as his subject *The Validity of Presbyterian Ordination*.[29]

He aimed in this lecture to demonstrate, from his study of the early church fathers, that neither scripture nor history supported Anglican claims for an order of bishops superior to presbyters. The episcopal form of government, he argued, could not be justified from scripture. It was not apostolic, nor was it even as ancient as Anglicans contended, since it appeared only in the third century. Christ founded one order of ministry, synonymously termed bishops and presbyters. The only evidence to the contrary resides in the writings of Ignatius of Antioch, and the bulk of his work is fraudulent.[30] Chauncy's sermon was an early salvo in the controversy, fired even before Mayhew went after the S.P.G. It demonstrated that Chauncy's objections were, at least on some counts, carefully considered and not entirely the result of blind prejudice.

A round from so heavy a gun as Chauncy's could not pass unnoticed. On January 7, 1763 Henry Caner of King's Chapel wrote urgently to Archbishop Secker, informing him of recent "provocations and Insults" in Boston. To prove his claim that Congregationalist zeal was "chiefly pointed at suppressing the Church of England," he mentioned that they "lately printed a sermon by Dr. Chauncy of this

Town, in support of the validity of Presbyterian ordination, not without hard and ungenerous reflections upon Episcopal Government." The "only reason" Caner could find for "that bitterness of spirit which seems thus of a sudden to break out among the Dissenters is, that they look upon the war as near a conclusion, and that a great part of the conquests made in America will probably be ceded to the British Crown." He continued: "So remarkable a Crisis, it is natural to imagine, will fall under such regulations as will either greatly establish the Church of England, or the Dissenting Interest, in this part of the world. Their activity is therefore employed to the uttermost, both here and in England, to secure the Event in their favor. And I am sorry to say, that their conduct in this matter is as disingenuous as their diligence is remarkable." Caner concluded the letter by explaining why Boston Anglicans had done nothing to oppose "these proceedings." They were, he said, a "Rope of Sand; there is no union, no authority among us; we cannot even summon a Convention for united Counsell and advice, while the Dissenting Ministers have their Monthly, Quarterly, and Annual Associations, Conventions, &c., to advise, assist and support each other. . . ."[31]

Although a rope of sand in America, the Church of England held close-knit power in Parliament. Mayhew and Chauncy knew that their rival to the S.P.G.—the Society for Propagating Christian Knowledge among the Indians of North America—stood no chance of success without government approval, and they knew that approval would be very hard to get. Mayhew, who had maintained a lifelong concern for the Indian missions, earnestly wanted the society to succeed. It is likely that Chauncy's interest in the organization grew from his association with the younger pastor. At any rate, in 1762 Chauncy busied himself with the problems of the western Indians. He had several motives. First, he believed in the gospel promise that "all nations of the earth would be blessed in Christ, the seed of Abraham."[32] Thus the Indians merited a chance for salvation, and they deserved ministers to help them.

Second, the imminent conclusion of the war would bring Indians out of French dominion into English hands, thus offering a perfect chance to wean them away from Catholicism and into a belief in Christ.[33] Chauncy had other, more earthly aims. "Gospelizing" would benefit both the souls of the Mohawks and the safety of the colonists; converting them, Chauncy remarked, would be the "least expensive method to make and keep them our good friends and peaceable neighbours."[34] Even more specifically, the church receiving rights to this missionary territory would greatly strengthen its position.[35] Since Mayhew and Chauncy believed the S.P.G. schemed to "episcopize" the colonies anyway, they could ill afford to yield this prize. Thus

132

they and some other influential Bostonians had taken the initiative and formed their own local society. James Bowdoin was president. They shrewdly opened membership to all denominations. The general court granted them a charter, but the act still required the approval of England's Privy Council.[36]

Chauncy and Mayhew knew that Church of England pressure could be brought to bear at this point. Anticipating a fight, they worked hard to install one of their own men as Massachusetts agent in Great Britain. In April 1762 the veteran agent, James Bollan, vacated the post; after much maneuvering the position went to Jasper Mauduit, an English Dissenter.[37] Chauncy and his friends immediately informed Mauduit that his job was to assist the incorporating act. In a letter to the new agent Chauncy dropped broad hints about the answer he should give to Archbishop Secker's objections:

Tis strange to us here, that the Arch-Bishop, or Society of which he is president, should be in a disposition to oppose our incorporating act. We have no interest of our own in view. We have no intention to oppose the Church of England, or do anything that may tend in the least to disserve it. Our sole aim is, to be under advantage to carry the Gospel of the blessed God to the Indian Natives on our western borders. And such a design, one would think, should be agreable to all who wish well to the name of Christ, and would be glad to see his kingdom settled in these dark corners of the earth. We are not so disaffected to the Church of England but that we should rejoice to see Missionaries sent from the society of which the Arch-B'p is *praeses* to promote the knowledge of Christ among the Indian tribes. The harvest is great. There is full room for Missionaries from them, as well as from us; and should they send them, we should not only wish them Godspeed, but do all in our power that their mission might turn out to good effect.

Chauncy then politely but firmly warned Mauduit against the temptation to let the matter ride:

You intimate as tho', in consequence of the opposition you are like to meet with, you tho't it best not to push an immediate confirmation of the act, but to let it lie by to receive its confirmation of course. For my self, I am clearly of the mind, tis best to press the matter now, be the event what it will. None of the money subscribed to our fund is payable till the act has received the Royal sanction; and if we must wait for this three years, we shall lose the benefit of the income of the subscribed money the whole of that time. And further, which is of more importance, the Spirit which has happily been excited in so many to promote the cause of Christ among the Indians will probably subside, and we shall lose the special opportunity we now have of collecting yet large sums in addition to what we have already got. If the confirmation of the act is delayed, I shall look upon it as nearly equal to its being negatived; and all the pains we have taken to collect monies, and raise a fund to serve the most valuable end . . . will come to nothing. . . . Tis not likely, if we fail in our present attempt, in which we have exerted ourselves beyond all that could be expected, that we shall ever make another. How they who set themselves to oppose so generous, so pious and christian a design will be able to give a good account of their conduct in the day of the appearing of Jesus Christ, is beyond me to say.[38]

The letter alludes to Chauncy's activities on behalf of the society during 1762 and 1763. Indeed he had taken great pains to set the project upon sound financial and organizational footings. Obtaining missionaries, prayers, and money were his primary concerns; to see all this wasted would be a crushing disappointment. He had especially encouraged one missionary, Mr. Eli Forbes. Forbes visited the Chauncys in 1762 and preached to the First Church about his experiences and the need for more help among the western Indians. Later he kept Chauncy informed about affairs in the "dark corners of the earth."[39] Chauncy also assisted another young man, Joseph Bowman, to work in the missions. In August 1762 he preached Bowman's ordination sermon, asking both for prayers of the people and funds to provide a *"perpetual* income for the service of Christ among the Indians."[40] While approval of the incorporation was pending, friends of the society collected several thousand pounds for its support. But they could not use the money without royal sanction.

Despite high initial hopes for Mauduit, Chauncy and other Congregationalists soon realized that he lacked aggressiveness. Acting upon the Board of Trade's negative opinion, the Privy Council disallowed the act in May 1763; during the crucial board meeting, Mauduit was at home with an attack of the gout.[41] It is questionable, however, whether any amount of lobbying could have secured approval of the incorporation act. Following this tremendous disappointment, Mayhew launched his series of attacks on the S.P.G., claiming until his death that Secker had sabotaged the colonial plan.

After Mayhew's death Chauncy stepped into the battle to answer strong proposals by the advocates of episcopacy. Bostonians knew from forty years' experience to expect flying sparks whenever an adversary collided with Charles Old-Brick. They were not disappointed. Newspaper publishers were delighted to fan the flames and ships carried bundles of inflammatory pamphlets and letters to both shores. Before the flurry subsided, Chauncy tangled with the British bishop of Landaff and the American Anglican Dr. Thomas Bradbury Chandler; he contributed nearly a thousand pages to the literature of the controversy.

In 1767 an address to the S.P.G. by John Ewer, Bishop of Landaff, spurred Chauncy to action. Carl Bridenbaugh states that no "Anglican prelate of the eighteenth century committed as great an indiscretion" as did Ewer in this sermon.[42] The bishop held the shortage of native ministers responsible for terribly inadequate religious instruction in the colonies. He concluded that one could trace this shortage to the lack of resident bishops, and that the establishment of bishops would solve the problem. The American Church would then "go out of its infant state; be able to stand upon its own legs; and without foreign help support and spread itself. Then the business of this society will have been brought to the happy issue intended."[43] He stressed the hardships suffered by candidates for ordination: distance, inconvenience, danger, expense, and the prospect of arriving unknown in a strange land. The descendants of the Puritans bristled at these opinions; incredibly, Ewer made matters worse by turning the Pilgrim legend completely on its head, asserting that since the earliest days the colonists had neglected the Christian faith altogether and turned heathen themselves—becoming "Infidels and Barbarians."[44]

Andrew Eliot received a copy of the sermon from Thomas Hollis. In a letter to his benefactor he explained the circumstances of Chauncy's reply:

When I received Dr. Ewer's Sermon, I intended to have published some remarks upon it in the public prints, as you advised.—But my good friend Dr. Chauncy, to whom I lent the Sermon, expressing an inclination to write something at large, I gave my copy to him. . . . From what he has communicated to me, his remarks appear to be written with freedom and manly sense. It is in the Press & if it is out in season, I shall send you some Copies. . . . When I knew the Dr.'s design I gave up the thought of publishing in the Papers—He might think it interfered with him.—[45]

Chauncy's answer immediately became a best seller. Eliot thought it "solid and just."[46] One admirer suggested that every minister and representative in Massachusetts receive a free copy.[47]

To answer the bishop, Chauncy revived one of his favorite literary vehicles, the "Letter to a Friend."[48] A tone of weary contempt pervades the piece. In Chauncy's judgment, to attack the early settlers simply revealed immense ignorance; Ewer's arguments were equally misinformed. For fifty-six pages Chauncy carried on a relentless polemic, even belittling the difficulties involved in going to England for orders. (What he hoped to accomplish by this tack is a puzzle. Everyone could easily see that hardships actually existed.) His main point—and one he reiterated often during the next four years—was that the plan to send bishops actually concealed a more sinister scheme. Using the bishop's comment about "THE BUSINESS OF THE SOCIETY" as a springboard, Chauncy jumped to this conclusion: "The conduct of the Society has, for many years, given us reason to suspect their MAIN VIEW was to EPISCOPISE the Colonies; but we were never before, that I know of, told so in direct terms."[49] Episcopacy, Chauncy contended, would be forced on the colonies; once they were "episcopised," the Church of England would have a majority in the land.[50] Like Mayhew, Chauncy never abandoned his belief in the plot, and it colored every aspect of the debate that followed.

During 1766 and most of 1767, fear of the impending takeover reached such a pitch that many ministers seriously considered a plan to unify North America's non-Episcopal churches in a loose association, hoping thereby to thwart the Episcopalians and to assist the Congregational cause. Ezra Stiles had proposed such a program for several years, and Chauncy had long been interested in it.[51] After the Stamp Act, the idea caught hold among New York and Pennsylvania Presbyterians, who felt especially threatened by the alleged Anglican plot. In May 1766 eighty ministers, meeting in New York at the United Synod of New York and Philadelphia, voted to approach the consociated churches of Connecticut at their general meeting in June. Accordingly two Presbyterian representatives, John Ewing and Patrick Alison, presented to the Connecticut convention copies of the Anglican proposal for a bishop, and suggested a union—ultimately of all American non-Anglican Protestant churches. The Connecticut meeting agreed to a conference in November to work out the arrangements. In the meantime, Alison, Ewing, and Stiles approached the New England Congregationalists. Stiles himself rode to Boston at commencement time in July to lobby for the scheme at the annual gathering of Massachusetts ministers. New England reaction was mixed. Some favored the idea, but many Congregationalists feared that the united assembly would assume authority; others declined to join with Presbyterians. Some feared repercussions in England. Stiles took these objections into account. Upon his return to Rhode Island he drafted articles for union which he thought broad enough to assure freedom for individual churches and yet strong enough to permit effective work against episcopacy.

Chauncy liked the plan and tried to win support for it in Massachusetts. He envisioned not only a colonial association, but a union of all Congregational and Presbyterian churches in North America and Great Britain. He thought that even the Quakers and Baptists might want to join against the Anglican threat. By late 1767, however, Chauncy saw that not enough Massachusetts Congregationalists shared his ecumenical ardor. The old divisions were too great to overcome. Realizing that this plan would bring strife and discord rather than union to his province, Chauncy settled for what he had: general cooperation in the struggle against a common foe. The Presbyterians in the middle colonies and the consociations of Connecticut New-Lights did, however, unite, and their organization operated effectively well into the 1770s.[52]

While plans for union went forward, Chauncy battled Thomas Chandler, the next controversialist to appear. In his *An Appeal to the*

Public, in Behalf of the Church of England in America (1767), Chandler forthrightly admitted that an episcopacy plan existed, but he hastened to add that the bishops' power would be limited and no one's liberty would be threatened. He aimed to prove colonial fears unfounded: the bishops would come only to govern, confirm, and ordain; they would enjoy spiritual and ecclesiastical authority only, and this solely over Church of England clergy. His proposals resembled those advanced earlier to Mayhew by Archbishop Secker. Chandler, however, committed several indiscretions in his *Appeal*. First, he did not rule out entirely the possibility of future civil power for bishops: "Should the government see fit hereafter to invest them with some degree of civil power, worthy of their acceptance, which it is impossible to say they will not, yet it is inconceivable that any would thereby be injured." Second, he qualified his statement about taxation, remarking that should the colonists be taxed, it would only be for a small amount, since the society already had funds to maintain the bishops.[53] Third, he scoffed at Chauncy's Dudleian lecture on the validity of Presbyterian ordination, and questioned the doctor's scholarship.[54] Finally, attempting to strike a note of fairness, he invited objectors to voice their views before "the tribunal of the public."[55] Chauncy seized upon these tactical errors. One did not challenge the Old-Brick with impunity in an area in which Chauncy felt supremely competent. The predictable pamphlet war ensued.

Chauncy wrote 205 pages to answer Chandler's *Appeal*. Chandler came back the next year with *The Appeal Defended*.[56] Chauncy countered in 1770 with 180 pages of *Reply to Dr. Chandler's 'Appeal Defended'*;[57] and then followed with his mammoth 474-page volume, *A Compleat View of Episcopacy* (1771).[58] Chandler's return volley was *The Appeal Farther Defended: In Answer to the Farther Misrepresentations of Dr. Chauncy* (1771),[59] but by then the force of the *Compleat View* was simply too much to combat. At the end of 1771 the debate was over.

Most of old Doctor Chauncy's adversaries felt as weary and ground-down as did Samuel Seabury, who sighed, "I am tired and beat out. Had I suspected there was so much Nonsense, so much trifling, so much Falsehood in the Way, I believe I never should have medled with him. Tis like suing a Beggar, or shearing a Hog or fighting a Skunk."[60]

Chandler struggled to convince the "opposers" that the bishops would be purely spiritual rulers. But Chauncy looked suspiciously at Chandler's incautious admissions about civil power and taxation. He doubted Anglican sincerity even more when Chandler conceded (in *The Appeal Defended*) that the plan included spiritual courts—albeit to try Church of England clergy only.[61] From the outset Chauncy scorned Chandler as a scholar. The man obviously spoke from igno-

137

rance of the ancient writers, or was "most evidently under the prevailing influence of Interest, or Malignity, or both, or something worse"[62] when he disagreed with the Dudleian Lecture. Such awkward attempts to disguise his true intentions convinced Chauncy that Chandler's *Appeals* could not be taken seriously. In fact Chauncy offered some counter suggestions that he surely meant sarcastically. If ordination is such a problem, have the ministers ordained either by the Roman Catholic bishop in the North or the Moravian in the South.[63] Furthermore, rather than waste money on an unworkable plan, spend it where it will do some good: send Anglican ministers to North Carolina—the same limbo to which he had assigned itinerants during the Great Awakening—where the price of one luxurious bishop could maintain numerous missionaries.

Nothing Chandler promised convinced Chauncy that American bishops would respect limitation, and he believed that once they discarded their limits they would rapidly become tyrants. The Old-Brick's principal objection was that the Anglicans wanted "nothing short of a COMPLETE CHURCH HIERARCHY, after the pattern of that at home, with like officers, in all their various degrees of dignity, with a like large revenue, for their grand support, and with the allowance of no other privilege to dissenters but that of a bare toleration."[64] Throughout the controversy Chauncy insisted strenuously that the colonies would forfeit their religious liberty if bishops settled in America. The Puritans had fled the old world to secure precisely this liberty; now the Anglicans wanted to snatch these liberties again. This was speculation about the future, but for proof one had only to study the nature of the bishop's office and consider Chandler's admissions.

Mayhew had made similar charges about Secker, but by the time Chandler and Chauncy clashed in the late 1760s, New Englanders believed they had further proofs besides the admissions of Anglican leaders. They could point to the actions of the British ministry itself, which seemed to have embarked since 1763 upon a determined campaign to deprive the colonists of their dearly held rights. It was not hard to believe that religious liberties would vanish, when everyone could see that the ministry was resolutely driving Americans into slavery. Emotions ran high in the mid-sixties; colonists were ready to believe that religious and civil liberties were two sides of the same issue, and that to attack one was to attack the other. Chauncy helped convince them.

To understand how Chauncy (and most of the other colonials) came to hold this severe view, we must look beyond his natural predisposition against Episcopacy, his training, and the admonitions of his great-grandfather, to the political events that rocked Boston and changed Chauncy's life between 1763 and 1767. The chief of these was of course the Stamp Act of 1765.

138

The Stamp Act followed upon five years of friction between the colonies and the British government. In 1760, when George III ascended the throne, the three-year administration of Massachusetts's popular governor, Thomas Pownall, yielded to Francis Bernard. Thomas Hutchinson held the posts of Lieutenant Governor and president of the Massachusetts Council. The year 1761 saw parties form around Hutchinson and James Otis during the writs-of-assistance controversy. With the end of the war in 1763 the ministry under Chancellor Grenville renewed its interest in the colonies and tried to tighten colonial administration and defense. The ministry restricted the settlement of the newly won Allegheny land, took control over Indian affairs, increased restrictions on colonial paper currency, settled a standing army of British regulars in the colonies, and taxed the colonists to maintain them. Part of the money was to come from taxing molasses imported from the West Indies—thus effectively regulating trade with those islands—and from requiring the colonists to buy government stamps for all newspapers, official documents, and commercial papers. Hitherto Parliament had taxed commodities only to regulate trade, not to raise revenue. The tax on molasses, or Sugar Act (1764), was met with alarm but only token resistance. It was assumed that the Stamp Act would also be accepted. But at its passage in 1765 the colonists virtually exploded; they refused to obey. While making life miserable for the stamp agents, they called a Congress to deny Parliament's right to levy internal colonial taxes and demanded repeal. The cause of colonial unity advanced immeasurably.[65]

Chauncy strongly opposed the Stamp Act. In a sermon discussing its repeal, he reviewed his objections. First, the measure worked against the commercial interests of the entire British dominion. Second, the colonies were too poor to pay the tax. "There is scarce a man in any of the Colonies, certainly there is not in the New England ones, that would be deemed worthy of the name of a rich man in Great-Britain," he claimed, and he argued further that the arduous labor of the colonists in subduing the new country and fitting it for profitable use should in itself be considered "a natural tax, which, though it has made way for an astonishing increase of subjects to the British Empire, greatly adding to its dignity and strength, has yet been the occasion of keeping us poor and low." To add to the burden, the colonists already paid heavy local taxes to support the recent war. Chauncy considered these taxes proportionally greater than those paid by Scotland, Ireland, or England. In short, "the STAMP-DUTY . . . would, in a few years, have taken away all of our money, and rendered us absolutely incapable, either of supporting the Government here, or of carrying on any sort of commerce, unless by an exchange of commodities." Chauncy feared even more the loss of "certain liberties and privileges, valued by us next to life itself," including the right to trial by one's peers and representation as a condition for taxation. Perhaps the British no longer considered the colonists Englishmen, he speculated, for without these rights Americans would no longer be brothers, but slaves. Chauncy's remarks on this point reveal a canny understanding of the colonial temper:

> Whether the Colonists were invested with a RIGHT to these liberties and privileges that ought not to be wrested from them, or whether they were not, tis the truth of fact, that they really thought they were: ALL of them as natural heirs to it, by being born subjects to the British Crown; and some of them, by additional charter-grants, the legality of which, instead of being contested, have all along, from the days of our fathers, been assented to, and allowed of, by the supreme authority at home. And they imagined, whether justly, or not, I dispute not, that their RIGHT to the free and full enjoyment of these privileges was their righteous due in consequence of what they, and their fore-fathers, had done and suffered in subduing and defending these American lands, not only for their own support, but to add extent, strength and glory to the British-Crown. And as it had been early and deeply impressed on their minds, that their Charter-privileges were RIGHTS that had been dearly paid for by a vast expence of blood, treasure and labor, without which this continent must have still remained in a wilderness-state, and the property of savages only; it could not but strongly put in motion their passion of grief, when they were laid under a Parliamentary restraint as to the exercise of that liberty, they esteemed their greatest glory. It was eminently this that filled their minds with jealousie, and at length a settled fear, lest they should gradually be brought into a state of the most abject slavery.[66]

Faced with such a situation, "we should have been stupid, had not a spirit been excited in us to apply, in all reasonable ways, for the removal of so insupportable a burden."[67] Most of Boston balked at the Stamp Act; many of Chauncy's friends applied for its removal. In some cases their applications were more passionate than reasonable. Among the organizations—generally called "Sons of Liberty"—that worked against the measure, Sam Adams's famous, long-established "Caucus Club" wielded the most power. Chauncy knew well at least two members, Adams himself and the Reverend Samuel Cooper, who was Adams's pastor and the club's unofficial chaplain. Chauncy's printer, Benjamin Edes of the Boston *Gazette*, led the influential "Loyal Nine." Whether Chauncy officially belonged to any of these societies is unknown, but he probably held membership in the Whig Club. John C. Miller comments that "scarcely a patriot club was without a divine who lent an odor of sanctity to what conservatives believed would otherwise have been rank treason."[68] A popular ballad, "The Boston Ministers," insisted in one version,[69]

140

                    And Charles Old Brick, if well or sick,
                    Will cry for Liberty

and in another version:[70]

                    That fine preacher, called a teacher,
                    Of old brick church the first,
                    Regards no grace to men in place
                    And is by tories curst.
                    At young & old he'll rave & scold
                    And is in things of State
                    A zealous whig than Wilkes more big,
                    In church a tyrant great.

A Whig more zealous than John Wilkes was very zealous indeed. Peter Oliver, who should have known, put Chauncy in James Otis's party;[71] Otis was a staunch member of the Boston Whig Club.[72] Chauncy also numbered among his friends John Hancock, John Adams, and Josiah Quincy, Jr., all prominent Whigs. The pastor of the First Church, then, probably worked with the Whig Club and other patriotic societies to nullify the Stamp Act.

He did not at this point, however, countenance the "violent outrages" upon the property of others which resulted in the destruction of the homes of Andrew Oliver and Thomas Hutchinson. He spoke against "villainous conduct" and "mobbish actions," realizing that the colonies would only suffer in the long run if they gained a reputation for mob rule.[73] On the other hand, although he favored redress through proper channels, he would fight for his "inalienable rights" if it came to that. "Dr. Chauncy," John Adams once said, "would not, for all the Commissions in the Gift of all the Potentates upon Earth, become the Tool of any Man alive."[74] Years after the crisis Adams recalled the mood of the colonies in 1766:

> It has been a question whether, if the ministry had persevered in support of the stamp act, and sent a military force of ships and troops to enforce its execution, the people of the colonies would then have resisted. Dr. Chauncy and Dr. Mayhew, in sermons which they preached and printed after the repeal of the stamp act, have left to posterity their explicit opinions upon this question. If my more extensive familiarity with the sentiments and feelings of the people in the eastern, western and southern counties of Massachusetts may apologize for my presumption, I subscribe without a doubt to the opinions of Chauncy and Mayhew.[75]

Chauncy's explicit opinion:

> The Colonies were never before in a state of such discontent, anxiety, and perplexing sollicitude; Some despairing of a redress, some hoping for it, and all fearing what would be the event. And had it been the determination of the King and Parliament to have carried the STAMP-ACT into effect by ships

141

of war and an embarkation of troops, their condition, however unhappy before, would have been inconceivably more so. They must either have submitted to what they thought an insupportable burden, and have parted with their property without any will of their own, or have stood upon their defence; in either of which cases, their situation must have been deplorably sad. So far as I am able to judge from that firmness of mind, and resolution of spirit, which appeared among all sorts of persons, as grounded upon this principle deeply rooted in their minds, that they had a CONSTITUTIONAL RIGHT to grant their own monies and to be tried by their peers, 'tis more than probable, they would not have submitted, unless they had been obliged to it by superior power. Not that they had a thought in their hearts, as may have been represented, of being an independent people. They esteemed it both their happiness and their glory to be, in common with the inhabitants of England, Scotland and Ireland, the subjects of King George the third, whom they heartily love and honor, and in defence of whose Person and Crown they would chearfully expend their treasure, and lose even their blood. But it was a sentiment they had imbibed, that they should be wanting neither in loyalty to their King, nor a due regard to the British-Parliament, if they should defend those rights which they imagined were unalienable, upon the foot of justice, by any power on earth.[76]

Providence operated in favor of justice, and the threat dissolved for a time.

Repealing the Stamp Act, however, did not dissolve the specter of episcopacy. Carl Bridenbaugh has shown that the threat of civil tyranny, symbolized by the Stamp Act, coalesced with the threat of ecclesiastical tyranny, symbolized by the episcopacy "plot," and that the union of the two issues in the colonial mind helps explain the bitterly intense reaction against the Grenville Acts.[77] For a short time after repeal Chauncy hoped that his fears had been groundless. In his sermon on that happy occasion, he sketched his vision of America:

> WE may now be easie in our minds, contented with our condition. We may be at peace and quiet among ourselves, every one minding his own business. All ground of complaint, that we are "sold for bond-men and bond-women," is removed away; and instead of being slaves to those who treat us with rigor, we are indulged the full exercise of those liberties which have been transmitted to us, as the richest inheritance, from our fore-fathers. We have now greater reason than ever to love, honor and obey our gracious King, and pay all becoming reverence and respect to his two houses of Parliament; and may with intire confidence, rely on their wisdom, lenity, kindness, and power, to promote our welfare.[78]

After the joy of celebration died down, however, the colonists learned that not everyone was minding his own business. The days of salutary neglect were over. Old fears did not die so easily. On the religious side, such Anglicans as Ewer, Chandler, and Samuel Johnson began to discuss the arrival of bishops in America; and it appeared to

142

many that civil tyranny had merely stepped aside momentarily, to return again in the shape of further, thinly disguised revenue taxes. The Townshend Acts of 1767 imposed duties on tea, paper, glass, painter's colors, and lead. The new acts also established a Board of Customs Commissioners in Boston. The money collected, furthermore, was to pay royal officials. As Bridenbaugh remarks, the "Great Fear of Episcopacy reached its highest intensity during the years 1767–70 when Anglican missionaries, encouraged and assisted by prelates in England, persisted in their attempts to procure bishops for America at the same time that Charles Townshend and the ministry ventured for the second time to reorder the British Empire."[79] Thus, by the time Chauncy clashed with Chandler, the two issues had become inseparable in colonial thinking; for Chauncy to insist that they came hand-in-glove was not merely a debater's trick, although the old pastor of the First Church certainly knew the pragmatic value of stressing their connection to an audience that wanted to believe in it.

CHAPTER TEN

Divinity, Zeal, Rancor, and Revenge

From the time of the Stamp Act until the outbreak of the Revolutionary War Chauncy caught the public eye more than at any time since the Great Awakening. Mayhew was dead; some other ministers, such as Ezra Stiles, had withdrawn from the political scene after concluding that politics and religion did not mix. Chauncy, however, had always assumed that they did mix. In the 1770s he became recognized by the Congregationalists as their defender against "Anglican scheming" and by the people of Boston as a pugnacious champion of political liberty— even rebellion—in the face of governmental tyranny. During this time Chauncy became politically radicalized.

This is remarkable, for Chauncy was no wild young Turk in 1770. He had completed forty-three years as pastor of the First Church. He was the senior Boston clergyman. His health was not good, partly because of the various ailments that had nagged him for thirty years, but also because he had begun to have trouble with his legs.[1] And he did not think of himself as young at heart. "My old friends and acquaintance," he wrote Ezra Stiles, "are almost all gone to the other world, and it is now too late to contract new friendships with former intimacy. I am well acquainted with many of our younger clergymen, as well as many of other orders, but age and youth do not so well match together. I expect no such friendships as former ones, till I go into another state."[2] In 1769 three old friends and his eldest daughter died within a period of six weeks. Edward Holyoke, the president of Harvard, died on June 1, 1769. Thomas Foxcroft, Chauncy's associate for forty-two years, died on June 18, after suffering greatly since a serious

144

stroke in 1762. Nine days later Joseph Sewall, his friend for half a century, was dead.[3] As if three deaths within a month were not enough, on July 12 Elizabeth Greenleaf, Chauncy's daughter, died at Newburyport.[4] The lessons to be learned from their deaths, Chauncy said, "I would consider as particularly applicable to my self. I am now approaching towards the time" beyond which "I cannot dwell in this my fleshly tabernacle, unless I had 'great strength,' which I know I have not." He considered himself the last representative of a great generation, shortly to be laid in his grave.[5]

But Chauncy lived on to help construct a new country. When he marked his sixty-fifth birthday on January 1, 1770 the Boston he had known just ten years before was gone forever. The America he had envisioned after the repeal of the Stamp Act—a state of "peace and quiet," with "everyone minding his own business," loving, honoring and obeying the king and respecting Parliament—had been only a dream. Now two regiments of His Majesty's troops paraded on Boston Common in answer to the town's vigorous resistance to the Townshend Acts; the king's representatives in the customs houses relied on British bayonets to assure the honor and obedience of the colonists; the governor himself had fled. Moreover Chauncy's characterization of his fellow Bostonians—"good friends to Government," and "peaceable loyal Subjects"—not overly accurate in 1766, certainly applied no longer in 1770. The Whigs had questioned the very authority of Parliament and the people had developed a powerful pride in their self-sufficiency and national identity.[6] The brilliant Boston propagandists and politicians on the one hand, and the severe policy of the ministry on the other, strengthened colonial pugnacity.

Even in the dead of the Boston winter of 1770 the town simmered with resentment. Between 1766 and 1770 Chauncy's political views had grown more radical, until at times it was hard to distinguish his sentiments from those of Samuel Adams. The specter of episcopacy fed the nationalism and pride in self-sufficiency that had always lain near the front of his store of emotions; the organized resistance to the Townshend Acts seems to have been the agent needed to bring them into the open. And with the springtime came the "Boston Massacre" of March 5, 1770, an event that launched some of the most flamboyant years of Chauncy's career.

On that day five members of the Boston mob died at the hands of British soldiers. The Sons of Liberty blamed the troops and the officer of the day, Captain Preston. They elevated the dead men to martyrdom and demanded a speedy trial and punishment of the murderers. Lieutenant Governor Hutchinson, now acting head of the government in the absence of Governor Bernard, managed, however, to delay the trial for six months. Chauncy badgered the governor relentlessly during

145

these months, and, because of the delay, delivered in May one of his most remarkable orations, the election day sermon of 1770, a speech demonstrating how far toward fanaticism he had allowed chauvinism to lead him.

In his own lively style Tory Peter Oliver relates an almost incredible incident leading up to this speech. If true it suggests that Chauncy had gone wholeheartedly to the Adams camp. After describing how the clergy blew up "the Coals of Sedition," Oliver narrates:

> One of those zealous Divines, Dr. *Chauncy*, who was the Head Master of the School of the Prophets, had heard that a Gentleman was wounded, on that unhappy Night when the Soldiers had fired. He waited upon the Gentleman, & asked him, whether he did not design to prosecute Capt. *Preston* in damages? The Gentleman replied, "No Sir! It will be of no Advantage. Capt. *Preston* is to be tried for his Life. If he should be convicted he will suffer Death, & then I cannot recover any Damages; & if he is acquitted I shall be in the same Circumstances"; to which this hoary-headed Divine, in the true Spirit of the Inquisition, said—"if I was to be one of the Jury upon his Trial, I would bring him in guilty; *evidence or no Evidence.*" What a noble Instance this of Divinity, Zeal, Rancor & Revenge, jumbled together into one Mass! But he had imbibed more of the Temper of *James & Peter*, than that of his & their Master. He was always for calling down Fire from Heaven to destroy his political Opposers.[7]

In the light of Chauncy's strictures against Davenport, Oliver's final comment is particularly ironic.

The letters of Ann Hulton, sister of Customs Commissioner Henry Hulton, offer another example of the frenzy that seized Chauncy in 1770. On June 19 a mob attacked her brother's house and threatened his life. The following Sunday, according to Miss Hulton, "Dr. Ch--cy preached a Sermon on that occasion & told his people plainly out of the Pulpit, that the Commissr broke his own windows to cast an odium on the Country & the next day this Rev. Dr. went all about, impressg this opinion on the People & However ridiculous it may seem, it was actually believed by two thirds of the People in Boston."[8] A letter from Chauncy to Richard Price lends credence to this account. After Hulton arrived in Boston, Price wrote to Chauncy, recommending the new commissioner as a man of integrity. Chauncy trusted no commissioner. Two weeks after the Boston massacre Chauncy replied to Price:

> If he was in England a man of "integrity," he has been greatly corrupted since he came here. He, with the other commissioners, have transmitted home cargoes of the most flagrant lies . . . and these abominable falsehoods have been the occasion of greater mischief to this town of Boston, both in a civil and religious sense, than it ever suffered fm the day of its first settlement by our fathers. I never yt saw Mr. Hulton, and happy would it have been for this poor distressed town, if it had never seen these commissioners.[9]

146

With tempers so high, and with normally temperate men willing to believe any rumor, it is no wonder that General Gage and Governor Hutchinson feared a lynch mob. Hutchinson worked diligently to postpone the trial until Boston cooled down. His opponents worked equally hard to keep the matter before the public. The illness of two judges forced postponement until June; in May Hutchinson delayed the trial again until the August session of the court. He wrote to Gage:

> I have given constant attention to the case of Captain Preston and the Soldiers by taking the advantage of a number of accidental occurrences have procured without any Tumult a continuance of the Trial to the next Term, which begins the last Tuesday in August, before which time I hope for some express orders from the Ministry. I never could be reconciled to the Trial's being brought on this Term, but the Temper of the people was such that it was necessary to keep them in expectation of it until they were somewhat cooled and could be diverted by some other Subject for their attention.[10]

Hutchinson's diversionary tactic was to get the general court out of Boston; accordingly he moved the session to Cambridge. Howling that this was unconstitutional, the Sons of Liberty organized a protest meeting for May 30, the day appointed for the election of counsellors. Samuel Cooke was to preach the traditional election sermon in Cambridge; the Liberty Boys countered with an election sermon of their own—thus, they trumpeted, preserving the "antient custom" of praising God in Boston on election day. Chauncy was the obvious choice for preacher. On May 28 their delegation asked him to honor the town with an address at the Old Brick.[11] In two days Chauncy prepared his thirty-five-page sermon, *Trust in God, the Duty of a People in a Day of Trouble*,[12] which he delivered "to a very crowded Auditory" on Election Day morning.[13]

The crowd came to the First Church hoping that the sermon would set a tone of high spirits for the day. Adapting his oration expertly to his audience and the occasion, Chauncy did not disappoint them. He took as his text a phrase from the Twenty-second Psalm, "Our fathers trusted in thee: they trusted, and thou didst deliver them." This brilliant choice provided Chauncy with ready-made parallels with the Jews of old, the fathers of New England, and the situation of eighteenth-century Bostonians. Trust in God, days of trouble, and providential deliverance—these three themes said neatly what the people wanted to hear. The text also enabled Chauncy to speak in several voices. At the outset he was the venerable old New Englander, solemnly reciting the saga of his holy oppressed forefathers, once again dwelling on their heroic courage, recounting the legendary parallel between New Englanders and Israelites, the chosen people of God; then he stood as a simple and honored representative of an afflicted and misunderstood people, articulating for them the hurt and bewilderment they felt at

147

the harsh treatment imposed at the hands of a distant government; as he progressed, he spoke as a mighty prophet, thundering at the people for their sins and demanding repentance; then he assumed the gentler voice of the urbane and rational gentleman, graciously spelling out the eminently fair and reasonable claims of American political theory; finally he ranted like a modern soapbox orator, sending his audience away with cries for blood and vengeance ringing in their ears.

The lessons for the present day, Chauncy told them, should be obvious. Surely New England faces a day of trouble. The mother country flounders in confusion; Americans are "called to put on sackcloth" and are unable to exercise the rights which "were the purchase of our fathers at the risque of every thing near and dear to them, their lives not excepted." For the terrible expense of "blood and treasure" suffered in the war the country has been rewarded with new duties, imposed "without any to represent our persons in parliament." New officers "and a numerous train of them too, with enormous stipends," paid "out of our pockets," patrol the streets. Not only this—we have been "treated as tho' we were rebels." Otherwise why is the town "garrison'd with the King's troops, to the infinite hurt of the morals of the inhabitants, and to their being in a variety of ways insulted, injured, and abused?"[14]

Our duty is clear. Like our forefathers, we must trust in God to deliver us, never forgetting that repentance must accompany trust. Even in calling sin "our worst enemy" and the true cause of New England's troubles, Chauncy ensured that his listeners recognize their proximate foes as well. In this passage he emphasized resentment more than religious humiliation:

> We may ascribe the ill state of our affairs to this or the other second cause. We may ascribe it to misrepresentations sent to the mother-country by those, in this, who seek their own, not the welfare of the public; We may ascribe it to the pride, the resentment, the hatred of men at home, clothed with dignity and honor; . . . to a malignant spirit in some, who cannot be easie without having the purses of the colonies subjected to their arbitrary pleasure. But if any should suppose our difficulties may, in any measure, be owing to these, or such like causes, it must be said, they are only secondary ones, superintended and governed by the great Ruler of the world. . . . God . . . would neither inflict, or permit the infliction of them, but on account of the sins of those who suffer by them.[15]

The present occasion invited discussion. Hutchinson thought he could distract attention from the trial by providing a different cause for complaint, but Chauncy so arranged his discourse that if his listeners remembered anything, it would be the fact that those responsible for the Boston massacre still awaited justice. At the climax of his sermon he delivered this severe admonition:

Who the sheders of this blood were may possibly appear, upon the tryal of those who are under confinement, as being supposed to be the guilty persons. We wish them as fair and equal a tryal as they themselves can desire. And should they all, or any of them, be found guilty, though their sin be as "scarlet, and red like crimson," we heartily wish their repentance, that, of the mercy of GOD in Jesus Christ, they may escape the second death; though our eye is restrained from pitying them so as to wish their deliverance from the first death. For the supreme legislator has said, "whoso sheddeth man's blood, by man shall his blood be shed"—"life shall go for life"— No satisfaction shall be taken for the life of a murderer.—He shall surely be put to death."

SOME have whispered a suspicion, as though a reprieve from death would be granted, should the guilt of blood be fastned upon some who are supposed to have been actors in this horrid wickedness—But it is an high indignity offered to him, who has the power of giving a reprieve, so much as to suspect he would do it in the case of BLOOD GUILTINESS, clearly proved upon any, in consequence of a fair and impartial tryal. Surely, he would not counter-act the operation of the law both of GOD and man. Surely, he would not suffer the Town and Land, to lie under the defilement of blood! Surely, he would not make himself a partaker in the guilt of murder, by putting a stop to the shedding of their blood, who have murderously spilt the blood of others![16]

Surely Chauncy knew that by the time he reached this part of his sermon he had convinced his listeners that they were one with the Israelites of old, true heirs of the Puritan fathers, and justified—if not sanctified—in throwing off tyranny and oppression. In this rhetorical context the tirade must have been explosive. Although Chauncy concluded his address with formulas calling for order and caution against rebellion,[17] he had placed the most inflammatory section at the climax. Chauncy knew his rhetoric: those were the words the people would remember.

A festive air prevailed for the rest of the day. John Boyle reports that "An Ox was roasted in the Common, and at two o'Clock carted to Faneuil-Hall"; "Several Hundreds of the Sons of Liberty dined at the Hall"; "Many loyal and patriotic Toasts were drank."[18] Two days later Hutchinson wrote triumphantly to Gage that the Court had adjourned in Cambridge on Election Day, "when the minds of the people had been much engaged in a jovial celebration of the Festival at Boston in opposition to me for carrying the General Court to Cambridge. . . . I expect some inflammatory Remarks in the News papers and, it may be, from the Pulpits but I hope it will end there."[19]

The inflammatory remarks followed quickly. For example the *Boston Evening Post* on June 18 approvingly quoted Chauncy's sermon (which had swiftly been put through Daniel Kneeland's press), speculated that no trial was intended, and demanded an inquiry into the

149

delay. "The blood of the innocent victims still calls aloud for vengeance."[20] Chauncy harped on the matter. As the trial date approached, Justice of the Peace James Murray wrote to Lt. Colonel Dalrymple of the Fourteenth Regiment: "After the pains taken by the Revd. Doctr. Chauncey and others to prejudice the People of Boston against Capt. Preston, there is too much room to suspect that the Captain will pass his time but badly at and after his Trial."[21]

When the soldiers finally came to trial in October even Chauncy's efforts failed to obtain a conviction. John Adams and Josiah Quincy, Jr. defended the soldiers before a lackluster Crown prosecution and a jury which may have been packed with pro-Preston sympathizers; they won acquittal for Preston and all but two of the soldiers. Those men stood guilty of manslaughter and suffered burning on the hand as punishment. Damaging evidence that the Whigs had agitated the riot hurt the party, although they arranged an annual March fifth ceremony to commemorate the massacre.[22]

Whig stock also declined when the colonists set aside the nonimportation agreements, in effect since 1767 and responsible in great measure for the ministry's decision—on March 5, 1770, the same day as the Boston massacre—to back down and repeal all the Townshend duties except that on tea.[23] When late 1770 brought a decline in the discipline needed to maintain the boycott of English goods that Sam Adams had engineered, Chauncy was dismayed.

For years he had supported home manufacture. He thought that nonimportation and nonconsumption agreements would not only squeeze the British economy but also encourage American crafts and industry. His *Reply* to Chandler and *A Compleat View of Episcopacy* had remained unpublished in 1769 and a part of 1770 because the province lacked enough paper to print them. Chauncy chafed at the shortage but blamed the "carelessness of our people in saving their rags,"[24] not the nonimportation restrictions. Convinced that New England could support itself, he delighted in evidence of native skill and ingenuity. When Abel Buell of Killingworth, Connecticut, designed and manufactured (without previous training) a set of printer's type, Stiles sent the type to Chauncy, who took it down to Edes and Gill and excitedly "had three copies of the advertisement that was set struck off, not for the public, but to gratifie my own curiosity." Chauncy declared Buell's work extraordinary. He proudly speculated that "the man that was capable of that, must be capable of making his letters still more perfect."[25] The nonimportation movement required vigorous enforcement by the Sons of Liberty, for the merchants, seriously threatened economically, tended to cheat; but in the long run it neatly pinched the British pocketbook. One observer estimated that trade to America fell off £700,000 in a year.[26] The Townshend Acts cost the government more than they were worth. A major goal of the repeal was to stop the boycott. Boston politicians, however, considered nonimportation a political weapon as well as an economic sanction. By maintaining the boycott they hoped to force Parliament to renounce its right to tax the colonies.[27] The merchants wanted none of that; despite threats from the Liberty Boys they broke down nonimportation. Chauncy never forgave their perfidy. He wrote to Richard Price: "We have found by experience, that no dependance can be had upon *merchants*, either at *home*, or in *America*, so many of them are so mercenary as to find within themselves a readiness to become slaves themselves, as well as to be accessory to the salvery of others, if they imagine they may, by this means, serve their own private separate interest. Our dependance, under God, is upon the *landed interest*, upon our freeholders and yeamonry."[28] Whatever sympathies he might previously have had for the merchant class, from this time onward he was suspicious of them.

Throughout 1771, with only the duty on tea remaining, Boston regained a measure of tranquility. The plan to establish episcopacy had sputtered, especially after the death of Archbishop Secker in 1768. Outspoken opposition in New England and the shaky course of political events dissuaded its advocates. With prospects so slim, many Anglicans agreed with Samuel Seabury that the cost in time and effort exceeded the chances of success when it came to "meddling" with Doctor Chauncy. For the moment, at any rate, Chauncy had won. One of the twin threats to liberty, he believed, had been quelled.

It was now time to concentrate attention upon the political front, where surprising threats to civil liberty were likely to arise at any time. Whereas Chauncy had been a commander in the ecclesiastical fight against the Anglican leaders, he relinquished that role in the political arena and served more as a staff officer in the skirmishes that led to revolution, making few command decisions but working closely with the radical leaders. Privy to strategic and tactical plans, he was continually called upon to advise, persuade, propagandize, comment on the times, and lend the influence of his position to the cause. He had a part in most of the important crises that jolted New England from 1771 to 1775, such as the development of the Committees of Correspondence, the revelation of the Hutchinson-Whately letters, the Boston Tea Party, the Coercive Acts, the forming of the Continental Congress, the blockade of Boston harbor, and the siege of Boston. They were exciting and dangerous days, and as they rolled by Charles Old-Brick plunged into the excitement and the danger.

The excitement began again in the summer of 1772, when the ministry moved to pay royal officials from the revenue collected by the customs commissioners. For years a favorite colonial gambit with re-

151

calcitrant officials had been simply to withhold their salaries until they revised their views. Convinced by this time of a plot to enslave the colonies, Chauncy believed that the governor and judges, if independent of the people and dependent upon the ministry, would cooperate in the scheme; "and what aggravates our unhappiness," he wrote to Richard Price, is "that the money, by which these officers . . . are tempted to be tools to carry into execution the arbitrary designs of those who hate us, is unconstitutionally taken out of our pockets and wickedly made use of to annihalate our privileges by charter and rights as Englishmen." Chauncy saw only two alternatives: "a submission to slavery, or an exertion of our selves to be delivered from it. Which of these will take place, and in what way or manner, I know not."[29] Three weeks later, the Boston Town Meeting drafted a petition of protest to Hutchinson.[30] Samuel Adams followed with the Committees of Correspondence, linking each town in the province with Boston and providing an effective machine to work against the British "tyranny."[31] Before the end of 1772 many Americans had gone so far as to assert that the colonies actually existed as independent states, subject to the king but not to Parliament's authority.

Thomas Hutchinson, having been appointed governor, challenged this claim when he spoke to the assembly on January 6, 1773. He denied any line between Parliament's supreme jurisdiction and colonial independence. Two supreme legislative bodies in the same state could not work. Therefore the colonies, if they counted themselves part of the kingdom, must grant their subordination to Parliament. John Adams drew the opposite conclusion from the same premises. In a reply to Hutchinson he granted that no line exists between Parliament's authority and colonial independence. Hence, he reasoned, the colonies must either be slave states or independent states; since the signers of the original charters had no intention of reducing the colonies to vassalage, they must therefore be independent states. In later years Adams claimed that "The Governor's reasoning, instead of convincing the people that Parliament had sovereign authority over them in all cases whatsoever, seemed to convince all the world that Parliament had no authority over them in any case whatsoever. Mr. Hutchinson really made a meagre figure in that dispute."[32]

Before the year passed Chauncy was involved in another attempt to discredit the governor. Five years earlier, in 1768, Hutchinson had corresponded with Thomas Whately, a former member of Parliament, about conditions in Massachusetts. Although critical of Samuel Adams and favorable toward strong British control, Hutchinson's views in these letters were moderate and relatively harmless. Benjamin Franklin obtained a number of the letters and shipped them to Boston, insisting that only a few people—members of the Committees of Corre-

152

spondence, James Bowdoin, Thomas Cushing, Samuel Cooper, James Pitts, John Winthrop, and Chauncy—should see them. The recipients, however, soon secured permission from Franklin to open the letters to wider private circulation. As more and more people read them or heard about them, wild rumors about them began to circulate. After Samuel Adams had them read aloud to the House of Representatives, it was inevitable that they would be published, at least in enough copies for the members of the assembly. In June 1773 Edes and Gill printed and published the letters. Thomas Hutchinson was now the scapegoat. Adams insisted that the letters proved the Governor the true instigator of the Stamp Act, the Townshend Duties, the Boston Massacre, and the grand scheme to enslave the colonies. The fact that the letters had come to light was taken as a special gift of divine Providence. Adams urged the House of Representatives to petition for Hutchinson's removal, but the house refused. Nonetheless New England branded Hutchinson a villain.[33]

Oddly enough the ministry chose this moment, when the governor's stock had tumbled, to announce a new tax measure—the Tea Act. The colonists loved their tea, but rather than pay a duty they smuggled it from Holland. The East India Company, in sad financial condition and unable to find markets, had jammed English warehouses with tea. The ministry therefore agreed to remit the twelvepence per pound duty charged on all teas imported into England and permit the East India Company to reship its tea to the colonies. Here the ministry would cut the duty to threepence per pound. Thus the East India Company, with a virtual monopoly in America, could undersell the smugglers and wipe out its surplus.[34] Boston patriots, however, realized that if the colonies succumbed to the lure of cheap, but taxed, tea, they would abandon their argument against the very principle of taxation. The amount of tax mattered little; the Sons of Liberty shouted that Britain wanted to trick them into easy submission.[35] When the patriots tried to frighten the tea importers out of the country, and then insisted that the tea-laden ships return to England, Governor Hutchinson took a stand. He refused to permit the ships to sail until, as the law required, the commissioners of customs gave him a receipt that the duty had been paid. With mobs of threatening Sons of Liberty lurking about, no one dared pay the duty and risk a bath in tar. The result was the Boston Tea Party of December 16, 1773, during which fifty or sixty men disguised as Indians emptied 342 chests of tea, worth approximately £9,000, into the icy waters of Boston harbor.[36]

King George and Lord North retaliated forcefully with a series of "Coercive Acts." Parliament closed the Boston port in the spring of 1774 until the citizens reimbursed the East India Company. They also moved the customs house to Salem. A month later Parliament passed

153

an act making the provincial council appointive, not elective; granting the governor power to appoint all law enforcement officers; restricting town meetings; and changing the system of jury selection. Another measure gave the governor authority to quarter troops in uninhabited houses and other buildings. Finally an act tolerant of Roman Catholics was passed in an attempt to devise a workable government for Quebec. The one bright spot amid these troubles for the radicals was the recall of Governor Hutchinson to England. His replacement, General Thomas Gage, arrived in May 1774 to keep the Massachusetts colonists in line.[37]

The Coercive Acts enraged Chauncy. He wrote furiously against them and cooperated happily in the unceasing efforts to make life miserable for General Gage. He published another *Letter to a Friend* and increased his correspondence with Richard Price in England, seeking avenues at home and abroad to advance the causes of colonial unity, nonimportation, and home manufacture. His pamphlet, clearly intended for English eyes as well as colonial readers, concerned the closing of the port; the letters to Price were really essays designed for British circulation. Taken as a whole they provide a good sense of Chauncy's frame of mind as well as a running account of Whig views after the Coercive Acts.

In his *Letter to a Friend* Chauncy argued that the town suffered cruel and unfair punishment. The act reduced to starvation fifteen thousand citizens who depended upon trade for a living. So far as anyone knew, none of them "had any more an hand in the destruction of the East-India company's tea, [than] Lord North himself." Why did Parliament punish the town? Either the British leaders knew nothing of America or they wanted "to enlarge our distress by the exercise of sovereign power." Chauncy clearly accepted the latter explanation. "The design of the British administration" to "oblige America, by the iron hand of power, to submit to sovereign pleasure" is "obviously visible," and "extends to the whole American continent." But force is no answer. It may "for a while keep the people under restraint; but this very restraint may, in time, be the occasion of the out-breaking of their passions with the greater violence; and what the consequence, in that case, will be, God only knows."[38]

One consequence of the Port Bill, Chauncy insisted, would surely be the unification of the colonies in a common cause, as the calling of a Continental Congress proved. To threaten Boston was to threaten every town; Chauncy asked all Americans "to frustrate the designs of those who would rule them with a rod of iron, instead of the laws of constitutional government." He advised everyone to begin an immediate boycott of English goods and to expand home industry.[39] In a letter to England two weeks later he could report unprecedented cooperation among the colonies: "The cause for which we in this

154

town are suffering, they look upon as the common cause of all North-America. . . . They sympathize with us, they offer us their help, and will chearfully join with us, as one, in such expedients as may be judged wise and proper to assist a redress of the grievances we are groaning under. . . . Their bountiful donations from one part of the country and another are daily flowing in upon us." Plans for the Continental Congress in Philadelphia continued, he told Price, adding that "So far as I can learn, 'tis not in the intention of the Deputies . . . to contend with Great-Britain. Their view is to bear with patience their treatment of us, however hard and cruel," substituting frugality for British goods. Armed resistance would be "highly grievous, and the last thing the Colonies would wish." But the Americans would take such a step, "should no other expedient be effectual."[40] Short of armed conflict, economic pressure seemed the best means of thwarting the British.

But Chauncy had not lost all faith in reason. Perhaps the ministry misunderstood the colonial situation. Perhaps Great Britain believed America would submit rather than fight. If powerful men in England could only learn the truth about the colonies, they might act rationally. Surely they would see the need to change their plans and press for conciliation. In July Chauncy helped a town committee prepare a "Declaration to be made by this town to Great Britain & all the World."[41] One could write such letters, declarations, and pamphlets, he knew—but time was short. A word in season directed to the right people might prove more efficient than the printed page. Thus Josiah Quincy, Jr. would be sent to London to serve his country as a highly unofficial Whig ambassador.

Quincy, the bright young law partner of John Adams, was temperate, well spoken, a keen student of history, and a quick thinker. Except for ill health, he exactly suited the job.[42] In August 1774 he agreed to sail for England.[43] Chauncy busied himself writing letters to Richard Price, John Temple, and others, introducing this emissary as "a young gentleman of good powers, a sprightly genius, and thorow acquaintance with the constitution of the American Colonies."[44] As a personal favor Chauncy asked his British friends to put the young man "into the company of those who may have it in their power to be serviceable to the Colonies in general and this Province in particular"—especially Lords Chatham and Temple.[45] Samuel and John Adams, along with Thomas Cushing, had already traveled to Philadelphia for the Congress, so Chauncy wrote to them there, asking Samuel Adams and the others to correspond on Quincy's behalf, "and the sooner the better."[46]

By September, when Quincy sailed, Massachusetts was clearly spoiling for a fight. A week before Quincy departed, Paul Revere rode from Boston to Philadelphia, bringing the Continental Congress news that

155

Suffolk County had adopted a set of resolutions urging disobedience of the Port Bill, warning the people to prepare for a defensive war, and directing the committees of correspondence to alert the citizenry when fighting erupted in Boston. Thanks in great measure to Samuel Adams, the Continental Congress adopted nonimportation and nonconsumption pacts, endorsed the Suffolk Resolves, approved military preparations, and pledged the colonies to assist Massachusetts if the province suffered attack.[47] "I think," wrote Adams to Chauncy, "I may assure you that America will make a point of supporting Boston to the utmost."[48]

To Chauncy this unity of the colonies seemed a miraculous gift from God. Benjamin Franklin's sister Jane Mecom heard the minister tell his fellow citizens that unity, along with the generosity of other colonies towards suffering Bostonians, betokened "Gods Design to deliver us out of all our trobles."[49] During the winter British troops fell victim to an epidemic of "malignant fever"; the fact that the townspeople escaped it was further evidence to Chauncy that God was on the American side.[50]

Congressional resolutions, the presence of troops in town, and the political exhortations of such men as Chauncy, Samuel Cooper, and Samuel Adams, kept martial spirits high during the fall and winter of 1774. An advertisement printed in the *Boston Evening Post* for September 19 indicates the temper of the time. It is addressed "To the Officers and Soldiers of his Majesty's Troops in Boston."

It being more than probable that the King's standard will soon be erected, from rebellion breaking out in this province, it is proper that you soldiers should be acquainted with the authors' thereof and of all the Misfortunes brought upon the province, the following is a list of them, viz. Mess. Samuel Adams, James Bowdoin, Dr. Thomas Young, Dr. Benjamin Church, Capt. John Bradford, Josiah Quincy, Major Nathaniel Barber, William Mollineaux, John Hancock, Wm. Cooper, Dr. Chauncy, Dr. Cooper, Thomas Cushing, Joseph Greenleaf, and William Downing.—the friends of your King and Country, and of America, hope and expect it from you soldiers, the instant rebellion happens, that you will put the above persons immediately to the sword, destroy their houses, and plunder their effects; it is just that they should be the first victims to the mischiefs they have br't upon us.

A Friend to Gr. Brit. & America

N.B. Don't forget those trumpeters of sedition, the printers Edes and Gill, and Thomas.

Whether or not the Whigs planted this notice as propagandistic nose-thumbing, as Clifford Shipton suspects,[51] it is clear that tempers ran high and that Chauncy's allegiances were well known. It was also clear that the colonists would fight. Chauncy told Samuel Adams, "The Spirit in all our Towns rises higher and higher, since the arrival of the last two parliamentary Acts respecting the Massachusetts Province. I fear lest some, by their precipitancy, will hasten that wch it would be wisdom shd be deferred for a while, and forever unless necessity shd drive to it."[52]

General Gage sniffed the storm. He sent worried reports home and prepared for battle. During the winter Chauncy watched eleven regiments fill the town with their red coats and gleaming boots. Warships circled Boston and blocked the harbor. In his first report to Quincy, Chauncy remarked: "Our sufferings in the town increase as the winter comes on; and our situation is the more distressingly difficult as we are so guarded both by sea and land that we may be restrained from going out of town, and may be at the mercy of those who are sent on purpose to distress us. Would our circumstances permit it, the town would be immediately evacuated of its proper inhabitants; and this will certainly be the case should administration determine to proceed in an hostile manner against us."[53]

"Can it in reason be thot that Americans, who were freeborn, will submit to such cruel tyranny?" Chauncy asked in a letter to Price. "They will sooner lose their heart's blood." If the soldiers were not British, and "subjects of the same sovereign with ourselves," they would never have set foot in town alive. The old pride in New England swelled in Chauncy's heart as he continued his letter. "The people in England have been taught to believe that five or six thousand regular troops would be sufficient to humble us." But England had underestimated the colonists, Chauncy warned. All the men between twenty and sixty years of age were forming companies; by spring the American forces, trained by veterans of the French and Indian wars, should number a hundred thousand. "A number of companies, in many of our towns, are already able to go thro the military exercise in all its forms with more dexterity and a better grace than some of the regiments which have been sent to us." In fact, Chauncy boasted, "we have in this town a company of boys, from about 10 to 14 years of age, consisting of 40 or 50, who, in the opinion of the best judges, can go thro the whole military exercise much more dexterously than a very great part of the regulars have been able to do since they have been here."[54]

While Chauncy applauded the colonial militia and companies of boys, he sought opportunities to harass Governor Gage. For example, at the meeting of the Associated Pastors of Boston on November 28, 1774 he proposed that the ministers refuse to read any proclamations "which may, in the future time, be issued, by the Governour and council, for days of public thanksgiving," since frequently paragraphs "very displeasing to us, and many of our people" appeared in them.[55] Peter Oliver summed up Gage's predicament: "Genl. *Gage* as a Soldier, preferred the engaging an Enemy in the *European* Mode, of an open Field. As Governor, he must engage an Enemy in the Mode of Bush fighting, which they have been bred in, but which he disdained."[56]

Four days later the nonimportation and nonconsumption agreements of the Continental Congress took effect. Those—especially merchants—who violated the pledges faced social pressure and often physical violence. The Sons of Liberty had plenty of tar and feathers; ugly mobs made Loyalists miserable. By now only the king was recognized as a bond with England; for all practical purposes British authority had ceased.[57] Instead Massachusetts towns sent representatives to a Provincial Congress, unrecognized by the governor, which managed the province by means of recommendations. During the winter other colonies followed suit. John Winthrop reported that seven thousand Bostonians depended upon contributions from neighboring districts "for their daily bread," and that their hopes rode on the petitions sent to the king by the Continental Congress.[58] Yet George III —despite warnings from Gage, the king's man on the spot—committed himself to force and sent reinforcements to America. He ordered the governor to crack down on the rebellious leaders of the Provincial Congress. These orders reached the general on April 14, 1775.[59] Four nights later Paul Revere and William Dawes rode to Lexington to warn the militiamen that the British were coming.

CHAPTER ELEVEN

Exile and Return

More than fifteen thousand New Englanders massed outside Boston immediately after the battles of Lexington and Concord, effectively sealing off the town from the countryside. Boston was a city besieged. Besides the usual problems of a besieged commander, Gage faced other difficulties, for he had thousands of anti-British patriots, Chauncy among them, shut up within the town. If he decided to engage the provincial army, disorganized as it was, who could tell what these citizens of Boston would do in the absence of his troops? It seemed best at first to sit tight, letting no one in or out, and wait for reinforcements.

Within a few days, however, Gage had to abandon this course. In the first place, the supply problem quickly became acute, for the soldiers and Tories as well as for the provincials. Gage also recognized that a strong hostile element in his midst could only hurt him in the long run. He decided therefore to negotiate with the Boston selectmen, and he offered to issue safe-conduct passes for Bostonians wishing to leave, provided they surrendered their weapons and pledged not to bear arms against the British after they left town. Meeting in Faneuil Hall on April 22 and 23, the citizens agreed. Many families gathered their possessions, marked their weapons, deposited them in Faneuil Hall, and left immediately.[1] Those who could not leave so suddenly, however, soon encountered difficulties getting out at all, for the evacuation plan quickly broke down. Strongly influenced by Tory fears that the city faced bombardment once the patriots departed, Gage put obstructions in the way and soon refused passes altogether.[2]

Chauncy and his wife did not leave town in the first wave, and consequently they were among those "shut up in Boston."[3] They finally obtained a pass, however. After they had satisfied the Governor's inspectors that they had no provisions or merchandise in their possession, they made their way to Brookline, the home of Mrs. Chauncy's sister, Mehatable Hyslop.[4] "Mr. Gage," said Chauncy, "has rendered himself the object of universal hatred and contempt, by his perfidy, cruelty, and oppressive conduct."[5] The next month they shifted their headquarters to Medfield, about twenty miles from Boston.[6] They were to remain exiled from their city for almost a year.

At seventy years of age, in shaky health, and far from his pulpit, Charles Old-Brick could do little for the patriot cause during the siege except keep abreast diligently of the news, assist in the amazing intelligence network operating throughout the colonies, and send accounts of the state of affairs to his correspondents in England. He also advised the colonial generals whenever he found the opportunity. From May 1775 until April 1776 he visited friends, relatives, and fellow refugees, exchanged news, speculated upon the outcome of hostilities, and cooperated with the Provincial and Continental Congresses. Whenever he rode to Andover or Watertown to visit John Winthrop,[7] or dined with the Reverend Mr. Cooper, John Adams, Colonel Quincy, Deacon Jeffries, Mr. Hunt, Mr. Hill, and the many others who stopped to visit,[8] he collected news of Boston and the war. He sought opportunities to speak with men who had seen action.

By July 18 he had gathered enough information through hearsay and personal interviews (including a conversation with General Israel Putnam)[9] to send Price a lively account of the Boston siege and the battles at Lexington, Concord, Hog Island, and Bunker Hill.[10] Of course his story tallies with the standard Whig report—the Provincials have much the better of it—but the prose is clear and effective; at seventy he retained his sure touch with the pen. He tried to correct false reports and to impress British readers with unbounded American confidence. "Our people," he said, "are firmly united and resolutely fixt to defend their rights, whatever opposition they meet with. And instead of being disheartened by what is done against them, they rise continually in the strength of their determination to die rather than live slaves." They will not relax their boycotts: "Not a shilling's worth" of British goods "will be sold except to the Tories in Boston, who have at present other things to mind than that of purchasing English commodities." American troops have proved themselves brave and able, "not such cowards as they are said to be in England," and the "King's troops, both officers and privates, now say that our men will fight like devils." American numbers and supplies grow every day: "It is intended our army shall be increased to thirty thousand; besides

160

which, our minute-men are so numerous, that upon an alarm fifty thousand of them might come to the help of the army. . . . We have a sufficiency of powder . . . and before next year we shall have a full supply within ourselves. We can make what cannon, shot, shells, bombs &c, we want." In short, only at their peril should Englishmen believe that the colonists will abandon the boycotts and that the American army consists of a handful of cowardly rabble:

> Tis astonishing to us that the people in England are so blind as not to see that every thing that is done against us is done against them. They may be ruined; but this will not be our case, tho we may suffer greatly. The ministry may imagine we can't live without commerce with England, but they are greatly mistaken. We have all the necessaries, and many of the comforts and conveniences of life within ourselves; and shall perhaps be better able to go thro the war than they are. You may rely upon it as truth that, instead of discord and faintheartedness, the Colonies are all united and couragiously resolute to suffer death, rather than submit to arbitrary, despotic government.[11]

Chauncy's letter was not all bravado; British Whigs enunciated many of his points in Parliament.[12] Price himself wrote a stirring defense of the Colonial cause.[13] Coercion, however, was the watchword in Britain, and the policy was inflexible. In the autumn the government decided to wage war against the Americans. In the spring Parliament supported the decision. Thousands of redcoats, augmented by hired mercenaries from Germany, soon sailed for America. As John Richard Alden writes, this policy "could have only one result—to force hundreds of thousands of Americans who had wished for no more than what they considered their rights within the empire to take the road to independence."[14] Chauncy was one of these thousands. Although a friend to the radical cause, bellicose in his pronouncements, he had clutched the slim hope of reconciliation if Britain would guarantee the colonists' rights. Once convinced, however, that the road to independence was unavoidable, he strode down its center with characteristic gusto, scattering Tories and Britishers from his path.

In October 1775 the king and cabinet replaced General Gage with General William Howe, and the British and American armies eyed each other for the rest of the fall and winter. Neither Howe nor the American General George Washington could act decisively: Howe for lack of manpower and transportation; Washington for lack of organization, training, and artillery. During that winter, however, Henry Knox made his famous march to Ticonderoga and carried back fifty-nine cannon and mortars. On March 4, 1776 Washington dug in his big guns on Dorchester Heights overlooking Boston. When the fog cleared the next day, General Howe discovered that the Americans now held the high ground with enough firepower to demolish his forces. To attack

161

would have been folly; he decided to get out and hope to fight another day. On March 17 the British evacuated Boston and sailed for Halifax, Nova Scotia.[15] Within the week thousands of exiled Bostonians trooped back to the homes they had left nearly a year before.

Shortly before the return to Boston Chauncy fell ill and did not come home. Thus he missed the "handsome entertainment" staged for Washington by the General Court on March 28.[16] Dr. Eliot preached in Chauncy's stead at the Old Brick,[17] and Samuel Cooper occupied the pulpit for him the next two Sundays.[18] By mid-April Chauncy felt well enough to return to Boston, preaching at the First Church on April 28.[19] He preached regularly thereafter during 1776, both on the Sabbath and at the various public lectures.[20] He also preached on May 17, 1776, the Continental Fast Day,[21] and attended the meetings of the Boston Ministers' Association.[22] He quickly renewed his customary visits to the sick;[23] the backlog of baptisms and marriages[24] and the ever-present burden of funerals filled out his time.

During May, while Chauncy settled back into pastoral routine, excited Bostonians clamored for copies of a pamphlet printed that winter. Entitled *Common Sense*, it had caught the interest and stirred the spirits of all America. Its author, Thomas Paine, shouted not for reconciliation, but for independence.[25] On June 7, 1776 Richard Henry Lee urged the delegates to the Second Continental Congress to declare independence. They should establish a confederation of American states and begin to negotiate alliances with the European powers.[26] After a month of serious consideration and debate Congress declared the independence of the colonies and formed the United States of America.

The printed Declaration arrived in Boston on July 18.[27] Not since the repeal of the Stamp Act had the town enjoyed a celebration like the one that greeted the Declaration of Independence. After Colonel Thomas Crafts, sheriff of Suffolk County, finished reading the document in public, the assembled citizens gave him three huzzas, the batteries on the surrounding hills fired thirteen rounds, thirteen infantry units fired in succession, and the church bells pealed. Bostonians held banquets, drank toasts, ripped the King's Arms from the state house, and that evening tossed all signs of royalty in Boston into an immense bonfire in front of the Bunch of Grapes Tavern.[28] "Thus ends royal authority in this State," wrote Abigail Adams to her husband, "and all the people shall say Amen."[29]

Not all the people joined the jubilation. In some colonies Loyalist strength grew after the declaration,[30] but in Boston the outnumbered Tories faced harassment and persecution from the Whigs. Should a man be not only a Tory but an outspoken Congregationalist minister as well, his position was precarious: he contended not only with the mob, but also with the Black Regiment. In July and August the newly

162

independent patriots, led by Chauncy and eager to prove their loyalty to the United States, centered their attention on just such a man: Mather Byles, pastor of the Hollis Street Church.[31]

Witty and friendly with British officers, Byles stayed in Boston during the seige. The army converted his church to barracks, and he held services in the First Church. When his parishioners returned to find their meetinghouse much the worse for wear, they were unhappy; when Dr. Byles proved sarcastic as ever about their cause, they were furious. According to John Eliot, who was close to the situation, Chauncy instigated a movement among Byles's parishioners to remove him from his pastorate.[32] Three weeks after the promulgation of independence, when patriotic fervor had reached high intensity, the Hollis Street Church summoned Byles for a hearing. The people brought political charges against him: he had associated with British officers, and had lent them his spyglass to observe American positions; he had not taken the "public calamity" seriously; he had neglected his people and prevented inhabitants from leaving town; he had refused to preach on a fast day appointed by the Continental Congress; he had prayed publicly for American submission; and he had permitted the "fences belonging to the society" and the "seats of the pews" to be removed when the soldiers moved in.

Byles refused to honor these charges with a defense, and his congregation, without calling an ecclesiastical council as New England tradition demanded, dismissed its pastor.[33] Chauncy, doubtless thinking Byles a traitor, defended the action. "Byles," he told John Eliot, "is not fit for a preacher."[34] Many Whig clergymen agreed, but they protested the failure to summon a council. "Notwithstanding I despise Dr. Byles as much as a man can hold another in contempt," wrote Eliot to Jeremy Belknap, "yet I think the proceedings of that church with him were irregular & unwarrantable, & hath held up a precedent for a practise that will cause the ruin of our ecclesiastical constitution, weaken the hands of the ministry, & lay such discouragement before candidates as will prevent their settling. . . ."[35] Chauncy lamely answered these critics by asserting that "it was an irregular time & we must expect thing[s] irregular."[36] For years ministers who believed themselves unfairly dismissed had sought Chauncy as an advocate. All his life he had upheld the traditional procedures, insisting upon charity towards settled ministers. But now the flames of patriotism licked high enough to obscure these principles, and he was willing to blink at ecclesiastical procedures in order to silence a political enemy of the new country. It was an astonishing reversal of form. Few of the younger men could remember that Byles had stood by Chauncy in the early days of the Awakening; Bostonians of an older generation would have noticed the irony of the situation.

On Sunday, August 11, two days after Byles left Hollis Street Church, Chauncy seized a chance to advertise his own patriotism. The Provincial Council had ordered every Massachusetts congregation to read the Declaration of Independence. With his unfailing sense of the dramatic, the aging Doctor Chauncy kept the people after morning service that Lord's Day and read them the Declaration of Independence, delivering with a practiced voice its measured cadences and resounding series of accusations against the king. Chauncy, who had stood in the same meetinghouse almost fifty years before to receive the right hand of fellowship from Cotton Mather, now carefully read the final sentence of the revolutionary document: "And for the support of this Declaration, with a firm Reliance on the Protection of divine Providence, we mutually pledge to each other our Lives, our Fortunes, and our sacred Honor." He paused; then, lifting his hands and eyes to heaven, he implored, "God bless the United States of America!" and bade the people answer with a solemn *Amen*.[37]

Chauncy was certain that God *would* bless the United States. The American cause was just, he told his friends. If human efforts could not win the war, he had no doubt that God would send a host of angels to assist the American soldiers.[38] He answered those who smiled at this assertion by stating that Providence would deflect bullets aimed at American troops![39] Trust in God was the duty of a people in a day of trouble. However confident, he carefully avoided charges of presumption. Sin caused the suffering of the war, he told his congregation in November: "Tis our sins that have bro't us into this very alarming State, and Till our Sins are repented of, and our Wicked Ways are reform'd, We are taught in Gods Word not to look for Deliverance from our Distresses."[40]

During these months, as the center of action shifted from Boston and the American army struggled for existence at Long Island and Morristown, Chauncy had little direct contact with the progress of the war. He stayed active politically, however, although he did not have the opportunity to play a dramatic role until four years after the Declaration of Independence, when he became embroiled in a controversy over the Declaration of Rights drafted by the Constitutional Convention.

The Americans could hardly claim to have won the war in 1780. France had entered the conflict on the American side, but that alliance had brightened only slightly the dark days of Valley Forge. Clinton, General Howe's replacement, controlled the South, and Washington was stalled along the Hudson. The total failure of the Penobscot expedition further discouraged Massachusetts, for all of Maine east of the Penobscot was now in British hands. Nonetheless the Americans, trusting in eventual victory, had tackled the job of recasting their social and political institutions: "They created written constitutions both for the several states and for the United States; made careful provision for the protection of personal liberties; struck at religious privilege; assailed barbarous punishment for crime; moved haltingly in the direction of political democracy; redistributed land; and even ventured to attack the institution of Negro slavery. They initiated an 'Internal Revolution' which continued beyond the war and exercised an enduring influence."[41]

In three hectic sessions, from September 1779 to March 1780, the Constitutional Convention drafted a document and submitted it to the people for discussion. Like most of the towns Boston approached the task vigorously, considering and voting on each clause. But Article III of the Declaration of Rights, concerning religious privilege, required special attention. As William McLoughlin has ably pointed out, Americans "did not want the Anglican system," which they took to be "a system in which the State prescribed an official creed, ritual, and mode of worship for all inhabitants and enforced them through a hierarchy, spiritual courts, and civil law,—that is, a confessional state on Erastian principles." Yet "in the confusion of social theory surrounding America's transition from a colony to an independent republic and from an outpost of European thought and practice to a unique experiment in republican self-government, Americans were no longer sure precisely what the relationship between church and state should be." They also did not want "the complete separation which Jefferson and 'the Enlightened' deists of the Age of Reason wanted. Jefferson and Madison had failed in their initial effort even in a state which had good reason to favor disestablishment. In New England, where the established clergy were among the most fervent patriots, it was even clearer that total separation was too radical a break with the old ideal of the corporate Christian state."[42] In May 1780 the town unanimously accepted the constitution except for the article on religious privilege, and called a town meeting to debate it. The meeting put Chauncy in a tight spot.

The article required each town to provide for the worship of God and the support of "public protestant teachers of piety, religion and morality"; the towns and religious groups would have the right to choose their own ministers, but they were also required to "enjoin upon all the subjects an attendance upon the instructions" of such ministers, "if there be any on whose instructions they can conscienciously and conveniently attend." Every citizen, however, churchgoer or not, was to be taxed for the support of the ministers. If he chose, he might specify that his money go to the minister of his own denomination; otherwise his taxes went to the Congregational church. Finally, "no subordination of any one sect or denomination to another shall ever be established by law."[43]

Objections to the article abounded. First, its loose wording made the nonsubordination proviso virtually meaningless. Second, although its intention may have been liberal,[44] its provisions were reactionary. Many Americans considered it a reversion to early Puritan days—it seemed to establish Congregationalism as the state religion. Formerly, Baptists, Quakers, and Episcopalians were exempt in most cases from religious taxation; now everyone would be taxed. Baptists, Quakers, and Episcopalians could earmark their money for their own men, but nonbelievers, nonchurchgoers, and minorities too small to have a minister were to support the Congregationalists. Many feared that in practice the law shut out all minority groups by enabling the town treasurer to direct the money as he saw fit. Looking ahead, others realized that new denominations would face a nearly impossible task in becoming established in Massachusetts.[45] The chief objection, however, was a matter of principle; the chief objectors were the Baptists. For several years, under the leadership of the brilliant Isaac Backus,[46] they had struggled against compulsory support for a religious establishment; now the commonwealth intended to fix precisely that principle as a fundamental law of the land.

The town meeting, held at the Old Brick, provided some awkward moments for Chauncy. Over the preceding decade he had fashioned a reputation as the foremost American opponent of compulsory support. In his *Reply* to Chandler, the doctor had plainly said, "We are, in principle, against all civil establishments in religion.—It does not appear to us, that God has entrusted the state with a right to make religious establishments." Although by "establishments" Chauncy meant "a confessional state on Erastian principles," such as that represented by Anglicanism, and not the traditional New England system, the Baptists did not let him forget his remark. In 1778 Backus quoted it in support of freedom for the Baptists in America and as a prime argument for separation of church and state.[47] "And yet," Backus recalled in later years, Chauncy "published more, for thirty years, to uphold the Congregational establishment in New England than any other man."[48] Precisely. On these matters the revolutionary Chauncy was a Puritan to the core. When it came to supporting either the standing Congregational order or the accomplishments of God's chosen people in New England, he held out for the good old way. When the town meeting convened on May 8, 1780, Samuel Stillman, minister of the First Baptist Church in Boston, spoke against the article. Chauncy, Eliot reports, then "arose from the pulpit, & delivered

166

his sentiments in favor of the article. It was a great pity that he could not be heard."[49] The debate continued for two days until the town finally adopted the article, with the amendment that the religious taxes of anyone who could not in conscience attend the instruction of the ministers in town should be used to help the poor.[50] Doctor Chauncy could not be heard. How could the old man be so feeble as that? During the next five years he precipitated a theological flurry to rival the war.

CHAPTER TWELVE

Pudding and Pies

After Foxcroft had been left incapacitated by a crippling stroke in 1762, the burden of pastoral duties at the First Church fell almost exclusively upon Chauncy. Since that time he had begun to think seriously about his own successor. He arranged for stopgap help in case of his sickness or sudden death, asking the church to permit any ordained minister in regular standing to administer the sacraments in an emergency. Increasingly he sought help with the preaching duties.[1] In his younger days he boasted that he could write faster than any man alive, often composing his second sermon of the day during the recess between the morning and afternoon meetings.[2] Now that he had passed his allotted threescore and ten years, he no longer assumed he would be well enough each Sunday to handle both services.

Traditionally pastors met the need for preachers by exchanging among themselves to save preparing a fresh sermon. The champion exchanger of Chauncy's later years was Samuel Cooper, whose activities with the Whig Party frequently kept him away from his study. Cooper's Brattle Street congregation never lacked variety, for everyone knew that the pastor was likely to press any available preacher into service. The practice became something of a joke among the townspeople. On one occasion, according to family legend, Chauncy's black servant Scipio brought a threadbare coat to the doctor and asked for a replacement. "Go into my study, take one of my old coats, and put it on and wear it," said Chauncy. Scipio replied that he didn't dare. "Why not?" asked Chauncy. "Because," Scipio replied, "if Dr. Cooper sees me, I'm afraid he will ask me to change!"[3]

168

Although he regularly 'changed with Cooper,[4] late in 1776 Chauncy sought help on a permanent basis. For an assistant, he had in mind a man with many good years still ahead of him. Of course he must be a scholar (the First Church had always boasted scholars) and a man of piety; but besides a firm grasp of the Scriptures, he must also have a lively curiosity about the world. He should be aware of his American Puritan heritage, although he should disdain New-Lights and such fatalists as Samuel Hopkins or the younger Jonathan Edwards. Politically only a staunch patriot would do; it would help if he had also crossed swords with the Episcopalians. And it would be nice to have a Harvard man. In short, Chauncy wanted another Charles Chauncy. Failing this, only one other man seemed suitable, and, providentially, he was available. On February 18, 1777 Chauncy wrote to Ezra Stiles, offering him a position at the Old Brick and assuring him that Boston was now the safest town in America.[5]

Stiles did not qualify on all counts—he was a Yale man, cordial to Hopkins, although disagreeing with him, and less zealous a patriot than either Chauncy or Cooper—but he came close enough. Since the British occupied his hometown, Newport, he currently served in Dighton, but he wanted a spot farther from the line of fire. Unfortunately for Chauncy, the First Church in Portsmouth also approached Stiles. Forced to choose between the two opportunities, he decided to visit both places. In April he rode to Boston and preached one Lord's Day at the Old Brick; then he continued to Portsmouth, where the offer was too munificent to refuse. Yet even if Stiles had picked Boston, Chauncy would have obtained merely a temporary assistant, not a successor, for only six months after Stiles settled in Portsmouth, he received another call—to become president of Yale College.[6]

While awaiting Stiles's decision Chauncy gave young John Eliot (Harvard, 1772) ten pounds every week "for half the day," but Eliot settled at the New North.[7] Later in the year John Clarke (Harvard, 1774) preached impressively at the Old Brick, and the congregation decided that he was their man. On January 18, 1778, the "question being put, whether they would take into consideration the choice of a pastor to carry on the work of the ministry, their present Pastor, Doctor Chauncy, being aged and infirm, it was unanimously voted in the affirmative. . . ." The next day the church selected Clarke; a week later the congregation concurred. They ordained the new assistant on July 8, 1778 and gave him seven pounds a week, plus firewood and the promise of a house if he should marry.[8]

Keenly sensitive to his age and weakness, Chauncy seemed amazed that he had lived to be seventy-five. He told his congregation that theirs was a day he had "not the most remote Expectation of living to See."[9] Discussing the death of John Winthrop, he wrote to Richard

169

Price that "I am also grown infirm as well as old, and very unable to write," asking Price to forgive the "blots" and the "almost illegible writing of the present letter." He was unsure that he would "live to see a settled state of things," but if he did, and if he should "have strength," he would "write you very largely upon our affairs."[10] Late in 1780 he began to ensure that Mary would be taken care of when he died. He told the church that he would "put the parsonage house in which he now lives, in tenantable repair, provided Madam Mary Chauncy his present wife be assured the possession and improvement of the same (rent free) during her natural life, she keeping the same in like good repair."[11] With the assurance of a home for the rest of her life, along with her inherited property on Noddle's Island[12] and a share in an Antiguan sugar plantation,[13] Chauncy could leave Mary well provided for. But Chauncy outlived his wife by nearly four years.

Two months after the town meeting thrashed out the Massachusetts Constitution, the legislature pleased Chauncy greatly by chartering the new American Academy of Arts and Sciences.[14] Justly proud of his charter membership, Chauncy almost certainly helped organize the academy. The society was the brainchild of John Adams, who in France had heard scores of compliments on the work of Franklin's American Philosophical Society and had decided that Massachusetts should form a similar group. He mentioned his idea to Samuel Cooper, who "did diffuse the project so judiciously and effectually that the first legislature under the new constitution adopted it and established it by law."[15] The academy named James Bowdoin its president and numbered John and Samuel Adams, John Hancock, Edward Wigglesworth, and John Winthrop—all close friends of Chauncy's—among its more famous charter fellows.[16] Thereafter Chauncy took great satisfaction in signing his publications "Fellow of the American Academy of Arts and Sciences."[17] The Americans wanted to show the world that they were a force to be reckoned with in intellectual circles as well as on the battlefield.

With the appointment of Clarke, Chauncy found time to stir the pudding again. He had kept his ideas about universal salvation simmering at the back of his mind for years, meanwhile collecting a select group of sympathetic protégés from among the younger ministers. Stiles certainly had tasted the pudding in the 1760s, although he probably did not read the complete work until it was published in 1784.[18] Chauncy had hinted at the recipe in several sermons;[19] Richard Price had been sent a sample as early as 1770.[20] During the 1770s younger men such as Eliot, Clarke, and Jeremy Belknap gained admission to the society. As Belknap wrote to his friend Ebenezer Hazard, "The doctrine of universal restitution has long been kept as a secret among learned men."[21]

170

After the episcopacy plans died Chauncy probably considered publishing his treatises, but he drew back once more when John Murray, another threat to good order, appeared in New England in 1772. During the 1770s and early 1780s Chauncy believed that publication of his views would only lend support and prestige to Murray's false doctrines. A young itinerant, Murray had known Wesley and Whitefield in England and was strongly influenced by the thought of James Relly. He preached a brand of universalism, holding that since Christ had already atoned for all our sins, the debt to God was satisfied and sinners therefore faced no more punishment.[22] Chauncy's theory of universal salvation differed markedly from Murray's: for Chauncy, we must be saved from sin as well as from guilt. Only when we rid ourselves of moral corruption do we become meet for heaven; this requires discipline in life and perhaps terrible purging in the afterlife. Eventually, through the mediation of Christ, each of us *will* be reformed; in the meantime the wicked face suffering and misery in proportion to their depravity.

Chauncy disapproved of Murray on several counts. First, Murrayism was unscriptural. Chauncy's lengthy struggles with the Scriptures convinced him that only his own system accorded with both reason and revelation. Second, since Murray's theory removed sanctions against immoral conduct, it encouraged "*Libertinism*";[23] such a doctrine naturally appealed enormously to young people. At a time when Boston seemed infatuated with dancing and gambling,[24] one could hardly have the town's ministers advocate loose living. Third, Murray was an itinerant. He drew great crowds; he encouraged the people to abandon their traditional moral standards in favor of an easier way; he attracted people away from established churches; he threatened the standing clergy. In short, when Chauncy looked at Murray he saw the avatar of Whitefield with a new theology.

Yet they were both Universalists. Here was the problem. Chauncy's scheme differed from Murray's, but the old man had learned during the Awakening that people were uninterested in subtle distinctions; they needed a simple *yea* or *nay*. In the 1740s, despite many points of agreement with the Awakeners, Chauncy finally had to abandon his middle course in favor of a resounding *nay*. The questions were cut sharply in the episcopacy controversy and the struggle for colonial rights; Chauncy thoroughly opposed episcopacy and thoroughly supported the Whigs, and that was that. Here, however, the problems were subtler. He agreed with Murray's conclusion of universal salvation; he opposed Murray's assumptions, theory, methods, and goals. How could he make his own position clear? How could he avoid misunderstanding?

Chauncy was no leveler. Experience had taught him that the person in the streets wanted results and was reluctant to think through carefully reasoned arguments, especially when he was preoccupied, as he then was, with political matters. Chauncy feared that the common reaction would be this: Does the Reverend Doctor Chauncy believe in universal salvation? Yes? So does the Reverend Mr. Murray. Then they believe the same thing. Look—Murray must be right; even wise old Doctor Chauncy agrees with him. John Eliot rhapsodically summarized Chauncy's predicament in a letter to Jeremy Belknap: "It will not do to publish it at once, if proper to expose it at all. It is too sublime for the soaring of vulgar imaginations, & would dazzle, if not blind, the eyes of the populace. It would be like the rays of the noonday sun to persons who had never before seen the light."[25] And in another place Eliot wrote: "Murray has tended to irritate the passions of those whom we call worthy men, rather than to mollify their minds with ointment to receive a doctrine any ways similar to what he hath propagated. They are not able to distinguish between the restitution of all things upon his plan, and the other scheme which employs the attention & arrests the assent of so many of the wise & learned of the modern New England clergy."[26] Too risky for both populace and clergy, his scheme, Chauncy knew, also invited attack from the New Divinity men. They would hardly miss the chance to link him to Murray. The disadvantages of publication far outweighed the advantages. Chauncy could still teach his people to lead a moral life without troubling them too much about the final outcome. For example, in his 1778 sermon *The Accursed Thing*, he borrowed a page from his manuscript on divine benevolence to posit sin as the cause of disorder, pain, and trouble.[27] Obviously countering Murray, he carefully pointed out that unrepentant sinners face punishment in the bottomless pit. He strongly reaffirmed the necessity of the good life and the threat of future punishment; there was no need to discuss the duration of the punishment.[28] "Our Saviour," Eliot explained, "said to his followers: 'I have many things to tell you, but ye cannot bear them now.' And this Dr. C. quotes to excuse his own conduct in concealing his sentiments from the people under his charge, as well as the world in general."[29]

By 1780, however, Chauncy could hardly avoid discussing Universalism any longer. Murray had attracted public attention; all the ministers were buzzing about him. He had even gained a nickname: he was known as Salvation Murray, to distinguish him from a strict Calvinist in Newburyport, also named John Murray, and appropriately dubbed Damnation Murray![30] Some who had "relished the pudding" began to press Chauncy to publish his manuscript. Belknap, for instance, argued that New England needed a strong statement advocating moral living and future punishment to counteract the laxity of

Murrayism. He also considered Chauncy duty bound as a minister to instruct the people in the truth. Yet other friends, such as Eliot, argued that publication was imprudent.[31]

During 1780 and 1781, while Chauncy weighed the question, other serious problems—the war, the new constitution, his own advancing years—competed for his attention. The end of 1781 saw the war decided. French money, troops, leadership, and sea power helped Washington move quickly that fall to Virginia, where General Cornwallis was building a base at Yorktown. When French warships, under Admiral De Grasse, slipped behind Cornwallis to cut off his escape, the British were forced to surrender. No chance remained for Great Britain to conquer the new states in armed conflict. After Yorktown the major battles took place around the negotiating tables. Franklin, and later Jay and John Adams, carried on the business of negotiation throughout 1782 until the peace treaty at Paris in November 1783.

In 1782 Chauncy decided, rather reluctantly, to publish his views on salvation. By this time they were an open secret anyway. Narrow escapes grew more frequent, and Chauncy more short-tempered, as he was forced to back and fill rather than speak his mind. The closest call came at the ordination of the Reverend Oliver Everett to the New South Church. Gossipy John Eliot told the story to Jeremy Belknap:

> It was agreed upon by the delegates of your mother church to sift the candidate, Mr. Everett, very closely. And as soon as he had read his confession, Dn. Jeffres began the business by asking what he thought of the God head of Jesus Ct? Brother Howard was opposed to this, & insisted that he declared in his confession every thing which the Scripture had pointed out. Mr. Eckley & others joined in the debate, some with the greatest vociferation (brother Sam's voice was heard among the rest). At last Dr. Chauncy grew mad, told Dn. Jeffres he was a fool, & Dn. Greenough that he knew nothing, & was fit only to lift up his hand, which was all any body expected from him. So we continued for an hour, & the ordination was upon the point of being sett aside, when Dr. Aquinas Cooper with a very mellifluous tone begged to ask one question: "Do you believe, Mr. Everett, that there are 3 persons, &c., &c., & that these 3 are one?" "Yes, Sir." A vote passed upon this, that the Council were satisfied, except the Old South elder & delegates, who drew off, & left us with the meeting to ourselves. . . . It was lucky the dispute turned upon the article of the trinity & exhausted the patience of the Council, for this was only a prelude to other matters which would have set us all aghast. We might have been obliged to eat the pudding, bag & all.[32]

During the summer Chauncy and Clarke dispatched a "scouting party, to make discoveries and try the temper of the public."[33] They put together a pamphlet entitled *Salvation for all Men, Illustrated and Vindicated as a Scripture Doctrine*, consisting of a preface by Chauncy

173

condemning Murrayism and a collection by Clarke of scriptural texts and selections from theologians supporting universal salvation.[34] Their little scouting party drew a crossfire of pamphlets, sermons, and letters-to-the-editor. Even their allies complained. Eliot, who had unfailingly opposed publication, called it "a meer castrated edition of the whole work" and predicted it would "admit of more bad than good consequences at such a time & in such a manner."[35] Upon its publication he wrote to Belknap: "Dr. Chauncy & Clarke have let the cat out of the bag. They begun by printing a sermon, or rather essay, containing the opinion of others upon this subject, which by no means served their cause, for it is not well done. Clarke then opened the subject in the pulpit, & in conversation with his people, and it hath given universal disgust."[36] Belknap, who had urged Chauncy to publish the entire manuscript, considered the pamphlet weak because it argued chiefly from authority.[37] Chauncy's old colleague Samuel Mather dashed off a pamphlet attacking Clarke for holding "the *Popish* doctrine of *purgatory*";[38] Clarke countered with *A Letter to Doctor Mather* claiming that Mather had not distinguished between his doctrine and Murrayism, and accusing the old gentleman of saying one thing in private and the reverse in print.[39] The New Divinity men also sniped at the scouting party. Early in 1783 Samuel Hopkins, Joseph Eckley, and William Gordon circulated pamphlets defending the traditional doctrines of damnation.[40] "None but the Murrayites among my acquaintance are satisfied," wrote Eliot, and "they not by being converted over to these notions of future happyness in Dr. C. MS., but only as they think that they have made a prize of the ministers. They are bold to say that they will be Murrayites soon, that they have given up the main point & are coming over as fast as they can. It will be a rich harvest for the Baptists likewise."[41]

Public reaction decided the matter: the complete work should be published. About this time Chauncy decided to publish *The Benevolence of the Deity* and his writings on original sin as well. This proved difficult. In the hectic postwar days, paper was scarce and subscriptions hard to collect for scholarly, nonpolitical critiques of theological problems. Another snag developed when no Greek or Hebrew type could be found in Boston or Philadelphia. "'Tis probable the Pudding will be boiled in England," wrote John Eliot in October 1783.[42]

In December 1783, while the 406 pages of *The Mystery* were in the press, Mary Chauncy died in Boston. Tradition says that Chauncy's reaction was typically stoical. Burial services on December 21 were to begin at three o'clock. When the clock struck that hour only a few parishioners had arrived. Chauncy turned to Clarke, who was to conduct the the funeral.

"It is time to begin," he said.

Clarke objected, "Will it not be well to wait a little while, as so few persons are present?"

"Mr. Clarke," replied the Doctor, "she is to be buried. Begin!"

In his funeral sermon, Clarke, dwelling on her gentleness and forebearance, portrayed Mary Chauncy as a remarkable Christian. Doubtless he believed she needed these qualities to live with Dr. Chauncy.[43]

Chauncy paid for the English publication of *The Mystery*, but he could not let the challenges of his fellow New England ministers remain unanswered while London printer Charles Dilly brought the pudding to a boil. Murrayism remained off limits for the moment, yet he could still hunt down the New Divinity men. Joseph Eckley had fired on the scouting party with his pamphlet, *Divine Glory, Brought to View, in the Condemnation of the Ungodly*. Chauncy returned the fire with a bigger gun. He loved to parody his opponents; thus he called his reply *Divine glory brought to view in the final salvation of men.*[44]

The essay stated the tenets of *The Mystery* coolly and briefly. Chauncy disagreed with Eckley chiefly on grounds of consistency. Like Chauncy, Eckley posited universal atonement. Once you do so, Chauncy argued, universal salvation inevitably follows as a logical conclusion. "You allow the former," Chauncy asked; "Why would you dispute the latter? . . . What should hinder the future accomplishment of the divine will; or the final success of Christ's mediatorial undertaking? *Our* wishes are often frustrated: but God cannot be disappointed. Inasmuch as the saviour of the world has atoned for the sins of every creature, and God earnestly desires the salvation of *all*, it is inconceivable that any should perish everlastingly. His infinite power, wisdom and goodness forbid such a dishonourable supposition." To deny this is to misread Scripture, especially the Epistle to the Romans, and to entertain a mistaken idea of God. The Calvinists' God is "destitute of goodness and sincerity," Chauncy objected: "The God you portray is only deficient in wisdom and power." To contend that damnation manifests God's glory leads only to this chilling conclusion:

> *You* expect to look down from heaven upon numbers of wretched objects, confined in the pit of hell, and blaspheming their creator forever. *I* hope to see the prison-doors opened; and to hear those tongues, which are now profaning the name of God, chanting his praise. In one word, *you* imagine the divine glory will be advanced by immortalizing sin and misery; *I* by exterminating both natural and moral evil, and introducing universal happiness. Which of our systems is best supported, let reason and scripture determine. Of this I am certain, we equally differ from the ORTHODOX sentiments of our country; and for this reason, *I* ought to be heard with the same candour which hath been exercised towards you.[45]

175

Divine Glory outshone *Salvation for all Men* at every point and prepared the way for the complete work, which crossed the Atlantic in the summer of 1784.[46] Like Chauncy's other theological treatises this ran to bulk—406 pages, plus an introduction—and to thoroughness. Chauncy tried to consider every facet, answer each objection. Reading it demanded an expense of time, but those who made the effort came away impressed with his scholarship; some were convinced by his arguments. Ebenezer Hazard took several weeks to read it. He decided: "His reasoning is clear and satisfactory, and his criticisms are just. . . . He has placed many texts and passages of Scripture in a light altogether new to me, and I cannot help thinking his system not only rational, but Scriptural, and that it reflects more honor on the divine character than I have yet met with."[47] New Divinity men thought less of it: Jonathan Edwards, Jr. "threatened to discipline for heresy a parishioner who had been converted by Chauncy's volume."[48] Bezaleel Howard met Chauncy on the street shortly after *The Mystery* appeared.

"Howard," Chauncy said, "have you seen my book?"

"Yes, Sir."

"Have you read it?"

"Yes, Sir."

"And do you believe it?"

"No, Sir."

"Ah! If you had faith as a grain of mustard seed, you would believe it!"

Howard loved Chauncy, but never forgave him for his Universalism. In 1833 he wrote: "And his own errors, although they may have injured thousands, did not appear to do him any harm, but rather increased his love to God and man; and how far he is accountable to God for the injury his book has done, is an awful question which none but God can answer. But it is a question which ought to fill the mind of every author, and every preacher with great anxiety, lest the blood of others should be required of them."[49]

Printed responses, surprisingly, were few in number and slow to appear. By far the most important, Jonathan Edwards, Jr.'s *The Salvation of all Men examined* . . . ably subjects Chauncy's idea of temporary punishment to searching criticism.[50] But Chauncy had been dead three years when Edwards's tract appeared.

In June 1784 Chauncy sent to England for publication the manuscript of his work on the Fall.[51] Later that year Boston printers Powars and Willis brought out *The Benevolence of the Deity*; 1785 saw all three treatises in print. A heretic in his old age, Chauncy encountered the inconvenience of attack, but at eighty, one more inconvenience could not matter much. After all, the manuscripts that had "lain by" in his study and had occupied his mind for decades

176

were now between boards. The bloody war had been won, and a new country had been born.

After the publication of *The Mystery* Chauncy deservedly adopted an attitude of mellow resignation. One suspects that he delighted in Boston's puzzled reaction to his new pose. "What will there be next?" asked an incredulous John Eliot. "The Dr. says he never will shew any more zeal, or scold, except at vice and immorality."[52] For the first time the unfamiliar luxury of an assistant allowed him leisure to visit his friends, smoke a pipe with his cronies, and take a glass of wine with a widow or two in the neighborhood. He enjoyed clattering across Boston's cobblestones "in a heavy, yellow-bodied chaise, with long shafts, a black boy perched on the horse's tail." He made a handsome figure "in his dignified clerical costume, with three-cornered hat, gold cane and laced wrists, bowing gracefully to citizens as he passed. His grinning young driver in the meanwhile exchanged his compliments with young acquaintances of his own color by touching them up with his long whip from his safe perch."[53]

Chauncy relinquished his grip on the Old Brick and gave Clarke his head with parish affairs, even when the young man proposed buying an organ for the meetinghouse. An organ? In a Congregationalist Church? "The Doctor was against it," Stiles jotted in his diary, "but Mr. Clark his Collegue & the Congrega. in general were for it."[54] In fact, Clarke even wrote to New England's greatest benefactor, Thomas Hollis, asking for £500 to buy the instrument. Hollis thought Clarke had lost his wits. He not only turned down the request, he had a "Tractate on Church Music" printed, dedicated it to Chauncy and Clarke, and sent a bundle of copies to New England as a blunt reminder of Puritan opposition to instrumental music in church services.[55] Undissuaded, the people insisted. In August 1784 they voted to repair the meetinghouse; it seemed a perfect chance to install the organ while the Church underwent remodeling.[56] A delegation appeared before Chauncy with this proposal. To their surprise, he wearily agreed, telling them "that it would not be long before he was in his grave—he knew that before his head was cold there, they would have an Organ—and they might do as they pleased."[57] In March, when the First Church met again at the Old Brick, they had their organ, and Chauncy had conceded even more. "Everything is strange," John Eliot reported. "Dr. Chauncy hath an organ fixed up in his meetinghouse; hath consented Clarke shall have a gown."[58]

Chauncy preached his final published sermon on the day the First Church returned to its refurbished meetinghouse. The house was "remarkably crouded both parts of the day," reported Joseph Russell, "and is repaired in a very neat and beautiful manner, and I think is equal to any in town, the Old South excepted." The meeting took place on March 13, 1785. "The solemnities of the day," recalled Russell, were "opened with an anthem composed by Billings, 'I was glad when they said unto me, we will go into the house of the Lord.' This was performed by the best masters in town, and, accompanied with the organ which we have introduced into the meeting, is a most delightful piece of musick, and is a very great help in singing. It is pleasing to almost every one of the society, excepting a few who retain their ancient prejudices, and who had rather hear this pleasing part of devotion performed by a small number of screaming voices, without order or decency, than have any tuned instrument as a help, however harmonious and agreable." After Clarke's opening prayer, "Dr. Chauncy then gave an excellent sermon suitable to the occasion, which was by unanimous vote printed."[59]

He chose a passage from III Kings: "But will God in very deed dwell on earth? Behold the heaven, and heaven of heavens, cannot contain thee; how much less this house that I have built?" It complemented nicely the text of his ordination sermon: "Lo, I am with you always." In his usual fashion he "opened" the text plainly and logically, discussing the nature of omnipresence, then considering the rational and scriptural arguments for attributing this quality to God, and finally "applying" the text to the affairs of his congregation. It was the old Puritan sermon style done by a practiced hand. For this occasion Chauncy permitted himself a personal—and surprisingly figurative—digression, in which he summed up his years at the Old Brick.

NEARLY sixty years, are now compleated, my beloved brethren, since I have been with you in the service of the Gospel; and my labours, I trust, have not been wholly in vain, notwithstanding my manifold infirmities and imperfections. Need I an epistle of commendation from you? Ye are yourselves, some of you, I have abundant reason to believe, my epistle, yea rather the epistle of Christ, through a divine influence, accompanying my ministrations, however unworthy, written not with ink, but with the spirit of the living God; not in tables of stone, but in fleshy tables of the heart. Such trust have I through Christ, Godward. And it is my joy now, and may it be my crown of rejoicing in the presence of the Lord Jesus Christ at his coming!

I am now grown old, and unable, through manifold infirmities, to go on with the work of the sacred ministry. Thanks be to God you have my son in the gospel to supply my place, and he will do it much to your advantage, as he is now in the prime of life, and singularly qualified to serve the interest of Christ among you. I am decreasing, and shall decrease still more and more, but he will increase; God grant it may be in all spiritual wisdom and understanding, that he may be more and more furnished for a masterworkman in the kingdom of Christ.[60]

Characteristically Chauncy concluded with "a few words of advice, which you may look upon as the last and dying words of your aged pastor from this desk, as he does not expect to be much longer with you." He told his people to love the Lord's Day and attend it faithfully with both inward and outward reverence; to "pay all due honour to the ordinance of the supper"; but not to make religion a mere Sabbath affair:

> Whether you eat or drink, whether you buy or sell, or whatever you do, you should do all to the glory of God, and in the name of Christ: so may you hope, and upon just and solid grounds, that your sacrifices of prayer and praise, and all your acts of devotion, whether they are offered to God from your closet, families, or his house of worship, will be acceptable to him; and that, from worshipping and serving him here on earth, you shall, in proper season, have entrance granted to you into the temple of God above, where you shall join, with that innumerable company which have been selected from the rest of mankind, in singing–HALLALUJAHS, TO HIM THAT SITTETH ON THE THRONE, AND TO THE LAMB, FOR EVER AND EVER. AMEN.[61]

Words in season indeed, and surely words that came from his heart.

While Clarke held forth in his gown, and the congregation sang at meeting, Chauncy did not simply retire to the seclusion of his study; God expected man to improve his time while he had life in him. Increasingly, his friends noticed, he spent a great part of his time in "religious exercises,"[62] but even that term suggests the energy with which he attacked every situation. Although his pastoral work diminished, he seemed busy as ever. In the afternoons of early 1786 he rode out in his carriage, dressed in his very best, to sit for his portrait. What artist took his likeness is unknown, but Joseph Woodward, who donated the painting to the Massachusetts Historical Society, commissioned the work and was pleased with the result.[63] Indeed, Chauncy, bewigged, stiff-backed, and dignified, hardly looks his years. His face and eyes are alert and clear, and his expression, although stern enough, is surely less severe than that which crossed his face one morning in 1742 when he glanced up to find James Davenport standing in his doorway.

If Chauncy spent his afternoons at the artist's studio, he apparently spent his evenings in still more pleasant pursuits. In 1785 Jonathan Jackson passed along this tantalizing piece of gossip to Richard Price: "Your friend Dr. Chauncy appears to be in good health for an old gentleman past eighty; he complains however of having arrived to his second dotage, and perhaps he is not mistaken, for he has been lately, since my return, paying his addresses to a widow of forty, to whom he would have given his hand had not she and her friends been possessed of more discretion. This communication is to excite you to a little merriment."[64] The identity of the discreet widow remains unknown.

179

If she and Doctor Chauncy exchanged letters, he probably burned them. Chauncy's papers have not turned up in nearly two hundred years; one can only assume that he carried out the promise he made to Ezra Stiles in 1768 and committed them to the flames. Let Chauncy tell the story as he wrote it to Stiles in his "Life of President Chauncy":

As I am the eldest son of Charles, the eldest son of Isaac, who was the eldest son of president Chauncy, I thought his papers properly belonged to me. Accordingly, after I was settled in the ministry, I was at considerable pains to recover them. I could not, for many years, find out which of his sons took possession of them upon his death, At length Mr. Chauncy of Durham informed me they were put into the hands of his father, the old gentleman's eldest son then living in this country, who kept them as a valuable treasure during his life; but, upon his death, his children being all under age, they were unhappily suffered to continue in the possession of his widow and their mother. She married sometime after a North-Hampton Deacon, who principally got his living by making and selling pies. Behold now the fate of all the good president's writings of every kind! They were put to the bottom of pies, and in this way brought to utter destruction. I was greatly moved to hear this account of them; and it has rivetted in my mind a determination to order all my papers, upon my decease, to be burnt, excepting such as I might mention by name for deliverance from the catastrophe; though I have not as yet excepted any, nor do I know that I shall.[65]

In 1750 Chauncy had carried out John Taylor's dying wish and burned all his close friend's papers.[66] During the revolution such men as Samuel Adams and James Otis destroyed their more incriminating letters.[67] Perhaps Chauncy decided to follow suit at this time, thus robbing history of an immense store of material.

It is probably just as well that the Boston widow and her friends decided against Chauncy's proposal, for health left him in the summer of 1786.[68] As one of his last official acts, he signed the "Declaration of Faith Subscribed by the Members of the First Church of Christ in Boston." The first such document in the church records since the original covenant, it reveals how far from the federal theology Boston's pioneer church had come. The text follows:

I. We, whose names are underwritten, declare our Faith in the one only living and true God.
II. We believe in the Lord Jesus Christ, that he was sanctified of the Father, and sent into the world, that he might "redeem us from all iniquity; and purify to himself a peculiar people zealous of good works."
III. We believe in that gospel, which was ratified by the death and resurrection of its author; and solemnly promise to make it the only rule of our faith and practice.

United by the ties of One Lord, one common Faith, and one Baptism, we promise to live in Christian love; to watch over each other as members of the same body; to counsel and assist, whenever there shall be occasion; to be faithful to our master, and faithful to each other, waiting in joyful hope of an eternal happy intercourse in the heavenly world.[69]

When the church composed its creed, it also set forth five requirements for communion. First, "all, who acknowledge the divine authority of the gospel, ought . . . to observe its positive institutions." Second, "Voted unanimously, that we remove every obstacle, which may prevent those who worship, from communing with us; and that we impose no other terms of communion than such as are found in the word of God, or may be clearly inferred from it." Third, "all who believe in Jesus Christ; profess this belief; and sustain a good moral character, have a right to commune at the Lord's Table: it appearing from sacred authority, that nothing more was required of the primative candidates for communion." Fourth, when any person thus qualified "shall desire stated communion, nothing more shall be required than subscription to the declaration of Faith to which we have set our hands; that this may be done in private, provided the Church be informed that such candidate has made application and his actual subscription be announced the first time he shall present himself to communion." Finally, when any person qualified to commune "but discouraged by scruples in his own mind" offers a child for baptism, "nothing further" will be required "than subscription to our common declaration of faith, assenting however to this additional article, that he will educate his child in the faith and practice of that religion to which he has solemnly set his hand."[70]

In a sense these articles illustrate the history and evolution of New England Puritanism. The end product of such burning issues as the covenant theology, visible saints, Stoddardeanism, the conversion experience, Arminianism, the nature of true virtue, spiritual relations, and the half-way covenant, they reflect the triumph of the Enlightenment and the decline of Puritan piety; they repudiate the rigors of John Cotton and anticipate the Unitarianism of William Emerson.[71]

With the body of his divinity published, the last of eight hundred sermons preached, his parting "words in season" delivered, and now his final manifesto signed, Chauncy entered in the summer of 1786 the concluding stages of his temporal sufferings. He bore "much bodily pain and weakness" with his customary courage and "exemplary patience." On February 10, 1787, slightly more than a month after his eighty-second birthday, he died in the parsonage on Summer Street.[72]

John Clarke preached his eulogy.[73] As a man who had spent his life praising the Godly, Faithful Man, Chauncy would have been pleased with Clarke's text: "Well done, Thou Good and Faithful Servant; enter thou into the Joy of the Lord."

181

Notes

Abbreviations

AAS. Proc.	*Proceedings of the American Antiquarian Society.*
AHR	*American Historical Review.*
AN&Q	*American Notes & Queries.*
AQ	*American Quarterly.*
CSM Pubs.	*Publications of the Colonial Society of Massachusetts.*
DAB	*Dictionary of American Biography.*
Hist. Mag.	*Historical Magazine.*
MHS Colls.	*Collections of the Massachusetts Historical Society.*
MHS Proc.	*Proceedings of the Massachusetts Historical Society.*
NEHG Reg.	*New England Historical and Genealogical Register.*
NEQ	*New England Quarterly.*
SHG	*Sibley's Harvard Graduates: Biographical Sketches of Those Who Attended Harvard College.* Ed. Clifford K. Shipton. 17 vols. Boston: Massachusetts Historical Society, 1933-75.
WMQ	*William and Mary Quarterly*

Notes

Preface

1. Paul Murray Kendall, *The Art of Biography* (New York: W. W. Norton, 1965), p. ix.

Introduction

1. Perry Miller et al., eds., *Major Writers of America* (New York: Harcourt, Brace & World, 1962), I, 83.

2. Benjamin Franklin, *The Autobiography of Benjamin Franklin*, ed. Leonard W. Labaree, Ralph L. Ketcham, Helen C. Boatfield, and Helene H. Fineman (New Haven and London: Yale University Press, 1964), p. 145.

3. Conrad Wright, *The Beginnings of Unitarianism in America* (Boston: Starr King Press, 1955), pp. 1–8.

4. A. C. McGiffert, *Protestant Thought Before Kant* (New York: C. Scribner's Sons, 1911), p. 189.

5. Conrad Wright, *The Liberal Christians: Essays on American Unitarian History* (Boston: Beacon, 1970), p. 6.

6. Franklin, *Autobiography*, p. 148.

7. William B. Sprague, *Annals of the American Unitarian Pulpit; or Commemorative Notices of Distinguished Clergymen of the Unitarian Denomination in the United States from its Commencement to the Close of the Year Eighteen Hundred and Fifty-Five* (New York: R. Carter & Bros., 1865), p. 12.

8. David Levin, ed., *Jonathan Edwards: A Profile* (New York: Hill and Wang, 1969), pp. 25–26.

9. Franklin, *Autobiography*, p. 113.

10. *Ibid.*, pp. 145–56.

11. *Ibid.*, pp. 114–15.

12. *The Writings of Benjamin Franklin*, ed. Albert Henry Smyth (New York: Macmillan, 1905–07), X, 84.

13. Michael Kammen, *People of Paradox: An Inquiry Concerning the Origins of American Civilization* (1972; rpt. New York: Vintage Books, 1973), pp. 169–79.

Prologue

1. The practices of having the new minister preach his own ordination sermon and holding a festive celebration after the ceremony were common in New England Congregational churches during the seventeenth century but had fallen out of fashion by the 1720s. Thomas Foxcroft, however, remained an outspoken proponent of the old customs and ensured that an ordination in his church would be done in the traditional way. See J. William T. Youngs, Jr., *God's Messengers: Religious Leadership in Colonial New England, 1700-1750* (Baltimore and London: The Johns Hopkins University Press, 1976), pp. 30-39, for the history of the ordination ceremony and Foxcroft's defense of seventeenth-century practices.

Chapter One: A Boston Lad

1. This scene has been constructed from details provided in various accounts of "Pope's Day," principally among them George Francis Dow, *Every Day Life in the Massachusetts Bay Colony* (Boston: The Society for the Preservation of New England Antiquities, 1935), p. 116; Samuel G. Drake, *The History and Antiquities of Boston* (Boston: Luther Stevens, 1856), pp. 661-65; Esther Forbes, *Paul Revere & the World He Lived In* (Boston: Houghton Mifflin, 1942), pp. 93-98; Robert H. Lord, John E. Sexton, and Edward T. Harrington, *History of the Archdiocese of Boston in the Various Stages of its Development 1604 to 1943* (New York: Sheed and Ward, 1944), I, 237-40; Annie Haven Thwing, *The Crooked and Narrow Streets of the Town of Boston, 1630-1822* (Boston: Marshall Jones, 1920), pp. 78-79, and Sherwood Collins, "Boston's Political Street Theatre: the Eighteenth-Century Pope-Day Pageants," *Educational Theatre Journal*, 25 (1973), 401-09.

2. Chauncy, "Life of the Rev. President Chauncy, Written At the Request of Dr. Stiles," *MHS Colls.*, 1st Ser., 10 (1809), 171.

3. *Ibid.*, p. 173.

4. William Chauncey Fowler, *Memorials of the Chaunceys* (Boston: Henry Dutton, 1858), pp. 55-56; Samuel Deane, *History of Scituate, Massachusetts, from its First Settlements to 1831* (Boston: James Loring, 1831), pp. 172-79.

5. Franklin, *Autobiography*, p. 56.

6. *Ibid.*, p. 55.

7. M. Halsey Thomas, ed., *The Diary of Samuel Sewall 1674-1729* (New York: Farrar, Straus and Giroux, 1973), II, 659.

8. Carl Bridenbaugh, *Cities in the Wilderness: The First Century of Urban Life in America, 1625-1742* (New York: Ronald Press, 1938), p. 143.

9. G. B. Warden, *Boston 1689-1776* (Boston: Little, Brown, 1970), p. 57.

10. Chauncy, *Man's Life Considered under the Similitude of a Vapour, that Appeareth for a Little Time, and then Vanisheth Away* (Boston: B. Green, 1731), preface.

11. Fowler, *Memorials of the Chaunceys*, p. 56. Judge Walley died on January 11, 1712. Sarah Chauncy was bequeathed "the land and tenement in the occupation of Capt. Nathl. Oliver, and £200." See Drake, *The History and Antiquities of Boston*, p. 491.

12. Clifford K. Shipton, *Sibley's Harvard Graduates: Biographical Sketches of Those Who Attended Harvard College*, VI (Boston: Massachusetts Historical Society, 1942), 569-71. This series is hereafter abbreviated *SHG*.

13. Chauncy, "A Sketch of Eminent Men in New-England," *MHS Colls.*, 1st Ser., 10 (1809), 158. Hereafter cited as "Eminent Men."

14. Shipton, *SHG*, VI (1942), 569-71. See also Pauline Holmes, *A Tercentenary History of the Boston Public Latin School 1635-1935* (Cambridge: Harvard University Press, 1935), pp. 258-60.

15. Robert Francis Seybolt, *The Public Schools of Colonial Boston 1635-1775* (Cambridge: Harvard University Press, 1935), p. 15, and *The Public Schoolmasters of Colonial Boston* (Cambridge: Harvard University Press, 1939), pp. 5-6.

16. Franklin, *Autobiography*, p. 53.

17. Samuel Eliot Morison, *The Puritan Pronaos: Studies in the Intellectual Life of New England in the Seventeenth Century* (New York and London: New York University Press, 1936), p. 103.

18. Kenneth B. Murdock, "The Teaching of Latin and Greek at the Boston Latin School in 1712," *CSM Pubs.*, 27 (1932), 23-25; Morison, *The Puritan Pronaos*, pp. 102-03.

19. Shipton, *SHG*, IV (1933), 15.

20. On Francis Willoughby, see Shipton, *SHG*, VIII (1951), 108.

Chapter Two: The Young Harvard Scholar

1. Samuel Eliot Morison, *Three Centuries of Harvard* (Cambridge: Harvard University Press, 1936), pp. 59, 66. See also Seymour Martin Lipset and David Riesman, *Education and Politics at Harvard* (New York: McGraw-Hill, 1975), pp. 20-28.

2. Morison, *Three Centuries of Harvard*, pp. 61-63.

3. Perry Miller, *The New England Mind: From Colony to Province* (1953; rpt. Boston: Beacon Press, 1961), pp. 456-63.

4. On the Pierpont case, see Shipton, *SHG*, VI (1942), 98-102, and Perry Miller, *The New England Mind: From Colony to Province*, pp. 455-56. The other matters are discussed at length in Miller and in Morison, *Three Centuries of Harvard*, pp. 54-75.

5. Morison, *Three Centuries of Harvard*, p. 71.

6. This is the famous epidemic in which Cotton Mather proposed that inoculation be tried. The story of his campaign for this new and unusual treatment is told in Perry Miller, *The New England Mind: From Colony to Province*, pp. 345-66, and in Otho T. Beall, Jr. and Richard H. Shryock, *Cotton Mather: First Significant Figure in American Medicine* (Baltimore: Johns Hopkins University Press, 1954), pp. 93-126.

7. Perry Miller, *The New England Mind: From Colony to Province*, p. 456.

8. Freshman Charles Chauncy was ranked eighth in the class at entrance. At this time "placing" of young scholars was more a question of social position than of intellectual promise or piety: a boy's rank depended largely upon the status of his father in the province, with preference given to public service. Classes were divided into three groups. Sons of magistrates comprised the highest group, followed by sons of graduates and then sons of farmers, artisans, merchants, and mariners. Chauncy probably owed his relatively high placement to several factors: although his father had been a merchant, his great-grandfather had been president of the college, his mother was the daughter of a judge, and his new stepfather, Francis Willoughby, had been Salem's representative to the General Court. Placement was important, for it established the order of preference at every college function, from meals in the dining hall to position in academic processions. The tutors of the college, notably Nicholas Sever, agitated unsuccessfully during Chauncy's college days for rankings based on academic promise. One could lose his place by misbehavior, and Chauncy lost his. He was fined for card-playing and in March 1720 was degraded in class rank for skipping the required "commons and sizings" in the dining hall for three quarters. The demotion was of rather long standing: he was not reinstated to his earlier rank until June 1722. Shipton, *SHG*, VI (1942), 569-71; Clifford K. Shipton, "Ye Mystery of Ye Ages Solved, or, how Placing Worked at Colonial Harvard & Yale," *Harvard Alumni Bulletin*, December 11, 1954, pp. 258-63; John Maynard Hoffman, "Commonwealth College: The Governance of Harvard in the Puritan Period," Dissertation, Harvard University 1972, pp. 526-27; Lipset and Riesman, *Education and Politics at Harvard*, pp. 23-24; and "Quarter Bill Books," March-June 1720, MS Harvard University Archives.

9. Shipton, *SHG*, VI (1942), 423.

10. See the biographies of the class of 1721 in Shipton, *SHG*, VI. On his friendship with Taylor and Sewall, see Chauncy, "Eminent Men," pp. 158-59.

11. Shipton, *SHG*, IV (1933), 15-17.

12. For sketches of Wigglesworth see Shipton, *SHG*, V (1937), 546-55, and *DAB*, XX, 191-92.

13. "Quaestio Sheet, Harvard College, 1724," MS in Harvard University Archives. A reproduction of this sheet appears in Harold Bernhard, "Charles Chauncy: Colonial Liberal," Dissertation, University of Chicago Divinity School 1945.

14. Chauncy, "Eminent Men," p. 160.

15. Shipton, *SHG*, V (1937), 548-49.

16. Shipton, *SHG*, VI (1942), 439-40; Chauncy, "Eminent Men," p. 160.

17. Morison, *The Puritan Pronaos*, p. 40.

18. Mary Latimer Gambrell, *Ministerial Training in Eighteenth-Century New England* (New York: Columbia University Press, 1937), p. 91.

19. "Harvard College Records," *CSM Pubs.*, 16 (1925), 470, 477, 504, 547.

20. Chauncy, "Eminent Men," p. 160.

21. Carl Bridenbaugh, *Mitre and Sceptre: Transatlantic Faiths, Ideas, Personalities, and Politics 1689-1775* (New York: Oxford University Press, 1967), p. 69.

22. *Ibid.*, p. 70.

23. Quoted in Kenneth B. Murdock, "Cotton Mather and the Rectorship of Yale College," *CSM Pubs.*, 26 (1927), 395.

24. William C. Lane, "Communication on a Manuscript Volume recently acquired by Harvard College," *CSM Pubs.*, 12 (1911), 220-31. Extracts from "The Telltale" and a discussion of the student society are included. In *Three Centuries of Harvard*, pp. 62-63, Morison includes a short discussion.

25. Hamilton A. Hill, *History of the Old South Church (Third Church) Boston, 1669-1884*, I (Boston and New York: Houghton Mifflin, 1890), 370-71, 417.

26. That had been a year of sorrow for the Sewalls: Elizabeth's mother died in 1716, her father followed in October 1717, and two weeks later her grandmother, Judge Sewall's wife, died; a fortnight later she lost her other grandfather, Judge Grove Hirst. This succession of deaths left Elizabeth and her sisters absolutely alone, except for old Judge Sewall, who took the children into his home. See Samuel G. Drake, "Researches Among Funeral Sermons, and Other Tracts, for the Recovery of Biographical and Genealogical Materials," *NEHG Reg.*, 8 (1854), 260. Drake draws his information from a funeral sermon, "rarely to be found" even in 1854, of Benjamin Colman's, entitled *Mr. Hirst's Remains* (Boston, 1717). Other references to these events may be found in the diary of Samuel Sewall, Jr., quoted in the "Introduction" to the *Diary* of Samuel Sewall, *MHS Colls.*, 5th Ser., 5 (1878), xxxvi.

27. Shipton, *SHG*, VI (1942), 440.

28. "Harvard College Records," pp. 513, 525, 540, 548.

29. Margery Somers Foster, *'Out of Smalle Beginings . . .': An Economic History of Harvard College in the Puritan Period (1636 to 1712)* (Cambridge, Mass.: Belknap Press of Harvard University Press, 1962), p. 140.

30. "Harvard College Records," p. 513. The scholars were paid a flat four pounds when the awards were renewed in 1725 and 1726.

31. From the College Laws of 1667, as cited by Foster, *'Out of Smalle Beginings,'* p. 140. In 1724 one of Chauncy's fellow scholars, Edward Huntting, was given the specific charge "to take care that the Doors upon the roofs of the several Colleges be kept Locked and the Gutters Troughs & Trunks be cleansed as there shal be occasion." "Harvard College Records," pp. 513-14. Apparently the nature of the job did not change drastically through the years.

32. He preached from Matthew, "If thou wilt enter into Life, keep the Commandments," on November 29, 1724. See "The Diary of Samuel Sewall," *MHS Colls.*, 5th Ser., 7 (1882), 345.

33. Rogers lived in Ipswich; the post was that of assistant to his own father; his grandfather and great-grandfather had occupied the Ipswich pulpit since the birth of the colony. Chauncy could not have been a very serious candidate. Shipton, *SHG*, VI (1942), 557.

34. Letter dated August 30, 1725, from William Waldron to Richard Waldron. MS Collection, Boston Public Library.

35. Richard D. Pierce, ed., "The Records of the First Church in Boston 1630-1868," *CSM Pubs.*, 39-41 (1961), 145.

36. *Ibid.*, p. 146.
37. *Ibid.*, pp. 148–49.
38. *Ibid.*, p. 149.
39. *Ibid.*, p. 150.
40. "Harvard College Records," p. 548; Shipton, *SHG*, VI (1942), 440.
41. Pierce, ed., "The Records of the First Church in Boston," p. 151.

Chapter Three: A "Godly, Faithful Man"

1. Diary of Joseph Sewall, quoted in Hill, *Old South Church*, I, 443. Chauncy told Ezra Stiles in 1768 that Judge Sewall "was so kind and good to his relatives and others in want, that he outdid his proper capacity for doing." *Extracts from the Itineraries and Other Miscellanies of Ezra Stiles, D. D., LL. D.*, ed. Franklin Bowditch Dexter (New Haven: Yale University Press, 1916), p. 446. Hereafter cited as *Itineraries*.
2. "Introduction" to *Diary of Samuel Sewall*, xxxvi.
3. Pierce, ed., "The Records of the First Church in Boston," pp. 144, 154–55.
4. *Ibid.*, p. 156.
5. *Ibid.*
6. *Ibid.*, p. 157.
7. Shipton, *SHG*, VI (1942), 441; Pierce, ed., "The Records of the First Church in Boston," p. 398.
8. H. B. Parkes, "New England in the Seventeen-Thirties," *NEQ*, 3 (1930), 397–419.
9. Pierce, ed., "The Records of the First Church in Boston," p. 395.
10. *Ibid.*, pp. 111–12.
11. Bernhard, "Charles Chauncy," p. 45, citing records of Harvard Overseers.
12. Robert F. Seybolt, "The Ministers at the Town Meetings in Colonial Boston," *CSM Pubs.*, 32 (1937), 300–04.
13. Thomas Foxcroft, *Observations Historical and Practical on the Rise and Primitive State of New-England, With a Special Reference to the Old or first gather'd Church in Boston* (Boston: S. Kneeland and T. Green for S. Gerrish, 1730), p. 1.
14. Perry Miller, *The New England Mind: From Colony to Province*, pp. 27–39.
15. See Shipton, *SHG*, VI (1942), 304–08 for a biographical sketch of Davenport.
16. Chauncy, "Eminent Men," p. 162.
17. *Ibid.*
18. *Ibid.*, p. 161.
19. May 30, 1734.
20. Photostat of MS letter to Zachary Grey, dated November 8, 1734, Massachusetts Historical Society. Cutler and Addington Davenport were close friends.
21. Chauncy, "Eminent Men," p. 162.
22. Chauncy, *Early Piety Recommended and Exemplify'd* (Boston: B. Gray, 1732), p.19.
23. Chauncy, *Nathanael's Character Display'd* (Boston: n.p., 1733).
24. Boston: B. Green, 1731, pp. 5–6.
25. Chauncy, *Prayer for Help a Seasonable Duty upon the Ceasing of Godly and Faithful Men* (Boston: T. Fleet, 1737), pp. 2–4.
26. *Ibid.*, p. 9.
27. *Ibid.*, pp. 5–7.
28. Chauncy, *Nathanael's Character*, p. 12. This conviction has a long history in New England. Cf., for example, Thomas Shepard, *The Sincere Convert*, "continuously in print from 1641 to 1812." See Perry Miller, *The American Puritans: Their Prose and Poetry* (New York: Doubleday, 1956), p. 22.
29. Chauncy, *Early Piety*, p. 21.
30. *Ibid.*
31. Pierce, ed., "The Records of the First Church in Boston," pp. 164–65.

189

32. Shipton, *SHG*, VI (1942), 441.
33. Pierce, ed., "The Records of the First Church in Boston," pp. 165-67.
34. Shipton, *SHG*, VI (1942), 441.
35. Pierce, ed., "The Records of the First Church in Boston," p. 166.
36. *Ibid.*, pp. 167-68.
37. "Diary of the Rev. Thomas Prince, 1737," *CSM Pubs.*, 19 (1918), 344.
38. *Ibid.*, p. 345.
39. Hill, *Old South Church*, I, 482.
40. Chauncy, *Prayer for Help*, p. 15.
41. "Diary of the Rev. Thomas Prince," p. 361.
42. Pierce, ed., "The Records of the First Church in Boston," pp. 173-76.
43. "Diary of the Rev. Thomas Prince," p. 351.
44. *Ibid.*, p. 356.
45. *Ibid.*, pp. 348, 361-62.
46. *A Report of the Record Commissioners of the City of Boston Containing the Records of Boston Selectmen, 1736-1742* (Boston: Rockwell and Churchill, 1886), pp. 114-15; 246.
47. Pierce, ed., "The Records of the First Church in Boston," p. 178.
48. *Ibid.*, pp. 178-79.
49. *Ibid.*, p. 179.
50. *New England Weekly Journal*, January 23, 1739.
51. *Ibid.*
52. Pierce, ed., "The Records of the First Church in Boston," pp. 184-85.
53. *Ibid.*

Chapter Four: After the Surprising Conversions

1. Robert Lowell, "After the Surprising Conversions," *Lord Weary's Castle* (New York: Harcourt, Brace & World, 1946), pp. 60-61, captures the intensity of these experiences in a powerful poem.

2. Ola Elizabeth Winslow, *Jonathan Edwards, 1703-1758. A Biography* (New York: Macmillan, 1940), pp. 152-74.

3. *Jonathan Edwards: The Great Awakening*, ed. C. C. Goen (New Haven and London: Yale University Press, 1972), pp. 22-25. Volume IV of *The Works of Jonathan Edwards*, ed. John E. Smith. Hereafter cited as Goen, ed., *The Great Awakening*.

4. *Ibid.*, pp. 109-10. The Boston clergy already knew Edwards, for they had invited him to preach at the Public Lecture of July 8, 1731. He spoke on *God Glorified in Man's Dependence*, and the ministers were so pleased with his sermon that they had it printed. Perry Miller, in *Jonathan Edwards* (New York: William Sloane Associates, 1949), contends that Chauncy, even in 1731, was a bitter opponent of Edwards and contrived to subvert the effect of his speech by having Samuel Whittelsey come to Boston three months before Edwards did and preach in the First Church, thus preparing the world for a contrast between the "free and catholic" Yale man, Whittelsey, and the rigorous opponent of liberalism, also a Yale man, Edwards. Miller, always ready to make Chauncy a villain, ignores the facts that the effect of such a calculated contrast would be rather dulled over a three-month time span; that it would require considerable prescience on the part of Chauncy in April to know the topic of Edwards's sermon in July; that it is quite likely that Whittelsey was, as Foxcroft and Chauncy state, "occasionally in Town," probably to arrange for his son's studies at Harvard; that Foxcroft in 1731 was still very much in charge of the Old Brick, and could have asked his visitor to preach from motives of simple courtesy; that Chauncy and Whittelsey had been close friends for years; and that Whittelsey's sermon, *The Woful Condition of Impenitent Souls in their Separate State*, is hardly remarkable and controversial. It is possible that Chauncy conducted a conspiracy against Edwards in 1731, but the evidence for such a theory is slight. (See Perry Miller, *Jonathan Edwards*, p. 26.)

5. Colman Papers, Massachusetts Historical Society. Cited in Edwin Scott Gaustad, *The Great Awakening in New England* (New York: Harper, 1957), pp. 22, 143.

6. C. C. Goen concisely reconstructs the publication history of *A Faithful Narrative* in his introduction to *The Great Awakening*, pp. 32–46.

7. Goen, ed., *The Great Awakening*, pp. 140–41.

8. "Diary of the Rev. Thomas Prince, 1737," pp. 331–64.

9. MS Diary of Joseph Sewall, quoted in Hill, *Old South Church*, pp. 469, 481.

10. *A Report of the Record Commissioners of the City of Boston, Containing the Records of the Boston Selectmen, 1736 to 1742* (Boston: Rockwell and Churchill, 1886), pp. 114–15. See also *A Report of the Record Commissioners of the City of Boston, Containing the Boston Records from 1729 to 1742* (Boston: Rockwell and Churchill, 1885), p. 246.

11. Diary of Joseph Sewall, quoted in Hill, *Old South Church*, pp. 481–82.

12. Edwards mentions the church of Chauncy's cousin Nathaniel Chauncy, in Durham, Connecticut, as one of those participating in the surprising conversions. (*A Faithful Narrative*, in Goen, ed., *The Great Awakening*, pp. 23, 110, 120, 154.) Because the cousins corresponded frequently, it is likely that Chauncy had detailed knowledge of the Awakening in Connecticut.

13. *Ibid.*, pp. 191–205.

14. Chauncy, *Early Piety*, p. 17. This is a common theme in New England devotional literature, extending back at least as far as Cotton Mather's memoir of his brother Nathanael (who died at nineteen), *Early Piety Exemplified in the Life and Death of Nathanael Mather . . .* (London: J. Astwood for J. Dunton, 1689).

15. Goen, ed., *The Great Awakening*, p. 199.

16. Chauncy, *Early Piety*, pp. 15–16.

17. Goen, ed., *The Great Awakening*, p. 202.

18. *Ibid.*, p. 203.

19. Chauncy, *Early Piety*, p. 17.

20. Goen, ed., *The Great Awakening*, pp. 202–03.

21. Chauncy, *Early Piety*, p. 16.

22. Goen, ed., *The Great Awakening*, p. 204.

23. Chauncy, *Early Piety*, p. 16.

24. *Ibid.*, p. 17.

25. Goen, ed., *The Great Awakening*, p. 196.

26. Chauncy, *Early Piety*, p. 18.

27. *Ibid.*

28. *Ibid.*, pp. 18–19.

29. Goen, ed., *The Great Awakening*, p. 198.

30. *Ibid.*

31. Chauncy, *Early Piety*, p. 19.

32. Edmund S. Morgan, *Visible Saints: The History of a Puritan Idea* (New York: New York University Press, 1963), p. 66.

33. "Legal troubles" here means the sinner's realization that he has failed in his duty to God and that his actions have offended against God's laws. Later the sinner should come to realize that his problems go deeper than mere disobedient behavior; his very personality is corrupt.

34. Goen, ed., *The Great Awakening*, p. 168.

35. *Ibid.*, p. 161.

36. Printed in Samuel Hopkins, *The Life of the Late Reverend, Learned and Pious Mr. Jonathan Edwards . . .* (Boston: S. Kneeland, 1765). Reprinted in Levin, ed., *Jonathan Edwards: A Profile*, pp. 1–86.

37. Chauncy, *Early Piety*, p. 5.

38. Goen, ed., *The Great Awakening*, p. 151.

39. Chauncy, *Early Piety*, p. 11.

40. *Ibid.*, p. 6.

41. *Ibid.*

42. Goen, ed., *The Great Awakening*, pp. 138-39.

Chapter Five: The Outpouring of the Holy Ghost

1. Gaustad, *The Great Awakening in New England*, p. 43. Gaustad dubs Whitefield, Tennent, and Davenport "The Grand Itinerants." Cedric Cowing, in "Sex and Preaching in the Great Awakening," *AQ*, 20 (1968), 642-44, suggests that the Awakening in Boston, New Haven, Portsmouth, and Essex County was "milder," more transient, and more appealing to women than that in Plymouth, northeastern Connecticut, Maine, and the Connecticut River Valley, where the Awakening revitalized "the male laity" and helped reestablish the old principles of Congregational church organization. Chauncy came to see the Awakening as a threat to traditional Congregational polity.

2. The background to the Osborn affair is discussed by Gustavus Swift Paine, "Ungodly Carriages on Cape Cod," *NEQ*, 25 (1952), 181-98, and by J. M. Bumsted, "A Caution to Erring Christians: Ecclesiastical Disorder on Cape Cod, 1717 to 1738," *WMQ*, 28 (1971), 413-38.

3. Enoch Pratt, *A Comprehensive History, Ecclesiastical and Civil, of Eastham, Welfleet and Orleans, County of Barnstable, Mass., from 1644 to 1844* (Yarmouth, Mass.: W. S. Fisher and Co., 1844), pp. 55-57.

4. Jacob Arminius, quoted in Perry Miller, *The New England Mind: The Seventeenth Century* (New York, 1939; rpt. Boston: Beacon, 1968), p. 368. At this time the doctrines of atonement and election had fallen into confusion. Men like Osborn had weakened the strict, Anselmic, covenant position, but had not devised any substantial substitute for it. With the passage of time two main positions emerged from a welter of theories advanced by New England theologians. Anselm's classic theory was reconstructed by Jonathan Edwards. This doctrine holds that God requires satisfaction for every sin. A sin against God is an infinite offense, since God is an infinite being. It therefore requires infinite atonement, which is beyond the power of the finite human. Thus Christ, as God and Man, assumed to himself the sins of humankind, and in sacrificing himself, provided infinite atonement. Justice having been done, God then imputed the righteousness of Christ to the chosen elect among humankind. The second theory, that of Hugo Grotius, treats God as a ruler, not a creditor. God administers justice according to law. Law carries with it punishment as a means of maintaining order and deterring crime. Christ died, not to satisfy a debt, but to serve as a perfect example to mankind of the highest veneration for God's law and obedience to its provisions. Jonathan Mayhew was perhaps the foremost New England exponent of the Grotian doctrine in the mid-eighteenth century. Osborn was getting at it in the 1730s. Its implications for the doctrine of election are obvious: the next step is universal atonement; following that, as we shall see, comes universal salvation. See Joseph Haroutunian, *Piety Versus Moralism: The Passing of the New England Theology* (New York: Henry Holt, 1932), pp. 157-76; Wright, *The Beginnings of Unitarianism in America*, pp. 197-98; 218-21.

5. Osborn recounts this story in *The Case and Complaint of Mr. Samuel Osborn, late of Eastham; As it was Represented in a Letter to the Reverend Dr. Colman, to be communicated by him to the Convention for their Consideration* (Boston: W. McAlpine, 1743).

6. Printed as "Appendix" to Osborn, *Case and Complaint.*

7. *Ibid.* The text (from v. 14): "I press toward the mark for the prize of the high calling of God in Christ Jesus. Let us therefore, as many as be perfect, be thus minded; and if in any thing ye be otherwise minded, God shall reveal even this unto you. Nevertheless, whereto we have already attained, let us walk by the same rule, let us mind the same thing." (King James Version.)

8. Preached September 2, 1739 at the Old Brick. Published by J. Draper for J. Edwards, Boston, 1739, pp. 2-3. Hereafter cited as *The Only Compulsion.*

9. *Ibid.*, p. 3.

10. *Ibid.*, p. 14.

11. *Ibid.*, pp. 14-15.

12. Chauncy, "Eminent Men," p. 160.

13. This account of Whitefield's first visit to Boston is derived chiefly from three sources: Gaustad, *The Great Awakening in New England*, pp. 25-31; C. C. Goen, *Revivalism and Separatism in New England, 1740-1800: Strict Congregationalists and Separate Baptists in the Great Awakening* (New Haven and London: Yale University Press, 1962), pp. 8-19; and Stuart C. Henry, *George Whitefield, Wayfaring Witness* (New York and Nashville: Abingdon Press, 1957), pp. 65-67.

14. *Boston Weekly News-Letter*, September 25, 1740.

15. Thomas Prince, *An Account of the Revival of Religion in Boston* (Boston, 1823), p. 9.

16. *The Works of the Reverend George Whitefield* (London: Edward and Charles Dilly, 1771-72), I, 220-21.

17. Gaustad, *The Great Awakening in New England*, p. 34.

18. Eugene E. White, "The Decline of the Great Awakening in New England: 1741 to 1746," *NEQ* 24 (1951), 36-37.

19. Thomas Prince writes that "evangelical writings" of both early Puritans and contemporary evangelists quickly became popular. "And the more experimental our preaching was, like theirs, the more it was relished." *An Account of the Revival of Religion in Boston*, p. 19.

20. Gaustad, *The Great Awakening in New England*, pp. 44-47.

21. George Whitefield, *A Continuation of the Reverend Mr. Whitefield's Journal from a Few Days after His Return to Georgia, to His Arrival at Falmouth, on the 11th of March, 1741* (London: J. Robinson and John Sims, 1744).

22. *Ibid.*, pp. 54-55.

23. Franklin, *Autobiography*, p. 180.

24. Boston: G. Rodgers for J. Edwards and S. Eliot, 1741. Hereafter cited as *The New Creature*. This sermon and Chauncy's other work during the Awakening prompted some Scottish friends to secure the honorary degree of Doctor of Divinity for him. A letter Chauncy wrote to Stiles in 1761 (Stiles, *Itineraries*, p. 439) indicates that the primary requirement was the payment of a fee, but the degree carried considerable prestige in the colonies.

25. Chauncy, *The New Creature*, pp. 5-7.

26. *Ibid.*, pp. 13-15.

27. *Ibid.*, pp. 19-20.

28. *Ibid.*, pp. 22-26.

29. *Ibid.*, pp. 34-47.

30. For a biographical sketch of Mather see Shipton, *SHG*, VII (1945), 216-38. Further information is available in Chandler Robbins, *A History of the Second Church, or Old North, in Boston. To Which is Added, A History of the New Brick Church* (Boston: John Wilson and Son, 1852), pp. 120-23.

31. Robbins, *A History of the Second Church*, pp. 121-22.

32. Stiles, *Itineraries*, p. 304. Stiles adds, "Dr. Chauncy opposed New Light—& a great posse arose against him. But he has lived to bury all his opposers, and to shine with Eminence to old Age."

33. *An Unbridled Tongue* was published by Rogers and Fowle "at the *Desire* of the *Hearers*," Boston, 1741.

34. Chauncy, *An Unbridled Tongue*, pp. 16-17.

35. *Ibid.*, pp. 18-19.

36. *Ibid.*, p. 12.

37. Delivered December 17, 1741 and published by Rogers and Fowle in Boston in 1742. Hereafter cited as Chauncy, *The Gifts of the Spirit*. William Chauncey Fowler reports that in this sermon Chauncy "is said to have put forth all his strength." "President Charles Chauncy, His Ancestors and Descendants," *NEHG Reg.*, 10 (1856), 325.

38. Chauncy, *The Gifts of the Spirit*, pp. 6-18.

39. *Ibid.*, pp. 19-32.

40. *Ibid.*, pp. 34-35.

41. Boston, 1741. Hereafter cited as Chauncy, *Distinguishing Marks*. Printed in Goen, ed., *The Great Awakening*, pp. 213-88.

42. *Ibid.*, p. 260.

43. Thomas Prince, *The Christian History, Containing Accounts of the Revival and Propagation of Religion in Great-Britain & America. For the Years 1743 and 1744.* II (Boston: S. Kneeland and T. Green for T. Prince, Junior, 1745), 386.

44. Chauncy, *The Outpouring of the Holy Ghost*, preached May 13, 1742, and published in Boston (T. Fleet for D. Henchman and S. Eliot, 1742).

45. *Ibid.*, pp. 12-27.

46. *Ibid.*, p. 13.

47. *Ibid.*, pp. 13-14.

48. *Ibid.*, p. 24.

49. *Ibid.*, pp. 34-47.

50. *Ibid.*, pp. 43-44.

51. "Diary of Jacob Eliot," ed. E. H. Gillett, *Hist. Mag.* 15 (1869), 33. Eliot's diary is filled with references to the "remarkables" of the New-Lights and his troubles with exhorters, one of whom told him he was worse than the pope.

52. *Ibid.*, entry for December 14, 1741.

53. I have drawn heavily on the accounts of Davenport in Gaustad, *The Great Awakening in New England*, pp. 37-41, Joseph Tracy, *The Great Awakening* (Boston, 1842), pp. 230-55, and especially Goen, ed., *The Great Awakening*, pp. 20-27.

54. *Boston Evening-Post*, July 5, 1742.

55. Gilbert Tennent, *The Danger of An Unconverted Ministry* (Philadelphia: Benjamin Franklin, 1740).

56. Goen, ed., *The Great Awakening*, p. 22.

57. Prince, *Christian History*, II (1745), 406.

58. *Ibid.*, p. 408.

59. *Ibid.*

60. *Ibid.* Also in Tracy, *The Great Awakening*, p. 242.

61. Quoted from the MS diary of Ebenezer Parkman in *ibid.*, p. 209.

62. Chauncy tersely recounts this adventure in "A Letter to the Reverend Mr. James Davenport, Pastor of the Church of Christ, in Southold, on Long Island, now in Boston," dated July 17, 1742, and prefaced to his sermon, *Enthusiasm Described and Caution'd Against* (Boston: J. Draper for S. Eliot and J. Blanchard, 1742). Hereafter cited as *Enthusiasm*.

63. This account is reconstructed from Chauncy's report of the interview in his open letter. The letter, of course, gives only Chauncy's side of the story.

64. "Letter to Davenport," p. i.

65. In *Seasonable Thoughts* (1743) Chauncy prints a report of this incident as he received it from a correspondent. It was a remarkable occasion, and was to be Davenport's final fling. Since it has stirred the imagination of more than one American author, it may be of interest here:

"The *Separatists* at NEW-LONDON sent a Boat over to LONG-ISLAND to invite the grand Enthusiast D—t over to Organize their Church (as they term'd it). He arrived on, or about the second Day of *March*. He was no sooner come to Town than he began to rectify some Disorders, he supposed were prevailing among the Children of God: He published the Messages which he said, he received from the Spirit in Dreams and otherwise, importing the great Necessity of Mortification and Contempt of the World; and made them believe that they must put away from them every Thing that they delighted in, to avoid the hainous Sin of Idolatry, that Wigs, Cloaks and Breeches, Hoods, Gowns, Rings, Jewels and Necklaces must be all brought together into one Heap into his Chamber, that they might, by his solemn Decree, be committed to the Flames; together with certain Books of Devotion, &c. which he determined to be unsafe to be in the Hands of the People. Accordingly, they seem'd to be in a Strife who should be first in this meritorious Action, and then was presently made a Pile of Men's and Women's Apparel and Ornaments to which the grand Director added a Pair of Plush Breeches which he wore to Town, and which now he would greatly want, were he not confined in Bed by a Distemper for which I want a Name. . . . [Among the books were one of Increase Mather's, one of Colman's, one of Sewall's, and, specifically, Chauncy's sermon on Enthusiasm]. . . . [T]hese being called over, were with much Noise and Outcry burnt on the Town Wharf in the Afternoon of the Sabbath Day, *March* 6th, just as People were coming from Meeting, who ran to see if Murder, or some other Mischief was not about to be done, and so were Witnesses of this their horrid Delusion, and heard them sing *Hallelujahs* and *Gloria Patri* over the Pile, and heard them with a loud Voice declare, *That the Smoak of the Torments of such of the Authors of the abovesaid Books, as died in the same Belief, as when they set them out, was now ascending in Hell in like Manner, as they saw the Smoak of these Books rise.*" (Pp. 220-23n.)

66. Chauncy, *Enthusiasm*, p. 3.
67. *Ibid.*, pp. 3-5.
68. Goen, ed., *The Great Awakening*, p. 206.

Chapter Six: Words in Season

1. *Ministers exhorted and encouraged to take heed to themselves, and to their Doctrine* (Boston: Rogers and Fowle for S. Eliot, 1744), p. 15.
2. Gaustad, *The Great Awakening in New England*, p. 55.
3. Shipton, *SHG*, VII (1945), 216-38.
4. For a biographical sketch of Byles see Shipton, *SHG*, VII (1945), 464-93; reprinted in Shipton, *New England Life in the 18th Century* (Cambridge, Mass.: Belknap Press of Harvard University Press, 1963), pp. 226-53.
5. Bezaleel Howard, in a letter to William B. Sprague. Quoted in Sprague, *Annals of the American Unitarian Pulpit*, p. 13.
6. Chauncy, "Eminent Men," p. 162.
7. *Ibid.*
8. P. 86. See above, p. 63.
9. Chauncy, *Seasonable Thoughts on the State of Religion in New England* (Boston: Rogers and Fowle for Samuel Eliot, 1743), p. xxix.
10. Letter to Ebenezer Pemberton, October 24, 1759. Printed in E. H. Gillett, "President Wheelock and Dr. Chauncy," *American Presbyterian Review*, 3 (1871), 473-75.
11. Chauncy, *Seasonable Thoughts*, pp. xxix-xxx.
12. Letter to William Pepperrell, February 14, 1745/6. Printed in "The Pepperrell Papers," *MHS Colls.*, 6th Ser., 10 (1899), 446-47.
13. Reprinted in *Clarendon Historical Society Reprints*, March 1883. Hereafter cited as *Letter to Wishart*. On authorship see Edwin Scott Gaustad, "Charles Chauncy and the Great Awakening: A Survey and Bibliography," *Papers of the Bibliographical Society of America*, 45 (1951), 128.
14. Goen, ed., *The Great Awakening*, pp. 289-530.
15. Fowler, "President Charles Chauncy," p. 332.
16. The table of contents continues: "I. Faithfully pointing out the Things of a BAD and DANGEROUS TENDENCY, in the *late*, and *present*, *religious Appearance*, in the LAND. II. Representing the OBLIGATIONS which lie upon the PASTORS of THESE CHURCHES in *particular*, and upon ALL in *general*, to use their Endeavours to suppress *prevailing Disorders*; with the GREAT DANGER of a Neglect in so important a Matter. III. Opening, in

many Instances, wherein the DISCOURAGERS of *Irregularities* have been INJURI-OUSLY TREATED. IV. Shewing what ought to be CORRECTED, or AVOIDED, in testifying against the *evil Things* of the present Day. V. Directing our Thot's, more *positively*, to what may be judged the BEST EXPEDIENTS, to *promote pure* and *undefiled Religion* in these Times. . . . ." The advertisement appeared in the *Boston Weekly News-Letter*, March 17, 1743; the published table of contents, cited above, differs only slightly from the advertisement.

17. March 25, 1743; March 31, 1743.

18. Perry Miller, *Jonathan Edwards*, p. 175.

19. Fowler, "President Charles Chauncy," p. 334.

20. *Journals of the Rev. Thomas Smith and the Rev. Samuel Deane, Pastors of the First Church in Portland: With Notes and Biographical Notices: And a Summary History of Portland*, ed. William Willis (Portland: J. S. Bailey, 1849), p. 104.

21. Published as *The Testimony of the Pastors of the Churches in the Province of the Massachusetts-Bay in New-England, at Their Annual Convention in Boston, May 25, 1743. Against Several Errors in Doctrine, and Disorders in Practice, Which Have of Late Obtained in Various Parts of the Land; as Drawn up by a Committee Chosen by the Said Pastors, Read and Accepted Paragraph by Paragraph, and Voted to be Sign'd by the Moderator in Their Name, and Printed* (Boston: Rogers and Fowle for S. Eliot, 1743).

22. For an account of the convention see Benjamin Prescott, *A Letter to the Reverend Mr. Joshua Gee, In Answer to His of June 3, 1743. Address'd to the Reverend Mr. Nathanael Eells, Moderator of the late Convention of Pastors in Boston* (Boston: Green, Bushell, and Allen for Samuel Eliot, 1743).

23. Joshua Gee, *A Letter to the Reverend Mr. Nathanael Eells, Moderator of the late Convention of Pastors in Boston; Containing Some Remarks on their Printed Testimony Against several Errors and Disorders in the Land* (Boston: J. Draper for N. Procter, 1743). Hereafter cited as Gee, *Letter to Eells*.

24. See Shipton, *SHG*, V (1937), 413-24; *SHG*, VI (1942), 180-81.

25. Prescott, *Letter to Gee*, p. 4.

26. Gee, *Letter to Eells*, pp. 7-8.

27. June 27, 1743, p. 2.

28. Prescott, *Letter to Gee*; John Hancock, *An Expostulatory and Pacifick Letter, By Way of Reply to the Revd. Mr. Gee's Letter of Remarks* (Boston: Rogers and Fowle, 1743).

29. In *The Boston Gazette, or, Weekly Journal*, July 5, 1743.

30. Gee, *Letter to Eells*, p. 15. See also *The Boston Gazette, or, Weekly Journal*, May 31, 1743.

31. *The Testimony and Advice of an Assembly of Pastors of Churches in New-England, at a Meeting in Boston July 7, 1743. Occasion'd by the Late Happy Revival of Religion in Many Parts of the Land. To Which Are Added, Attestations Contain'd in Letters from a Number of Their Brethren Who Were Providentially Hinder'd from Giving Their Presence* (Boston: S. Kneeland, T. Green, N. Procter, 1743).

32. Osborn, *Case and Complaint*, p. 8.

33. Advertised for sale in the *Boston Evening Post*, July 4, 1743.

34. Edwards, *Some Thoughts*, in Goen, ed., *The Great Awakening*, p. 293.

35. *Ibid.*, p. 330.

36. Advertised for sale as "just published" in the *Boston Evening Post*, September 19, 1743.

37. Chauncy, *Seasonable Thoughts*, p. 380.

38. Edwards, *Some Thoughts*, in Goen, ed., *The Great Awakening*, p. 331.

39. *Ibid.*, p. 323.

40. *Ibid.*, p. 344.

41. Edwards, *Distinguishing Marks*, in Goen, ed., *The Great Awakening*, p. 227.

42. *Ibid.*, pp. 249-59.

43. Edwards, *Some Thoughts*, in Goen, ed., *The Great Awakening*, p. 328.

44. *Ibid.*, pp. 325-30.

45. *Ibid.*, pp. 331-41. The "person" is probably his wife, Sarah Pierpont. See Perry Miller, *Jonathan Edwards*, pp. 204-05.

46. Edwards, *Some Thoughts*, p. 341.

47. *Ibid.*, p. 342.

48. *Ibid.*, p. 344.

49. Chauncy, *Seasonable Thoughts*, p. 329.

50. *Ibid.*, pp. 329-30.

51. *Ibid.*, p. 330.

52. *Ibid.*, pp. 93-200. Cowing, "Sex and Preaching in the Great Awakening," pp. 624-44, analyzes the pyschology of New-Light preaching.

53. Chauncy, *Seasonable Thoughts*, p. 99.

54. *Ibid.*, pp. 108-09.

55. *Ibid.*, pp. 242-85.

56. *Ibid.*, pp. 307-08.

57. *Ibid.*, p. 5.

58. *Ibid.*, p. 327.

59. *Ibid.*, p. 324.

60. Chauncy, *Enthusiasm*, p. 62. For a detailed and perceptive analysis of Chauncy's psychological beliefs see Norman Brantley Gibbs, "The Problem of Revelation and Reason in the Thought of Charles Chauncy," Dissertation, Duke University 1953, chapters four and five.

61. Edwards, *Some Thoughts*, in Goen, ed., *The Great Awakening*, p. 298.

62. *Ibid.*, p. 297.

63. *Ibid.*, pp. 296-97.

64. In the account that follows I have drawn upon my remarks in *Jonathan Edwards*, University of Minnesota Pamphlets on American Writers, No. 97 (Minneapolis: University of Minnestoa Press, 1971), pp. 24-27. Used by permission of the publisher.

65. John Locke, *An Essay Concerning the Understanding, Knowledge, Opinion, and Assent*, ed. Benjamin Rand (Cambridge: Harvard University Press, 1931), pp. 61-66; 119-20.

66. *A Treatise Concerning Religious Affections*, ed. John E. Smith, Vol. II of *The Works of Jonathan Edwards* (New Haven and London: Yale University Press, 1969), pp. 205-06. Hereafter cited as *Religious Affections*.

67. Described in *A Divine and Supernatural Light, Immediately Imparted to the Soul by the Spirit of God, Shown to Be Both a Scriptural, and Rational Doctrine* (Boston: S. Kneeland and T. Green, 1734).

68. Smith, ed., *Religious Affections*, p. 200.

69. *Ibid.*, p. 343.

70. *Ibid.*, p. 206.

71. *Ibid.*, p. 108.

72. Chauncy, *Seasonable Thoughts*, p. 384.

73. *Ibid.*, p. 422.

74. Chauncy always retained considerable respect for Edwards. In answering Ezra Stiles's request for his estimate of the greatest men in American history, he included Edwards and ranked him well above his famous grandfather, Solomon Stoddard. "I suppose this Mr. Stoddard to have been a gentleman of very considerable powers, though not so great as some have imagined. Mr. EDWARDS, his grandson was much the greatest man. I have read all Mr. Stoddard's writings, but was never able to see in them that strength of genius some have attributed to him." Chauncy, "Eminent Men," p. 157.

75. The complete text, with commentary, is printed in Edward M. Griffin, "Chauncy and *Seasonable Thoughts*: A New Letter," *AN&Q*, 11 (1972), 3-5.

76. "Letters of Isaac Watts," *MHS Proc.*, 2d Ser., 9 (1895), 400-06.

77. Perry Miller, *Jonathan Edwards*, pp. 176-77.

78. Griffin, "Chauncy and *Seasonable Thoughts*," p. 5.

79. Goen, *Revivalism and Separatism in New England*, p. vii.

80. *Ibid.*, p. 34.

81. The letter is dated September 3, 1744. Fowler, "President Charles Chauncy," p. 335.

82. Griffin, "Chauncy and *Seasonable Thoughts*," p. 4.

83. Boston: S. Kneeland and T. Green, 1744.

84. *Ministers cautioned against the Occasions of Contempt* (Boston: Rogers and Fowle for Samuel Eliot, 1744), pp. 45, 12. Hereafter cited as *Ministers Cautioned.*

85. For full title see note 1 to this chapter.

86. ii Titus, 15.

87. Chauncy, *Ministers Cautioned*, pp. 24-25.

88. See Shipton's account of Frink, *SHG*, VII (1945), 69-75, and of Leonard, *SHG*, VI (1942), 324-27.

89. Chauncy, *Ministers Exhorted*, pp. 34 ff.

90. William H. Sumner, *A History of East Boston with Biographical Sketches of its Early Proprietors, And an Appendix* (Boston: J. E. Tilton and Co., 1858), p. 266.

91. Chauncy, *Seasonable Thoughts*, pp. 36 ff.

92. *A Letter to the Reverend Dr. Chauncy, On Account of Some Passages relating to the Rev. Mr. Whitefield, in his Book intitled Seasonable Thoughts on the State of Religion in New-England* (Boston: S. Kneeland and T. Green, 1745).

93. *A Letter To the Reverend Mr. George Whitefield, Vindicating certain Passages He has excepted against, in a late Book entitled, Seasonable Thoughts on the State of Religion in New-England; and shewing that he has neither sufficiently defended himself, nor retracted his past Misconduct* (Boston: Rogers and Fowle for S. Eliot, 1745). The letter is dated January 31, 1744/45.

94. *Ibid.*, p. 3.

95. *Ibid.*, p. 10.

96. The correspondence is edited and printed in *MHS Colls.*, 4th Ser., 2 (1854), 238-39.

97. Henry, *George Whitefield, Wayfaring Witness*, p. 205.

98. Howard H. Peckham, *The Colonial Wars 1689-1762* (Chicago: University of Chicago Press, 1964), p. 224. Word reached America in May. *Ibid.*, p. 97.

99. "Benjamin Cleaves's Journal of the Expedition to Louisbourg, 1745," ed. F. A. Foster, *NEHG Reg.*, 66 (1912), 114.

100. Pepperrell married Mary Hirst, sister of Chauncy's first wife. See Fowler, *Memorials of the Chaunceys*, and Fowler's genealogy in "President Charles Chauncy," p. 324.

Chapter Seven: After the Great Awakening

1. Chauncy, "Eminent Men," p. 162.

2. *Ibid.*

3. Holyoke was keeping school there when Chauncy visited him on November 9, 1746. *The Holyoke Diaries*, ed. George Francis Dow (Salem, Mass.: The Essex Institute, 1911), p. 41.

4. Taylor, one of Chauncy's best friends, died at Milton on January 20, 1750. (See MS Diary of Jeremiah Wheelwright in the library of the Massachusetts Historical Society.) Chauncy was at Taylor's deathbed (Chauncy, "Eminent Men," p. 158). Chauncy helped with the pastoral affairs of the Milton church until Taylor's successor, Nathaniel Robbins, was installed. He baptized Nathan Phillips and Josiah Harris there on February 4, 1750; Benjamin Wadsworth, Abigail Vose, and Samuel Tucker on July 29, 1750. See William Blake Trask, "Milton (Mass.) Church Records.—1678—1754," *NEHG Reg.*, 24 (1870), 47-48.

5. MS Diary of Ebenezer Bridge, Houghton Library, Harvard University. Bridge's diary entry for May 4, 1751 reads as follows: "Rev. Dr. Chauncy & Mr. Edwd. Jackson of Boston came before dinr. to See us & spend Sabbath with us, in their Journeyings as Invalids." Chauncy

preached both sermons the next day. Bridge returned the visit in June when he had business in Boston, and he frequently stopped to see Chauncy when he had occasion to visit the town.

6. Shipton cites Robert Treat Paine's diary for 1752 and 1753 to this effect. Shipton also suggests that Chauncy visited Antigua. This is quite likely. *SHG*, VI (1942), 445. Chauncy also owned a farm in Quincy, which he probably used as a summer home. See the biographical sketch of Joseph Woodward (who eventually bought the farm from Chauncy) by Lemuel Capen in Thomas C. Simonds, *History of South Boston: formerly Dorchester Neck, Now Ward XII. of the City of Boston* (Boston, 1857; rpt. New York: Arno Press, 1974), p. 246, and Frederick A. Whitney, "A Church of the First Congregational (Unitarian) Society in Quincy, Mass., Built in 1732," *NEHG Reg.*, 18 (1864), 123.

7. Chauncy, "Eminent Men," p. 162.

8. Stiles, *Itineraries*, p. 442.

9. Chauncy, "Eminent Men," p. 156.

10. Chauncy, "Life of the Rev. President Chauncy," p. 179.

11. Chauncy, "Eminent Men," p. 157.

12. Sprague, *Annals of the American Unitarian Pulpit*, p. 12.

13. *Diary and Autobiography of John Adams*, ed. L. H. Butterfield, Leonard C. Faber, and Wendell D. Garrett (Cambridge, Mass.: Belknap Press of Harvard University Press, 1961), II, 70-71.

14. Sprague, *Annals of the American Unitarian Pulpit*, p. 13; John Adams, *Diary and Autobiography, ibid.*

15. *The Works of John Adams, Second President of the United States*, ed. Charles Francis Adams (Boston: Little, Brown, 1856), X, 220. Hereafter cited as John Adams, *Works*.

16. One of his earliest published sermons was preached at the annual election of officers in the Ancient and Honourable Artillery Company, of which his father had been a member. The young pastor delivered "A Caution against Security," improving upon the text, "And they . . . came to Laish, unto a people that were at quiet and secure, and smote them with the edge of the Sword, and burnt the city with fire. And there was no deliverer, because they were far from Zidon." Calling for increased preparedness, Chauncy "applied" the text by spelling out, with remarkable insouciance, the duties of each company officer from Captain General to the lieutenants, even offering pointers on conducting drill and on decreasing the AWOL rate. Chauncy, *Character and Overthrow of Laish considered and applied* (Boston: S. Kneeland and T. Green for D. Henchman, 1734).

17. "Pepperrell Papers," *MHS Colls.*, 6th Ser., 10 (1899), 257.

18. "Letters Relating to the Expedition against Cape-Breton," *MHS Colls.*, 1st Ser., 1 (1792), 49.

19. Chauncy, *Marvellous Things done by the right Hand and holy Arm of God in getting him the Victory* (Boston: T. Fleet, 1745).

20. Peckham, *The Colonial Wars*, p. 102.

21. Chauncy, *Marvellous Things*, p. 12.

22. *Ibid.*, pp. 11-12.

23. *Ibid.*, pp. 12-22.

24. "Letters Relating to the Expedition against Cape-Breton," p. 50.

25. *Ibid.*

26. *Ibid.*, pp. 50-51.

27. *Ibid.*, p. 51.

28. Byron Fairchild, *Messrs. William Pepperrell: Merchants at Piscataqua* (Ithaca: Cornell University Press, 1954), pp. 178-79.

29. *Ibid.*, p. 177.

30. "Pepperrell Papers," pp. 385, 446.

31. *Ibid.*, p. 385.

32. MS Letter dated 18 January, 1745/46, in the library of the Massachusetts Historical Society.

33. *Ibid.*

34. *Ibid.*

35. Fairchild, *Messrs. William Pepperrell*, p. 181.

36. "Pepperrell Papers," p. 345.

37. *Ibid.*, p. 385. Lyde graduated at Harvard in 1723. Shipton characterizes him as " a professional office-seeker." *SHG*, VII (1945), 206.

38. *Ibid.*, pp. 446-47.

39. Sumner, *History of East Boston*, pp. 264-65. Sumner states that Chauncy's "intercourse with other people" was characterized by "generous and benevolent feelings." He recalls Chauncy's collecting sufficient funds from friends to put "Samuel Sewall, who, on acccount of family misfortunes, was in needy circumstances," through college. In gratitude, Sewall named a son Charles Chauncy Sewall, later a minister in Medfield, Massachusetts. Joseph Woodward, who became an important figure in New England commerce and politics, was another grateful beneficiary of Chauncy's kindness. Woodward, born in 1758 in Hingham, Massachusetts, was put to board with the Chauncys as an adolescent after his mother had been left poverty-stricken upon the death of her sea-captain husband. "This," writes the nineteenth-century historian Lemuel Capen, "Mr. Woodward considered the most fortunate circumstance of his life. The discernment of Dr. Chauncy soon discovered his good points—the activity and force of his mind, and the open frankness and kindness of his disposition—and brought them into exercise. And no doubt he did what could then be done to check the violence of his temper." (Throughout Woodward's life, his temper made him notorious. Apparently he came to Chauncy as a "problem child.") "To the last he cherished the highest esteem and reverence for Dr. Chauncy. He regarded him as a father, and attributed all that was good in his own character to his influence." Capen's sketch of Woodward is in Thomas C. Simonds, *History of South Boston*, pp. 244-50.

40. Chauncy, *Cornelius' Character* (Boston: D. Gookin, 1745), pp. 11-15. Chauncy's views were probably influenced by those of Benjamin Wadsworth, his predecessor in the pastorate of the First Church and the president of Harvard during Chauncy's student days. John Taylor, Chauncy's close boyhood friend, had boarded with the Wadsworths while his father was in Jamaica on business. Wadsworth's treatise *The Well-Ordered Family* (Boston, 1712; rpt. in Wilson Smith, ed., *Theories of Education in Early America 1655-1819*. Indianapolis: Bobbs-Merrill, 1973) is a detailed consideration of the duties of husbands and wives, parents and children, and masters and servants in which moderate authoritarianism is preached.

41. See the sketch of his life by Shipton, *SHG*, XII (1962), 246-51.

42. *Ibid.* See also Fairchild, *Messrs. William Pepperrell*, pp. 189-90.

43. Fairchild, *Messrs. William Pepperrell*, p. 190.

44. Walter Muir Whitehill, *Boston: A Topographical History*, 2nd. ed., (Cambridge, Mass.: Belknap Press of Harvard University Press, 1968), p. 37.

45. Pierce, ed., "The Records of the First Church in Boston," p. 202.

46. William S. Sachs and Ari Hoogenboom, *The Enterprising Colonials: Society on the Eve of the Revolution* (Chicago: University of Chicago Press, 1965), p. 92.

47. Lindsay Swift, "The Massachusetts Election Sermons," *CSM Pubs.*, 1 (1895), 417.

48. Chauncy, *Civil Magistrates Must be Just, Ruling in the Fear of God* (Boston: House of Representatives, 1747).

49. *Ibid.*, p. 22.

50. *Ibid.*, pp. 63, 64-65.

51. Reported by William Emerson in *An Historical Sketch of the First Church in Boston from its Formation to the Present Period* (Boston: Munroe and Francis, 1812), p. 198.

52. Sachs and Hoogenboom, *The Enterprising Colonials*, p. 92.

53. *Ibid.*, p. 93. The authors note, "Parliament confirmed the settlement with passage of the Currency Act, which prohibited New England from making paper money a legal tender and imposed restrictions on future issues. This ended the controversy and vindicated the authors of a metallic standard." Pp. 92-93.

54. *The Diary of Ebenezer Parkman 1703-1782*, ed. Francis G. Walett (Worcester, Mass.: American Antiquarian Society, 1974), p. 234.

55. His sermon was *The Idle-Poor secluded from the Bread of Charity by the Christian Law* (Boston: Thomas Fleet, 1752).

56. *Ibid.*, pp. 7-8.

57. *Ibid.*, p. 7.

58. *Ibid.*, pp. 8-9.

59. *Ibid.*, p. 9.

60. *Ibid.*, pp. 10-11.

61. *Ibid.*, pp. 11-12.

62. *Ibid.*, pp. 11-15.

63. Quoted by Perry Miller in *The American Puritans*, p. 171.

64. *Ibid.*, pp. 171-72. Alan Heimert, in *Religion and the American Mind: From the Great Awakening to the Revolution* (Cambridge, Mass.: Harvard University Press, 1966), pp. 246-53, is less charitable to Chauncy, reading the sermon as a sinister instance of the Liberal desire to celebrate "the differences among men" and to "minimize the wealthy man's obligations to his fellows." Chauncy was attempting to squeeze the poor by restricting private philanthropy and public welfare payments only to the "hopelessly disabled," thus forcing such idlers as women and children into a grim life as factory hands. "What such Liberals as Chauncy come close to arguing is that men as individuals are under no explicit obligations to their fellows." (P. 251.) This is in stark contrast, Heimert says, to the views of Jonathan Edwards, who believed that "whatever worldly substance a man happened to accrue was 'an accident.' It was a reason neither for pride nor for contempt of one's fellow creatures, but rather an opportunity for serving the less fortunate." Heimert contends that fear that such a view might catch on "cemented Liberal affections for mother Britain. Not the least of the advantages of the empire was a power and an authority that could keep the American rabble diligent in their proper callings." (P. 253.) What Heimert says Chauncy and his fellows "came close to arguing" is not in fact what he did argue. To suggest that Chauncy felt contempt for the unfortunate, that he considered people under no obligations to their fellows, that he spoke from the standpoint of the privileged rich, and that he was antagonistic to the native American spirit is to overstate the case.

65. William De Loss Love, Jr., *The Fast and Thanksgiving Days of New England* (Boston and New York: Houghton Mifflin, 1895), p. 322.

66. Chauncy, *The Idle-Poor*, p. 19.

67. "Extracts from the Diary of Mary Fleet of Boston," *NEHG Reg.*, 19 (1865), 59.

68. Boston: Edes and Gill, 1755. For detailed and interesting accounts of the reaction to the earthquake see Charles Edwin Clark, "Science, Reason, and an Angry God: The Literature of an Earthquake," *NEQ*, 38 (1965), 340-62, and James West Davidson, *The Logic of Millennial Thought: Eighteenth-Century New England* (New Haven and London: Yale University Press, 1977), pp. 95-121.

69. Chauncy, *Earthquakes a Token*, pp. 16-23.

70. *Ibid.*, pp. 7-9.

71. Peckham, *The Colonial Wars*, p. 120; 142-48.

72. *A Letter To a Friend; Giving a concise, but just, Account, according to the Advices hitherto received, of the Ohio-Defeat; and pointing out also the many good Ends, this inglorious Event is naturally adapted to promote; or, shewing wherein it is fitted to advance the Interest of all the American British Colonies. To which is added, Some general Account of the New-England Forces, with what they have already done, counter-ballancing the above Loss* (Boston: Edes and Gill, 1755), p. 7. The letter is dated August 25, 1755.

73. *Ibid.*, p. 9.

74. *Ibid.*, p. 5.

75. Peckham, *The Colonial Wars*, pp. 148-50.

76. The title   ntinues: *Representing also the vast Importance of this Conquest to the American-British   olonies. To which is added, Such an Account of what the New-England*

Governments have done to carry into Effect their Design against Crown-Point, as will shew the Necessity of their being help'd by Great-Britain, in Point of Money (Boston: Edes and Gill, 1755). The letter is dated September 29, 1755.

77. *Ibid.*, p. 2.

78. *Ibid.*, p. 13.

79. *Ibid.*, p. 3.

80. *Ibid.*

81. Peckham, *The Colonial Wars*, p. 150.

82. *Ibid.*, p. 151.

83. Chauncy, *The Earth delivered from the Curse to which it is, at present, subjected* (Boston: Edes and Gill, 1756), p. 23. This sermon, occasioned by the earthquakes in Spain, Portugal, and New England, was preached as the Boston Thursday Lecture, January 22, 1756. Hereafter cited as *The Earth Delivered*.

84. *Ibid.*, p. 24.

85. *Ibid.*, p. 23.

86. Peckham, *The Colonial Wars*, pp. 173-95.

87. Shipton, *SHG*, VI (1942), 441.

88. Shipton, *SHG*, XII (1962), 246. Bridge noted in his diary for October 19 and 20, 1757, a visit from Chauncy on his way to Kittery.

89. He graduated from Harvard in 1741. See Shipton, *SHG*, XI (1960), 75-78; XII (1962), 508.

90. Shipton, *SHG*, IX (1956), 246-47.

91. Fowler, "President Charles Chauncy," pp. 329-30; Justin Winsor, *The Memorial History of Boston, Including Suffolk County, Massachusetts. 1630-1880* (Boston: J. R. Osgood, 1880-81), II, 348-49; "Boyle's Journal of Occurrences in Boston, 1759-1778," *NEHG Reg.*, 84 (1930), 270.

92. If one counts the Townsend children: Mary, b. May 6, 1750; Thomas, b. 1752; James, b. 1748. James "died young"; thus Chauncy may have had only six grandchildren at the time. The others were the Winthrop boys: John, b. 1747; Adam, b. 1748; James, b. 1752, and William, b. 1753. See entries for Townsend and Winthrop in Shipton, *SHG*, notes 89 and 90 above.

93. "Phyllis, Dr. Chauncy's Negro Woman," is listed under "Adult Persons baptized though not come into full Communion" in Pierce, ed., "The Records of the First Church in Boston," p. 440. Chauncy also had a male servant, reportedly named Scipio. Shipton, *SHG*, VI (1942), 452; A. B. Ellis, *History of the First Church in Boston* (Boston: Hall and Whiting, 1881), p. 194; Sumner, *History of East Boston*, p. 267. Whether these servants were in fact slaves I have been unable to determine.

94. Shipton, *SHG*, XII (1962), 246.

95. Sumner, *History of East Boston*, p. 268; Fowler, "President Charles Chauncy," p. 329.

96. Sumner, *History of East Boston*, p. 269.

97. *Records of the Church in Brattle Square, Boston, with Lists of Communicants, Baptisms, Marriages and Funerals, 1699-1872* (Boston: The Benevolent Fraternity of Churches, 1902), p. 249; see also Pierce, ed., "The Records of the First Church in Boston," p. 266.

98. Shipton, *SHG*, VI (1942), 441. The MS, dated June 12, 1761, is in the Washburn collection at the Massachusetts Historical Society.

Chapter Eight: A Body of Divinity

1. Bezaleel Howard applies this term to Chauncy's work (Sprague, *Annals of the American Unitarian Pulpit*, VIII, 12-13). It is an honorable term in New England religious history, signifying a thorough, systematic treatment of doctrine. The classic example is Samuel Willard's massive series of lectures on each article of the Westminster *Shorter Catechism*. Willard, who had been one of the prize pupils of Harvard's President Chauncy, was for decades

pastor at the Old South Church. After his death in 1707 Joseph Sewall and Thomas Prince assembled his lectures and published them in 1726 as *A Compleat Body of Divinity*, a folio volume of a thousand pages that became the *summa theologica* of New England Congregationalism.

2. This is also the tradition of Philip Doddridge, another of Chauncy's favorite writers. The line from Baxter to Doddridge is traced in Geoffrey F. Nuttal, *Richard Baxter and Philip Doddridge: A Study in a Tradition* (London: Oxford University Press, 1951). See also Gibbs, "The Problem of Revelation and Reason," especially pp. 111-18. Gibbs also demonstrates that John Taylor and John Tillotson influenced Chauncy strongly.

3. Chauncy, *The Mystery hid from Ages and Generations, made manifest by the Gospel-Revelation: or, the Salvation of All Men the Grand Thing Aimed at in the Scheme of God, As opened in the New-Testament Writings, and entrusted with JESUS CHRIST to bring into EFFECT* (London: Charles Dilly, 1784), p. 2.

4. Chauncy, "Eminent Men," p. 163.

5. *Ibid.*, p. 162. The fire referred to destroyed Harvard Hall on January 24, 1764, during the college's winter vacation. Harvard lost its dining hall, kitchens, library, scientific apparatus, and a great deal of personal property belonging to students. Chauncy was appointed to a committee of the Harvard Corporation to raise funds for the replacement of the scientific equipment. He undertook this task vigorously and also took a great interest in replenishing the library. See William C. Lane, "New Hampshire's Part in Restoring the Library and Apparatus of Harvard College after the Fire of 1764," *CSM Pubs.*, 25 (1924), 24-33; F. Apthorp Foster, "The Burning of Harvard Hall, 1764, and its Consequences," *CSM Pubs.*, 14 (1913), 2-43; and David P. Wheatland, *The Apparatus of Science at Harvard 1765-1800* (Cambridge, Mass.: The Stinehour Press; distributed by Harvard University Press, 1968).

The "writers recommended by Doct. Doddridge" is apparently a reference to a list of forty-eight "practical writers" endorsed by Philip Doddridge in his "Lectures on Preaching." Doddridge's *Works*, ed. E. Williams and E. Parsons (Leeds: Edward Baines, 1802-05), V, 428.

6. Fowler, "President Charles Chauncy," p. 335.

7. Chauncy, "Eminent Men," p. 163.

8. *Ibid.*, pp. 163-64.

9. Chauncy, *The Benevolence of the Deity, Fairly and Impartially Considered* (Boston: Powars and Willis, 1784), hereafter cited as *The Benevolence of the Deity; Five Dissertations on the Scripture Account of the Fall; and its Consequences* (London: C. Dilly, 1785), hereafter cited as *Five Dissertations*.

10. See Chauncy's remark above that the work was completed "many years ago." Furthermore a long section on p. 12 of Chauncy's sermon *The Earth Delivered*, preached January 22, 1756, is identical with a paragraph toward the end of *The Benevolence of the Deity* (p. 258). This suggests that the latter work was complete by early 1756. The paragraph begins, "It was, perhaps, highly expedient, if not absolutely necessary, that we should live in a world of *discipline* . . ."

11. Chauncy, *The Benevolence of the Deity*, pp. iv, ix, and viii-ix.

12. *Ibid.*, title page.

13. Published by S. Kneeland. Now, edited by Paul Ramsey, it is Volume I of *The Works of Jonathan Edwards* (New Haven and London: Yale University Press, 1957).

14. Chauncy, *The Benevolence of the Deity*, pp. 18, 38-39.

15. *Ibid.*, pp. 51-53.

16. A. O. Lovejoy, *The Great Chain of Being: A Study of the History of an Idea*. The William James Lectures Delivered at Harvard University, 1933 (1936; rpt. Cambridge: Harvard University Press, 1957), p. 52.

17. *Ibid.*, pp. 56-57.

18. *Ibid.*, p. 183.

19. *Ibid.*, pp. 183-85.

20. Chauncy, *The Benevolence of the Deity*, p. 86.

21. *Ibid.*, pp. 86-87.
22. *Ibid.*, pp. 92-119. Cf. Gibbs, 119-75.
23. Chauncy, *The Benevolence of the Deity*, p. 120.
24. *Ibid.*, p. 98.
25. *Ibid.*, p. 120.
26. *Ibid.*
27. *Ibid.*, p. 126.
28. *Ibid.*, pp. 129-30.
29. *Ibid.*, p. 142.
30. *Ibid.*, p. 141.
31. *Ibid.*, p. 144.
32. *Ibid.*, p. 183.
33. *Ibid.*, pp. 177-78.
34. Lovejoy, *The Great Chain of Being*, p. 215.
35. *Ibid.*, p. 212. Chauncy quotes Law's translation approvingly in *The Benevolence of the Diety*, pp. 184-85.
36. Chauncy, *The Benevolence of the Deity*, pp. 183-84.
37. *Ibid.*, pp. 185-86.
38. *Ibid.*, p. 191.
39. *Ibid.*, p. 193.
40. *Ibid.*, p. 205.
41. *Ibid.*, pp. 237-38.
42. *Ibid.*, p. 252.
43. *Ibid.*, pp. 252-53.
44. *Ibid.*, p. 254.
45. *Ibid.*, p. 255. Should this be thought näive, compare the following remark of Dr. Jonas Salk: "Man is at present the greatest obstacle to his own health. He is also the greatest single contributor as a cause of human disease and discomfort." Quoted in "This World," *San Francisco Examiner and Chronicle*, May 22, 1966, p. 2.
46. Chauncy, *The Benevolence of the Deity*, p. 256.
47. *Ibid.*, p. 258.
48. *Ibid.*
49. *Ibid.*, p. 288.
50. *Ibid.*, pp. 288-89.
51. Lovejoy, p. 208.
52. *Ibid.*
53. Chauncy, *The Benevolence of the Deity*, p. 288.
54. *Ibid.*, p. 203.
55. H. Shelton Smith, *Changing Conceptions of Original Sin. A Study in American Theology since 1750* (New York: Charles Scribner's Sons, 1955), p. 1.
56. *Ibid.*, pp. 1-10.
57. *Ibid.*, pp. 10-36.
58. *Ibid.*
59. Boston: S. Kneeland, 1758. The preface is dated Stockbridge, May 26, 1757. *Original Sin*, ed. Clyde A. Holbrook, is Volume III of *The Works of Jonathan Edwards* (New Haven and London: Yale University Press, 1970).
60. Smith, *Changing Conceptions of Original Sin*, p. 36.
61. *NEHG Reg.*, 10 (1856), 335.
62. New Haven: S. Parker, 1757.
63. Boston: S. Kneeland, 1758.
64. Clark, *The Scripture Doctrine of Original Sin*, p. 8. See Smith, *Changing Conceptions of Original Sin*, pp. 41-43.
65. Clark, *The Scripture Doctrine of Original Sin*, pp. i-ii.

66. Entitled *The Opinion of one that has perused the Summer Morning's Conversation, concerning Original Sin, wrote by the Rev. Mr. Peter Clark* (Boston: Green and Russell, 1758). Foxcroft's support of Clark may have been one reason for Chauncy's reluctance to publish his contrary views.

67. *Ibid.*

68. Chauncy, *The Mystery hid from Ages*, p. 122.

69. Chauncy, *Five Dissertations*, especially pp. 50–63. I have been assisted in my understanding of Chauncy's position by the analyses of both Gibbs and Smith. Gibbs has an illuminating section on the relationship of Chauncy's views to those of Taylor, Tillotson, and Baxter on this question (pp. 176–214). Smith has a truly excellent chapter on Chauncy and Samuel Webster (*Changing Conceptions of Original Sin*, pp. 37–59).

70. Chauncy, *The Earth Delivered*, pp. 6–7.

71. Chauncy, *Five Dissertations*, p. 208.

72. *Ibid.*, p. 298; Chauncy, *The Mystery hid from Ages*, pp. 22–80. Incidentally the twofold principle that children are not born morally corrupt (hence they must form their moral characters by their choices) but are born weak (hence they are prey to the many temptations brought on by our condition of mortality) provides some theoretical ground for Chauncy's insistence upon cultivating self-discipline in rearing children. By learning to place one's natural appetites (which are morally neutral) under the governance of one's reason and will, children will develop the strength to resist temptation, make correct moral choices, and thereby form a healthy character. Failing to learn self-discipline, they will be easy prey to temptation. In Chauncy's view the parent bears a weighty responsibility for charting the correct course during the formative years.

73. Chauncy, *Five Dissertations*, pp. 274–75; 298; 174–87. See also Gibbs, pp. 188–91n; Smith, *Changing Conceptions of Original Sin*, pp. 56–57.

74. King James Version.

75. Chauncy, *The Mystery hid from Ages*, pp. 120–21; 124–32. Chauncy's relationship to the history of modern Universalism is traced in Ernest Cassara, ed., *Universalism in America: A Documentary History* (Boston: Beacon Press, 1971), pp. 1–44.

76. *Ibid.*, p. 18. Cf. Chauncy, *The Benevolence of the Deity*, pp. 166–73; *Twelve Sermons*, pp. 150–52; 164–68; 265–68.

77. Chauncy, *The Mystery hid from Ages*, p. 324. My account is a summary of the arguments in this treatise.

78. *Ibid.*

79. *Ibid.*, p. 225.

80. Chauncy, *The Earth Delivered*, p. 15.

81. Chauncy, *The Mystery hid from Ages*, p. 122. In *The Logic of Millennial Thought: Eighteenth-Century New England*, pp. 109–11, James West Davidson locates Chauncy's theory in the tradition of New England millennialism. "By putting the new heavens and new earth after the Last Judgment, he rejected a postmillennialist eschatology," Davidson points out. That is, he rejected the belief that a thousand years of peace and prosperity would precede the physical Second Coming of Christ. By putting the new heavens and new earth after the general resurrection, moreover, he rejected the traditional eschatology of such theorists as Joseph Mede and the Mathers "which asserted that evil men would be condemned and sentenced to hell only after the thousand years had ended." Davidson calls "astonishing" Chauncy's conclusions "that the new heavens and new earth referred not to a millennial world but to the traditional heavenly paradise" and that heaven will be our own world perfected. He considers Chauncy's theory a major departure "from established millennial theories."

Chapter Nine: Liberty, Civil and Religious

1. Chauncy to Stiles, 14 June 1771, in Stiles, *Itineraries*, p. 451.

2. *Ibid.*

205

3. MS Letter, Chauncy to Richard Price, March 22, 1770. Boston Public Library.

4. Eliot to Belknap, 10 December 1780, Belknap Papers, *MHS Colls.*, 6th Ser., 4 (1891), 201; Eliot to Belknap, February, n.d., 1781, Belknap Papers (1891), p. 207.

5. *Ibid.*

6. *Magnalia Christi Americana: Or, the Ecclesiastical History of New England* (London: Thomas Parkhurst, 1702), bk. iii, p. 6.

7. Chauncy, "Life of the Rev. President Chauncy," pp. 171–80.

8. For the long history of the controversy, which stretches far back into the seventeenth century, see Arthur Lyon Cross, *The Anglican Episcopate and the American Colonies* (New York and London: Longmans, Green, 1902) and Carl Bridenbaugh, *Mitre and Sceptre: Transatlantic Faiths, Ideas, Personalities, and Politics 1689-1775.*

9. Cross, *The Anglican Episcopate*, pp. 3, 108–09; Bridenbaugh, *Mitre and Sceptre*, pp. 30–31.

10. Cross, *The Anglican Episcopate*, p. 248; Bridenbaugh, *Mitre and Sceptre*, pp. 5–6; 209–10.

11. Charles W. Akers, *Called Unto Liberty: A Life of Jonathan Mayhew, 1720-1766* (Cambridge, Mass.: Harvard University Press, 1964).

12. Chauncy and Hooper remained friends. Chauncy served as a bearer at Hooper's funeral on April 17, 1767. See MS diary of John Rowe at the Massachusetts Historical Society and *Letters and Diary of John Rowe, Boston Merchant, 1759-1762; 1764-1779*, ed. Annie Rowe Cunningham (Boston: W. B. Clarke, 1903), p. 128.

13. Boston: D. Fowle and D. Gookin, 1750. See Akers, *Called Unto Liberty*, pp. 66–78.

14. Akers, *Called Unto Liberty*, pp. 81–94.

15. *Ibid.*, pp. 138–43; 229.

16. Jonathan Mayhew, *Remarks on an Anonymous Tract* . . . (Boston: R. and S. Draper, Edes and Gill, T. and J. Fleet, 1764), p. 80.

17. *Ibid.*

18. Akers, *Called Unto Liberty*, p. 178.

19. Jonathan Mayhew, *Observations on the Charter and Conduct of the Society for the Propagation of the Gospel in Foreign Parts; designed to shew Their Non-conformity to each other* (Boston: Richard and Samuel Draper, Edes and Gill, Thomas and John Fleet, 1763), p. 103.

20. Mayhew, *Observations on the Charter*; *A Defence of the Observations* (Boston: R. and S. Draper, Edes and Gill, T. and J. Fleet, 1763); *Remarks on an Anonymous Tract* (Boston: R. and S. Draper, Edes and Gill, T. and J. Fleet, 1764).

21. London, 1764; Boston: R. and S. Draper, Edes and Gill, T. and J. Fleet, 1764. See Cross, *The Anglican Episcopate*, p. 147, and Bridenbaugh, *Mitre and Sceptre*, p. 240.

22. Secker, *An Answer to Dr. Mayhew's Observations* (London: 1764; rpt. Boston: R. and S. Draper, Edes and Gill, T. and J. Fleet, 1764), pp. 50–66.

23. Mayhew, *Remarks on an Anonymous Tract*, p. 62.

24. Chauncy, *A Discourse Occasioned by the Death of the Reverned [sic] Jonathan Mayhew, D.D. Late Pastor of the West-Church in Boston* (Boston: R. and S. Draper, Edes and Gill, T. and J. Fleet, 1766), p. 27. Akers, pp. 220–21.

25. *Ibid.*

26. Chauncy's prayer may have been the first of its kind ever made at a Boston funeral. See the dispute on this claim in the minutes of the October 1879 meeting of the Massachusetts Historical Society, *MHS Proc.*, 1st Ser., 17 (1880), 166–70.

27. Chauncy, "Eminent Men," p. 159.

28. *Ibid.*, p. 161.

29. Chauncy, *The Validity of Presbyterian Ordination asserted and maintained* (Boston:

Richard Draper and Thomas Leverett, 1762). Chauncy delivered the lecture on May 12, 1762. Judge Paul Dudley had founded the series to refute theological errors.

30. *Ibid*. Chauncy felt strongly about the equality of presbyters and bishops. He once told John Adams that if he were ever called upon to give the "charge" at an ordination, he would begin with the words, "We, Bishops." John Adams, *Diary*, p. 70.

31. William Stevens Perry, ed., *Historical Collections Relating to the American Colonial Church* (Hartford: Church Press Co., 1870–78), III, 489–90.

32. See his sermon, *All Nations of the Earth blessed in Christ, the seed of Abraham* (Boston: John Draper, 1762), p. 23.

33. *Ibid*., pp. 27–29.

34. *Ibid*., p. 46.

35. *Ibid*., p. 29.

36. Akers, *Called Unto Liberty*, p. 175.

37. Charles G. Washburn, "Preface," *Jasper Mauduit: Agent in London for the Province of the Massachusetts-Bay, 1762-1765*, in *MHS Colls.*, 74 (1918).

38. Chauncy to Mauduit, May 4, 1763. *MHS Colls.*, 74 (1918), 115–19.

39. "Diary of Rev. Eli Forbes," *MHS Proc.*, 2d Ser., 7 (1892), 389–90; 396–97.

40. Chauncy, *All Nations of the Earth*, p. 44.

41. Akers, *Called Unto Liberty*, pp. 176–77.

42. John Ewer, *A Sermon Preached before the Incorporated Society for the Propagation of the Gospel in Foreign Parts* (London: E. Owen and T. Harrison, 1767); Bridenbaugh, *Mitre and Sceptre*, p. 293.

43. Ewer, *A Sermon*, p. 17.

44. *Ibid*., pp. 6–7.

45. MS Letter, December 7, 1767, Houghton Library, Harvard University.

46. MS Letter, Andrew Eliot to the Rev. William Harris, December 1767, Houghton Library, Harvard University.

47. Bridenbaugh, *Mitre and Sceptre*, p. 295.

48. Chauncy, *A Letter to a Friend, containing, Remarks on certain Passages in a Sermon preached, by the Right Reverend Father in God, John Lord Bishop of Landaff . . . In which the highest Reproach is undeservedly cast upon the American Colonies* (Boston: Kneeland and Adams for Thomas Leverett, 1767).

49. *Ibid*., p. 51.

50. *Ibid*., pp. 46–47.

51. In 1761 Chauncy had guided Stiles's *A Discourse on the Christian Union* (Boston: Edes and Gill) through the press, arranging for publication and correcting the proofs. He told Stiles, "I doubt not, this your first, publication will be of great service to the Churches, as it reflects honor on you, and will propagate thro the Country that good reputation, you have justly merited." MS letters, Chauncy to Stiles, June 15, July 21, August 3, 1761, in Stiles Papers, Yale University. Quoted by Bridenbaugh, *Mitre and Sceptre*, p. 4. Extracts in Stiles, *Itineraries*, pp. 439–40.

52. See the account in Edmund S. Morgan, *The Gentle Puritan: A Life of Ezra Stiles, 1727-1795* (New Haven and London: Yale University Press, 1962), pp. 237–54, which I have followed.

53. Chandler, *An Appeal to the Public* (New York: J. Parker, 1767), especially pp. 28–35.

54. *Ibid*., pp. 8–9.

55. *Ibid*., p. 266. Chauncy responded with *An Appeal to the Public Answered* (Boston: Kneeland and Adams for Thomas Leverett, 1768).

56. *The Appeal Defended; Or, the Proposed American Episcopate Vindicated* (New York: H. Gaine, 1769).

57. *A Reply to Dr. Chandler's 'Appeal Defended': Wherein His Mistakes are rectified, his false Arguing refuted, and the OBJECTIONS against the PLANNED AMERICAN EPISCO-*

PATE shewn to remain in full Force, notwithstanding all he has offered to render them invalid (Boston: Daniel Kneeland for Thomas Leverett, 1770).

58. *A Compleat View of Episcopacy, as Exhibited from the Fathers of the Christian Church, until the Close of the Second Century: Containing an Impartial Account of Them, of their Writings, and of what they say concerning Bishops and Presbyters; With Observations, and Remarks, tending to shew, that they esteemed These One and the Same Order of Ecclesiastical Officers. In Answer to Those, who have represented it as a Certain Fact, Universally Handed Down, even from the Apostles Days, that Governing and Ordaining Authority was Exercised by such Bishops Only, as were of an Order Superior to Presbyters* (Boston: Daniel Kneeland for Thomas Leverett, 1771). Hereafter cited as *A Compleat View*.

59. New York: Hugh Gaine, 1771.

60. Quoted in Bridenbaugh, *Mitre and Sceptre*, p. 310.

61. Chandler, *The Appeal Defended*, p. 118.

62. Chauncy, *An Appeal to the Public Answered*, p. 25 n.

63. Chauncy, *Reply to 'Appeal Defended,'* pp. 91-93.

64. Chauncy, *Appeal to the Public Answered*, pp. 154-55. One may judge the extent of anti-episcopacy feeling among Congregationalists by the correspondence between Samuel Cooper and William Livingston regarding Chauncy's attacks on Chandler. Episcopalians called Chauncy too harsh; some of his fellow Congregationalists thought him far too mild! Livingston wrote, "Tho perhaps no Man hath a higher opinion of Dr Chauncy's learning or Judgment than myself, yet I think his writings exhibit some symptoms of the languor of old age." He also suggested that Cooper persuade Chauncy to let "some of his younger brethren" edit any future pamphlets. Cooper knew Chauncy better than to try this tack, but agreed that Chauncy should "more freely" consult some of his younger friends. MS Letters, Massachusetts Historical Society.

65. See John Richard Alden, *The American Revolution 1775-1783* (New York: Harper, 1954), pp. 1-11.

66. *A Discourse On "the good News from a far Country"* (Boston: Kneeland and Adams for Thomas Leverett, 1766), pp. 10-15. Reprinted in J. W. Thornton, *The Pulpit of the Revolution* (Boston: Gould and Lincoln, 1860), pp. 105-46; lengthy extract in *The World's Best Orations from the Earliest Period to the Present Time*, ed. David J. Brewer (St. Louis: F. P. Kaiser, 1900), III, 1089-95. Hereafter cited as *Good News*.

67. *Ibid.*, p. 13.

68. John C. Miller, *Sam Adams, Pioneer in Propaganda* (Boston: Little, Brown, 1936), pp. 37-38, 52-53. Such clergy were called the Black Regiment.

69. James Spear Loring, *The Hundred Boston Orators Appointed by the Municipal Authorities and Other Public Bodies from 1770 to 1852* (Boston: J. P. Jewett and Co., 1855), p. 10.

70. Harris manuscripts, American Antiquarian Society.

71. *Peter Oliver's The Origin & Progress of the American Rebellion: A Tory View*, ed. Douglass Adair and John A. Schutz (San Marino, Cal.: Huntington Library, 1961), p. xiii.

72. John C. Miller, *Sam Adams*, p. 86.

73. Chauncy, *Good News*, pp. 24-25.

74. John Adams, *Works*, II, 304.

75. *Ibid.*, X, 191.

76. Chauncy, *Good News*, pp. 18-20.

77. Bridenbaugh, *Mitre and Sceptre*, pp. 230-59.

78. Chauncy, *Good News*, p. 23.

79. Bridenbaugh, *Mitre and Sceptre*, p. 288.

Chapter Ten: Divinity, Zeal, Rancor, and Revenge

1. In May 1768 he sprained his right ankle; before it could heal, he sprained the other one. "I fear," he said, "whether I shall ever have the proper use of my legs again. Walking was my life, and it has been a great disadvantage to my health, that I have been obliged to so much

confinement." From May 1768 until March 1769 he could not travel as far as the First Church "without the help of my chaise," Chauncy to Stiles, March 20, 1769, in Stiles, *Itineraries*, p. 448.

2. Chauncy, "Eminent Men," p. 161.

3. On deaths of Holyoke, Foxcroft, and Sewall see Shipton, *SHG*, V (1937), 277; VI (1942), 54; and V (1937), 389, respectively. See also Chauncy, *A Discourse Occasioned by the Death of the Reverend Dr. Joseph Sewall* (Boston: Kneeland and Adams, 1769) and *A Discourse Occasioned by the Death of the Reverend Thomas Foxcroft* (Boston: Daniel Kneeland for Thomas Leverett, 1769).

4. Drake, *The History and Antiquities of Boston*, p. 760.

5. Chauncy, *A Discourse Occasioned by the Death of the Reverend Thomas Foxcroft*, p. 21.

6. Lawrence Henry Gipson, *The Coming of the Revolution, 1763-1775* (New York: Harper, 1954), p. 215; Bernard Bailyn, *The Ordeal of Thomas Hutchinson* (Cambridge, Mass.: The Belknap Press of Harvard University Press, 1974), pp. 156-57.

7. Oliver, *Origin & Progress*, pp. 91-92.

8. Ann Hulton, *Letters of a Loyalist Lady* (Cambridge, Mass.: Harvard University Press, 1927), pp. 38-39.

9. Chauncy to Price, 22 March 1770, Boston Public Library.

10. Printed in Randolph G. Adams, "New Light on the Boston Massacre," *AAS Proc.*, n.s., 47 (1938), 309-10.

11. Swift, "The Massachusetts Election Sermons," p. 424.

12. The title speaks for itself: *Trust in GOD, the Duty of a People in a Day of Trouble. A Sermon preached, May 30th, 1770. At the request of a great number of Gentlemen, friends to the LIBERTIES of North America, who were desirous, not withstanding the removal of the Massachusetts General-Court (unconstitutionally as they judged) to CAMBRIDGE, that GOD might be acknowledged in that house of worship at BOSTON, in which our tribes, from the days of our fathers, have annually sought to him for direction, previous to the choice of his Majesty's Council* (Boston: Daniel Kneeland for Thomas Leverett, 1770).

13. "Boyle's Journal of Occurrences in Boston," p. 266.

14. Chauncy, *Trust in God*, pp. 11-23.

15. *Ibid.*, p. 29.

16. *Ibid.*, pp. 35-36. Chauncy would seem to offer in this incident, and generally by his behavior after the Stamp Act, corroboration of Norman O. Hatch's contention that among New England Congregational ministers of the time, "explanations of the civil order by religious symbols became even more extensive and highly charged. Far from removing political culture from the domination of religious concepts, ministers extended the canopy of religious meaning so that even the cause of liberty became sacred." Remarkably this convergence transcended theological differences between New and Old Light Congregationalists. "Ministers of contrasting theologies defended the Revolution with the full force of religious persuasion because certain aging religious symbols common to both were revitalized as they became infused with the potent connotations of a Real Whig or 'Country' ideology." *The Sacred Cause of Liberty: Republican Thought and the Millennium in Revolutionary New England* (New Haven and London: Yale University Press, 1977), pp. 2, 7.

17. Chauncy, *Trust in God*, pp. 36-37.

18. "Boyle's Journal of Occurrences in Boston," p. 266.

19. Adams, "New Light on the Boston Massacre," pp. 309-10.

20. See Sparks MS. 10, New England Papers IV, 14, Houghton Library, Harvard University.

21. Adams, "New Light on the Boston Massacre," p. 324.

22. *Ibid.*, pp. 268-69; Hiller B. Zobel, *The Boston Massacre* (New York: W. W. Norton, 1970), pp. 243-46; 298.

23. Gipson, *The Coming of the Revolution*, p. 203; John C. Miller, *Sam Adams*, 193-226; Pauline Maier, *From Resistance to Revolution: Colonial Radicals and the Development of American Opposition to Britain, 1765-1776* (New York: Alfred A. Knopf, 1972), pp. 114-38.

24. Chauncy to Stiles, 23 October 1769, in Stiles, *Itineraries*, p. 449.

25. *Ibid.*, pp. 448-49.

26. Gipson, *The Coming of the Revolution*, pp. 193, 197.

27. John C. Miller, *Sam Adams*, pp. 206-26.

28. Chauncy to Price, 30 May 1774, Price Letters, *MHS Proc.*, 2d ser., 17 (1903), 267.

29. *Ibid.*

30. Gipson, *The Coming of the Revolution*, p. 211.

31. John C. Miller, *Sam Adams*, pp. 256-75.

32. Gipson, *The Coming of the Revolution* pp. 211-14; John Adams, *Works*, II, 313. For a detailed account of Hutchinson's position, see Bailyn, *The Ordeal of Thomas Hutchinson*, pp. 196-220.

33. Carl Van Doren, *Benjamin Franklin* (New York: Viking, 1938), pp. 443-44, Bailyn, *The Ordeal of Thomas Hutchinson*, pp. 221-73, and David Freeman Hawke, *Franklin* (New York: Harper & Row, 1976), pp. 305-20.

34. Gipson, *The Coming of the Revolution*, pp. 217-19.

35. Peter Oliver's comment sheds light both on the Tory reaction and on Chauncy's opinion of Hutchinson: "The Case of the Colonies with *great Britain*, at this Time, was similar to that Reverend & zealous Divine, Dr. *Chauncy*, his Expression relative to Govr. *Hutchinson*; upon its being said to him by a Friend, 'that he did not doubt that the Govr. would be the Savior of his Country,' the Doctor replied, that 'he had rather the Country should perish than be saved by him'." *Origin & Progress*, p. 101.

36. Bailyn, *The Ordeal of Thomas Hutchinson*, pp. 259-63; John C. Miller, *Sam Adams*, pp. 276-96.

37. For an extended analysis of these measures see David Ammerman, *In the Common Cause: American Response to the Coercive Acts of 1774* (Charlottesville: University Press of Virginia, 1974). Upon Hutchinson's arrival in England, King George subjected him to a searching interrogation in which the king declared that he knew about Chauncy by reputation. See "Extracts from the Journal of Thomas Hutchinson, Governor of Massachusetts," *MHS Proc.*, 1st Ser., 15 (1878), 326, and the minutes of the February 1878 meeting of the Massachusetts Historical Society in *MHS Proc.*, 1st Ser., 16 (1879), 36-49; see also Bailyn, *The Ordeal of Thomas Hutchinson*, pp. 275-78.

38. Chauncy, *A Letter to a Friend. Giving a concise, but just, representation of the hardships and sufferings the town of Boston is exposed to, and must undergo, in consequence of the late Act of the British-Parliament* . . . (Boston: Greenleaf, 1774), pp. 6, 9, 16-17, 24-25.

39. *Ibid.*, pp. 28, 34. Josiah Quincy, Jr., in his *Observations on the . . . Boston Port-Bill* (Boston: Edes and Gill, 1774), argues for precisely the same tactics.

40. Chauncy to Price, 18 July 1774, Price Letters, pp. 268-69.

41. *A Report of the Record Commissioners of the City of Boston, Containing the Boston Town Records, 1770 through 1777* (Boston: Rockwell and Churchill, 1887), p. 183.

42. Josiah Quincy, *Memoir of the Life of Josiah Quincy, Jun., of Massachusetts* (Boston: Cummings, Hilliard, and Co., 1825). See also the account in H. Trevor Colbourn, *The Lamp of Experience: Whig History and the Intellectual Origins of the American Revolution* (Chapel Hill: University of North Carolina Press, 1965), pp. 77-82.

43. Chauncy to Samuel Adams, 26 August 1774. New York Public Library.

44. Chauncy to Price, 13 September 1774, Price Letters, p. 270; MS Letter, Massachusetts Historical Society. Naturally Chauncy respected Chatham. Once the earl sent Chauncy some cheeses by way of James Bowdoin and John Temple. Chauncy replied that he would keep the cheese "for his best friends only, and shall let them know it is the produce of the Earl of Chatham's estate, & for that reason will deal it out to them very frugally," as he meant to "keep it as long as he can, as a memento of the man to whom the nation is under infinite obligations." Bowdoin and Temple Papers, *MHS Colls.*, 6th Ser., 9 (1897), 301; 375-76.

45. *Ibid.*, p. 301.

46. Chauncy to Samuel Adams, 26 August 1774. New York Public Library.

47. John C. Miller, *Sam Adams*, pp. 323-25; Ammerman, *In the Common Cause*, pp. 89-101.

48. *The Writings of Samuel Adams*, ed. Harry Alonzo Cushing (New York and London: G. P. Putnam's Sons, 1904-08), III, 155-56.

49. *The Letters of Benjamin Franklin and Jane Mecom*, ed. Carl Van Doren, Memoirs of the American Philosophical Society, 27 (Princeton: Princeton University Press, 1950), pp. 148-49. On June 22, 1774 "The General Association of Congregational Ministers in Connecticut" sent a long letter to the Boston ministers, in Chauncy's care, offering prayer and assistance. This was typical of the offers that pleased Chauncy so greatly.

50. Chauncy to Price, 10 January 1775, Price Letters, p. 278.

51. Shipton, *SHG*, VI (1942), 453.

52. Chauncy to Samuel Adams, 26 August 1774. New York Public Library.

53. Chauncy to Quincy, 3 November 1774. Massachusetts Historical Society.

54. Chauncy to Price, 10 January 1775, Price Letters, pp. 275-76.

55. MS Report of the Associated Pastors of Boston, November 28, 1774. Washburn Manuscripts, XIV, 11, Massachusetts Historical Society.

56. Oliver, *Origin & Progress*, p. 115.

57. Alden, *The American Revolution*, pp. 19-22.

58. Chauncy to Price, 10 April 1775, Price Letters, p. 284.

59. Alden, *The American Revolution*, p. 20. See also Howard H. Peckham, *The War for Independence: A Military History* (Chicago: University of Chicago Press, 1958), pp. 7-10.

Chapter Eleven: Exile and Return

1. Alden, *The American Revolution*, pp. 25-33; Richard Frothingham, *History of the Siege of Boston, and of the Battles of Lexington, Concord and Bunker Hill. Also, An Account of the Bunker Hill Monument* (Boston: Little, Brown, 1890), pp. 91-96; John Jennings, *Boston: Cradle of Liberty, 1630-1776* (Garden City: Doubleday, 1947), pp. 248-49.

2. Frothingham, *History of the Siege of Boston*, p. 96. See also Chauncy to Price, 18 July 1775, Price Letters, p. 297.

3. John Winthrop to Price, 6 June 1775, Price Letters, p. 291.

4. "Diary of Samuel Cooper, 1775-1776," ed. Frederick Tuckerman, *American Historical Review*, 6 (1901), 306.

5. Chauncy to Price, 18 July 1775, Price Letters, p. 297.

6. *Ibid.*, p. 294.

7. *Ibid.*, p. 299; Tuckerman, ed., "Diary of Samuel Cooper," p. 319.

8. Tuckerman, ed., "Diary of Samuel Cooper," pp. 306, 314, 319, 331.

9. Chauncy to Price, 18 July 1775, Price Letters, p. 297.

10. *Ibid.*, pp. 294-300.

11. Chauncy to Price, 22 July 1775, Price Letters, pp. 300-01.

12. Foremost supporters of conciliation were the Earl of Chatham and Lord Camden in the upper chamber; Edmund Burke, George Johnstone, the Marquis of Granby, and David Hartley in the Commons. Alden, *The American Revolution*, pp. 16-17; Dora Mae Clark, *British Opinion and the American Revolution* (New Haven: Yale University Press, 1930), pp. 152-80; 241-43.

13. Richard Price, *Observations on the Nature of Civil Liberty* (Boston: T. and J. Fleet, 1776).

14. Alden, *The American Revolution*, pp. 65-66.

15. *Ibid.*, pp. 40-41.

16. *Letters and Diary of John Rowe, Boston Merchant*, ed. Annie Rowe Cunningham, pp. 305-06.

17. *Ibid.*, p. 306.

18. Tuckerman, ed., "Diary of Samuel Cooper," p. 340.

19. *Ibid.*, p. 341.

20. *Ibid.*

21. *Ibid.*

22. *The Literary Diary of Ezra Stiles, D.D., L.L.D.*, ed. Franklin Bowditch Dexter (New York: Charles Scribner's Sons, 1901), II, 154.

23. John Clarke, *A Discourse, delivered at the First Church in Boston, February 15, 1787, at the interment of the Rev. Charles Chauncy, D.D. A.A.S., its senior pastor, who expired Feb. 10, 1787* (Boston: James D. Griffith and Edward E. Powars, 1787). Clarke stressed Chauncy's reputation for work among the sick.

24. Pierce, ed., "The Records of the First Church in Boston," pp. 425–26.

25. *The Writings of Thomas Paine*, ed. Moncure Daniel Conway (New York: G. P. Putnam's Sons, 1906), I, 67–120.

26. *Journals of the Continental Congress, 1774-1789*, ed. Worthington C. Ford et al. (34 vols., Washington: Government Printing Office, 1904-1937), IV, 258.

27. John H. Hazelton, *The Declaration of Independence: Its History* (New York: Dodd, Mead, 1906), pp. 263–67.

28. *Ibid.* See also *Familiar Letters of John Adams and His Wife Abigail Adams, During the Revolution*, ed. Charles Francis Adams (Boston and New York: Houghton Mifflin, 1875), pp. 204–05.

29. John Adams, *Familiar Letters.*

30. Alden, *The American Revolution*, p. 84.

31. For biographical sketch see Shipton, *SHG*, VII (1945), 464–93.

32. Eliot to Belknap, 19 March 1777, Belknap Papers (1891), pp. 106–07.

33. Shipton, *SHG*, VII (1945), 483.

34. Eliot to Belknap, 19 March 1777, Belknap Papers (1891), p. 107.

35. *Ibid.*, p. 106.

36. Eliot to Belknap, 17 June 1777, Belknap Papers (1891), p. 124. "When the church at Bolton made this innovation," Eliot commented (Eliot to Belknap, 19 March 1777, Belknap Papers [1891], p. 107), "Dr. Chauncy was so angry that he would have refused holding communion with the members." In 1771 the Congregational parish at Bolton, in Worcester County, dismissed its minister, the Reverend Thomas Goss. Chauncy moderated a council of seven churches, which met in Bolton the following August to try to force Goss's reinstatement on the grounds that no church had the right to dismiss its pastor without the direction of a council. Chauncy was unsuccessful; the council published its testimony against the Bolton parish. The fact that he blithely reversed his position in the Byles case three years later discredited him with a number of New England ministers. For a full account of the controversy see Shipton, *SHG*, X (1958), 173–85.

37. John Adams, *Familiar Letters*, p. 214.

38. William Tudor, *The Life of James Otis* (1823; rpt. New York: Da Capo Press, 1970), p. 148.

39. If one may judge from his account of the battle of Hog Island, *MHS Proc.*, 2d Ser., 17 (1903), 297–98.

40. MS. Sermon 871, November 13, 1776, New York Public Library, no. 1387.

41. Alden, *The American Revolution*, p. 150.

42. William G. McLoughlin, ed., *Isaac Backus on Church, State, and Calvinism: Pamphlets, 1754-1789* (Cambridge, Mass.: The Belknap Press of Harvard University Press, 1968), pp. 346–47. McLoughlin analyzes the convention in *New England Dissent 1630-1883: The Baptists and the Separation of Church and State* (Cambridge, Mass.: Harvard University Press, 1971), I, 591–612.

43. Samuel Eliot Morison, "The Struggle over the Adoption of the Constitution of Massachusetts," *MHS Proc.*, 3d Ser., 50 (1917), 353–411. Morison reprints the article.

44. As Allan Nevins contends in *The American States During and After the Revolution, 1715-1789* (New York: Macmillan, 1924), p. 422.

45. Morison, "The Struggle," pp. 371–72.

46. See Clair Eugene Tromsness, "Isaac Backus: Colonial Apologist for Religious Liberty," Dissertation Stanford 1964, pp. 27–37; and McLoughlin's introduction to *Isaac Backus on Church, State, and Calvinism*, pp. 1–61.

47. *Government and Liberty Described; and Ecclesiastical Tyranny Exposed* (Boston: Powars and Willis, 1778); reprinted in McLoughlin, ed., *Isaac Backus*, pp. 349–65.

48. Isaac Backus, *A Church History of New England from 1620 to 1804* (Philadelphia: Baptist Tract Depository, 1839), p. 186.

49. Eliot to Belknap, 23 May 1780, Belknap Papers (1891), p. 188.

50. Morison, "The Struggle," p. 372. See also the *Boston Gazette*, May 22, 1780.

Chapter Twelve: Pudding and Pies

1. In 1770 the church began regular allotments to Chauncy "for supplying the Pulpit." Pierce, ed., "The Records of the First Church in Boston," pp. 252–60.

2. Bezaleel Howard, quoted by Sprague, *Annals of the American Unitarian Pulpit*, p. 13.

3. Sumner, *History of East Boston*, p. 267.

4. Tuckerman, ed., "Diary of Samuel Cooper," p. 341.

5. Morgan, *The Gentle Puritan*, p. 289.

6. *Ibid.*, pp. 172–74; 255–76; 279; 288–89; 291. Stiles graduated from Yale in 1746. Although determined not to become involved in worldly affairs, he did become caught up in the spirit of patriotism and supported the American cause. Portsmouth offered him a house, firewood, moving expenses, and £110 per year.

7. Eliot to Belknap, 19 March 1777, Belknap Papers (1891), p. 106.

8. Pierce, ed., "The Records of the First Church in Boston," pp. 260–61. Clarke was to see his salary fluctuate wildly during the next few years, while the new states stumbled through a deep financial morass. The nation needed money badly; it decided to raise funds by issuing paper money. Not surprisingly, the paper dipped in value as fast as it was issued. By 1778 everyone knew that redemption of the money at face value was impossible. With each issue of currency, ministers on fixed salaries faced the same problem: they received so many pounds per week, but each week the pound was worth less. Chauncy had ripped into the General Court about the same predicament in 1747; in 1778 he spoke out again, in his lecture *The Accursed Thing*. The farmers, merchants, and manufacturers increased their prices in proportion to the depreciation of the currency, but the people were too greedy to provide for the poor, widows, orphans, and, of course, the clergy. (Chauncy acknowledged one good result: the freeholders and farmers had become rich enough to wage war without great strain, and they were increasingly determined to retain their independence.) The government, Chauncy concluded, must in justice provide tax relief for those injured by the depreciation. Of course such a situation could not long continue. In March 1780 Congress virtually repudiated the continental bills, called them in at forty to one, and brought out a new issue, redeemable in specie in six years, bearing five percent interest, and receivable as payment of taxes. Congress turned to the requisition system to finance the war. The repudiation wiped out thousands of holders of the now worthless continental bills. See Nevins, *The American States During and After the Revolution*, p. 471.

Chauncy's arguments carried weight at home, for the First Church took steps to counter depreciation by increasing the salaries of both ministers at regular intervals from 1778 to 1781. Chauncy accepted only a minimal salary, but during this time Clarke's pay jumped from £7 to a flat £300 per week. See *CSM Pubs.*, 39 (1961), 263–67.

9. MS Sermon, November 13, 1776. New York Public Library.

10. Chauncy to Price, 20 May 1779, Price Letters, p. 321.

11. Pierce, ed., "The Records of the First Church in Boston," p. 266.

12. For the details of this complicated arrangement, see Sumner, *History of East Boston*, pp. 220–59.

13. See Ulrich B. Phillips, "An Antigua Plantation, 1769-1818," *North Carolina Historical Review*, 3 (1926), 439-45. One correction should be noted. Phillips states that "by 1779 the plantation had become the property of William Hyslop, Charles Chauncey and Thomas Greenough as partners in equal interests" (pp. 439-40). Documents in the Greenough Collection, Massachusetts Historical Society, indicate that the property belonged to Mary Chauncy, not Charles, although Chauncy managed her business affairs. Chauncy gained possession of his wife's interest upon her death. See MS "Arbitral Award, 21 April 1785." Sumner's account of Mary Chauncy's inheritance seems to bear out my deduction.

14. Chartered May 4, 1780. See *The American Academy of Arts and Sciences* (Boston, n.p., 1940), p. 3.

15. John Adams, *Works*, IV, 260-61n.

16. *Memoirs of the American Academy of Arts and Sciences*, 11 (1888), 33 ff.

17. See title page to *A Sermon, Delivered at the First Church in Boston, March 13, 1785: Occasioned by the Return of the Society to their House of Worship, After Long Absence, To Make Way for the Repairs that were Necessary* (Boston: Greenleaf and Freeman, 1785). Hereafter cited as *Return of the Society*.

18. Stiles, *Literary Diary*, III, 143, 147. Chauncy's remarks in "Eminent Men," p. 164, suggest that he and Stiles had discussed the matter in the 1760s.

19. See *All Nations of the Earth* (1762), p. 22; *Twelve Sermons On the following seasonable and important Subjects. Justification impossible by the Works of the Law. The Question answered, "wherefore then serveth the Law?" The Nature of Faith, as justifying, largely explained, and remarked on. The Place, and Use, of Faith, in the Affair of Justification. Human Endeavours, in the use of Means, the way in which Faith is obtained. The Method of the Spirit in communicating the "Faith, by which the Just do live." The Inquiry of the young Man in the Gospel, "What shall I do that I may have eternal Life"? With interspersed Notes, in Defence of the Truth; especially in the Points treated on, in the above Discourses* (Boston: D. and J. Kneeland for Thomas Leverett, 1765).

20. Chauncy to Price, 22 March 1770, Massachusetts Historical Society. Chauncy outlined his theory and asked Price to consider it.

21. Belknap to Hazard, 19 December 1782, Belknap Papers, *MHS Colls.*, 5th Ser., 2 (1877), 171.

22. Conrad Wright, *The Beginnings of Unitarianism in America*, pp. 189-92.

23. [Charles Chauncy and John Clarke], *Salvation for all Men, Illustrated and Vindicated as A Scripture Doctrine, in Numerous Extracts from a Variety of Pious and Learned Men, who have purposely writ upon the subject. Together With their answer to the objections urged against it* (Boston: T. and J. Fleet, 1782), p. iii.

24. Foster Rhea Dulles, *America Learns to Play: A History of Popular Recreation, 1607-1940* (New York and London: D. Appleton-Century, 1940), pp. 46-50.

25. Eliot to Belknap, 31 July 1779, Belknap Papers (1891), p. 145.

26. Eliot to Belknap, 10 December 1780, Belknap Papers (1891), p. 201.

27. *The Accursed Thing must be taken away from among a People, if they would reasonably hope to stand before their Enemies* (Boston: Thomas and John Fleet, 1778), pp. 7-12. Cf. *The Benevolence of the Deity*, pp. 203 ff.

28. *Ibid.*, pp. 11-12.

29. Eliot to Belknap, 31 July 1779, Belknap Papers (1891), p. 145.

30. Michael Kammen, *People of Paradox: An Inquiry Concerning the Origins of American Civilization*, p. 175n.

31. Eliot to Belknap, February, n.d., 1781, Belknap Papers (1891), pp. 202-07.

32. Eliot to Belknap, 1 February 1782, Belknap Papers (1891), pp. 225-26.

33. Belknap to Hazard, 19 December 1782, Belknap Papers (1877), p. 172.

34. See above, note 23.

35. Eliot to Belknap, 14 August 1782, Belknap Papers (1891), p. 233.

36. Eliot to Belknap, 30 September 1782, Belknap Papers (1891), pp. 236-37.

37. Belknap to Hazard, 19 December 1782, Belknap Papers (1877), p. 171.

38. Samuel Mather, *All Men will not be saved forever: or, an attempt to prove, That this is a Scriptural Doctrine; and To give a sufficient Answer to the Publisher of Extracts in Favor of the SALVATION of all MEN* (Boston: Benjamin Edes and Sons, 1782), p. 8.

39. Boston: T. and J. Fleet, 1782.

40. Samuel Hopkins, *An Inquiry Concerning The future State of those who die in their Sins* (Newport: Solomon Southwick, 1783); Joseph Eckley, *Divine Glory, Brought to View, in the Condemnation of the Ungodly* (Boston: Robert Hodge, 1782); William Gordon, *The Doctrine of Final Universal Salvation Examined and Shewn to be Unscriptural* (Boston: T. and J. Fleet, 1783).

41. Eliot to Belknap, 30 September 1782, Belknap Papers (1891), p. 237.

42. Eliot to Belknap, 18 September 1783, Belknap Papers (1891), p. 263; Eliot to Belknap, 22 October 1783, Belknap Papers (1891), p. 265.

43. Ellis, *History of the First Church*, p. 194; Sumner, *History of East Boston*, p. 269.

44. Boston: T. and J. Fleet, 1783.

45. Chauncy, *Divine Glory*, pp. 4, 8, 9, 10.

46. Belknap to Hazard, 24 May 1784, Belknap Papers (1877), pp. 347-48. Apparently Eliot brought it with him from London.

47. Hazard to Belknap, 13 November 1784, Belknap Papers (1877), pp. 406-07.

48. Shipton, *SHG*, VI (1942), 459.

49. Quoted in Sprague, *Annals of the American Unitarian Pulpit*, pp. 12-13.

50. *The Salvation of all Men examined; and the endless Punishment of those who die impenitent, argued and defended against the Objections and Reasonings of the late Rev. Doctor Chauncy, of Boston* (New Haven: A. Morse, 1790).

51. Eliot to Belknap, 26 August 1784, Belknap Papers (1891), pp. 275-76.

52. Eliot to Belknap, 24 February 1785, Belknap Papers (1891), p. 287.

53. Charles Francis Adams, *Three Episodes of Massachusetts History: The Settlement of Boston Bay; the Antinomian Controversy; A Study of Church and Town Government* (Boston: Houghton Mifflin, 1892), II, 678.

54. Stiles, *Literary Diary*, III, 162.

55. Samuel Abbot Green, "Hollis's 'Tractate on Church Music'," *MHS Proc.*, 3d Ser., 44 (1911), 176-78.

56. Pierce, ed., "The Records of the First Church in Boston," pp. 271-74; Stiles, *Literary Diary*, III, 162.

57. Stiles, *Literary Diary*, III, 162.

58. Eliot to Belknap, 24 February 1785, Belknap Papers (1891), p. 287.

59. Russell to Belknap, 28 March 1785, Belknap Papers (1891), p. 291.

60. Chauncy, *Return of the Society*, pp. 17-18.

61. *Ibid.*, pp. 18-23.

62. "Memoirs of the life and character of the late Dr. Chauncy, of Boston," *The American Museum, or Universal Magazine*, 7 (1790), 77. Chauncy may also have spent some time in Quincy, where he had purchased a "country home." See *NEHG Reg.*, 18 (1864), 123.

63. *MHS Proc.*, 1 (1859), 479-80. On another portrait, probably of Chauncy in middle age, see Henry Wilder Foote, "False Faces. A Study of the Use and Misuse of Portraits as Historical Documents," *MHS Proc.*, 67 (1945), 573.

64. Jonathan Jackson to Price, Price Letters, p. 330.

65. Chauncy, "Life of the Rev. President Chauncy," p. 179.

66. Chauncy, "Eminent Men," p. 158.

67. Shipton, *SHG*, VI (1942), 454.

68. Chauncy was probably attended by Benjamin Waterhouse, Harvard's able young professor of medicine. In the early 1780s Waterhouse had given Chauncy a copy of Luigi Cornaro's *Long and Healthful Life*. Dissipated by youthful excesses, Cornaro had recovered by means of self-discipline. The *Long and Healthful Life*, written in Cornaro's hundredth year,

describes his system of sobriety, regularity, and dietary temperance. Chauncy discovered with delight that his own program, self-imposed during the 1740s after serious illness, closely paralleled Cornaro's. Confirmed in his belief that he owed his cure and longevity to regular habits, Chauncy urged the American publication of Cornaro's treatise; it appeared in this country shortly after Chauncy's death. See Henry Rouse Viets, "Benjamin Waterhouse on Luigi Cornaro's *Long and Healthful Life,*" *MHS Proc.*, 69 (1956), 3–56.

69. Pierce, ed., "The Records of the First Church in Boston," p. 474.

70. *Ibid.*, p. 473.

71. Cotton was installed October 10, 1633; he died December 23, 1652. Emerson was installed October 16, 1799; he died May 12, 1811.

72. *American Museum* 7 (1790), 77.

73. Clarke, *A Discourse . . . At the Interment of the Rev. Charles Chauncy* (Boston: James D. Griffith and Edward E. Powars, 1787).

The Works of Charles Chauncy

The Works of
Charles Chauncy

In the following list I have retained the spelling, punctuation, and capitalization of initial letters in Chauncy's titles, but I have not attempted to duplicate the typography found on the title pages. Most of Chauncy's works, having been published in the American colonies, are listed in Charles Evans, *American Bibliography: A Chronological Dictionary of All Books, Pamphlets, and Periodicals Printed in the United States of America from the Genesis of Printing in 1639 Down to and Including the Year 1820, with Bibliographical and Biographical Notes* (Chicago, 1903-59; rpt. New York: Peter Smith, 1941-67), and the *Supplement to Charles Evans' American Bibliography* by Roger P. Bristol (Charlottesville: University Press of Virginia, 1970). The American Antiquarian Society has performed an invaluable service by making the extant works listed in *American Bibliography* available on microcards in *Early American Imprints, 1639-1800; Evans Numbers 1-49197*, ed. Clifford K. Shipton (Worcester, Mass.: American Antiquarian Society, 1960-68).

A convenient guide to Chauncy manuscripts may be found in the second edition of *American Literary Manuscripts: A Checklist of Holdings in Academic, Historical, and Public Libraries, Museums, and Authors' Homes in the United States*, ed. J. Albert Robbins et al. (Athens, Ga.: University of Georgia Press, 1977). For this list I have selected those manuscripts and unpublished materials by and about Chauncy that I have found most useful in my study of his life.

PUBLISHED WORKS

The accursed Thing must be taken away from among a People, if they would reasonably hope to stand before their Enemies. A Sermon Preached at the Thursday-Lecture in Boston, September 3, 1778. And printed at the Desire of the Hearers. Boston: Thomas and John Fleet, 1778.

All Nations of the Earth blessed in Christ, the Seed of Abraham. A Sermon Preached at Boston, at the Ordination of the Rev. Mr. Joseph Bowman, to the Work of the Gospel-Ministry, More especially Among the Mohawk-Indians, on the Western Borders of New-England. August 31. 1762. Boston: John Draper, 1762.

The Appeal to the Public answered, In Behalf of the Non-Episcopal Churches in America; Containing Remarks on what Dr. Thomas Bradbury Chandler has advanced, on the four following Points. The Original and Nature of the Episcopal Office; Reasons for sending Bishops to America. The Plan on which it is proposed to send them. And the Objections against sending them obviated and refuted. Wherein the Reasons for an American Episcopate are shewn to be insufficient, and the Objections against it in full force. Boston: Kneeland and Adams for Thomas Leverett, 1768.

The Benevolence of the Deity, Fairly and Impartially Considered. In Three Parts. The first explains the sense, in which we are to understand Benevolence, as applicable to God. The second asserts, and proves, that this perfection, in the sense explained, is one of his essential attributes. The third endeavours to answer objections. Under one or other of these heads, occasion will be taken to view man as an intelligent moral agent; having within himself an ability and freedom to Will, as well as to do, in opposition to Necessity from any extraneous cause whatever:—To point out the Origin of Evil, both natural and moral:—And to offer what may be thought sufficient to shew, that there is no inconsistency between infinite benevolence in the Deity, which is always guided by infinite wisdom, and any appearances of evil in the creation. Boston: Powars & Willis, 1784.

The Blessedness of the Dead who die in the Lord. A Sermon Preached the Lord's Day after the Funeral of Mrs. Anna Foxcroft, The amiable and pious Consort of the Reverend Mr. Thomas Foxcroft, Who died October 9th 1749, in the 53d Year of her Age. Boston: Rogers and Fowle, 1749.

"Breaking of Bread," in remembrance of the dying Love of Christ, a Gospel institution. Five Sermons. In which the institution is explained; a general observance of it recommended and enforced; objections answered; and such Difficulties, Doubts, and Fears, relative to it, particularly mentioned, and removed, which have too commonly discouraged some from an attendance at it, and proved to others a source of discomfort, in the regard they have endeavoured to pay to it. Boston: D. Kneeland for Thomas Leverett, 1772.

Character and Overthrow of Laish considered and applied. A Sermon Preached at the Desire of the Honourable Artillery-Company, In Boston, June 3. 1734. Being the Anniversary Day for their Election of Officers. Boston: S. Kneeland and T. Green for D. Henchman, 1734.

"The Charge" at the ordination of John Hunt. Printed at pp. 29-32 of John Hunt, *A Sermon Preached September 25, 1771. At his Ordination, and at the Instal-*

ment of the Rev. John Bacon, to the joint Pastoral Charge of the South-Church in Boston. Boston: Kneeland and Adams, 1772.

Charity to the distressed Members of Christ accepted as done to himself, and rewarded, at the Judgment-day, with blessedness in God's everlasting Kingdom. A Sermon, Preached the Lord's-Day after the Death of Mr. Edward Gray. Who Departed this Life July 2nd, 1757, in the 84th Year of his Age. Boston: Green & Russell, 1757.

Christian Love, as exemplified by the first christian church in their Having All Things in Common, placed in its true and just point of light. In A Sermon, Preached at the Thursday-Lecture, in Boston, August 3d. 1773. From Acts 4. 31. Wherein it is shown, that christian churches, in their character as such, are strongly obliged to evidence the reality of their christian love, though not by having all things in common, yet by making such provision, according to their ability, for their members in a state of penury, as that none of them may suffer through want of the things needful for the body; and that Deacons are officers appointed by Christ to take care of his poor saints, making all proper distributions to them in his name, and as enabled hereto by the churches to which they respectively belong. Boston: Kneeland & Davis for Thomas Leverett, 1773.

Civil Magistrates must be just, ruling in the Fear of God. A Sermon Preached before His Excellency William Shirley, Esq; The Honourable His Majesty's Council, And House of Representatives, Of the Province of the Massachusetts-Bay in N. England; May 27. 1747. Being the Anniversary for the Election of His Majesty's Council for said Province. Boston: House of Representatives, 1747.

A Compleat View of Episcopacy, As exhibited from the Fathers of the Christian Church, until the Close of the Second Century: Containing An Impartial Account of them, of their Writings, and of what they say concerning Bishops and Presbyters; With Observations, and Remarks, Tending to shew, that they esteemed these One and the Same Order of Ecclesiastical Officers. In Answer To those, who have represented it as a Certain Fact, universally handed down, even from the Apostles Days, that Governing and Ordaining Authority was exercised by such Bishops only, as were of an Order Superior to Presbyters. Boston: Daniel Kneeland for Thomas Leverett, 1771.

Cornelius's Character. A Sermon Preach'd the Lord's-Day after the Funeral of Mr. Cornelius Thayer, One of the Deacons of the first Church of Christ in Boston; Who died, April 10. 1745. Aetat 60. Boston: D. Gookin, 1745.

The Counsel of two confederate Kings to set the Son of Tabeal on the Throne, represented as evil, in it's natural Tendency and moral Aspect. A Sermon Occasion'd by the Present Rebellion in Favour of the Pretender. Preach'd in Boston, at the Thursday-Lecture, February 6th. 1745,6. Boston: D. Gookin, 1746.

A Discourse On "the good News from a far Country." Deliver'd July 24th. A Day of Thanks-giving to Almighty God, throughout the Province of the Massachusetts-Bay in New-England, on Occasion of the Repeal of the Stamp-Act; appointed by his Excellency, the Governor of said Province, at the Desire of it's House of Representatives, with the Advice of his Majesty's Council. Boston: Kneeland and Adams for Thomas Leverett, 1766.

A Discourse Occasioned by the Death of the Reverend Dr. Joseph Sewall, Late colleague Pastor of the South-Church in Boston: who departed this Life, On the Evening of June 27. 1769. In the 81st. Year of his Age. Delivered the Lord's-Day after his Decease. Boston: Kneeland and Adams, 1769.

A Discourse occasioned by the Death of the Reverend Jonathan Mayhew, D. D. late Pastor of the West-Church in Boston: who departed this Life On Wednesday Morning, July 9. 1766, Aetatis 46. Delivered the Lord's-Day after his Decease. Boston: R. and S. Draper, Edes and Gill, and T. and J. Fleet, 1766.

A Discourse occasioned by the Death of the Reverend Thomas Foxcroft, M. A. late Colleague-Pastor of the First Church of Christ in Boston: who departed this Life On Lord's-Day Forenoon, June 18. 1769. In the 73d year of his Age. Delivered the Lord's-Day after his Decease. Boston: Daniel Kneeland for Thomas Leverett, 1769.

Divine Glory Brought to View in the Final Salvation of All Men. A Letter To the Friend to Truth. By One Who wishes well to all Mankind. Boston: T. and J. Fleet, 1783.

The Duty of Ministers to "make known the Mystery of the Gospel"; and the Duty of People to "pray for them", that they may do it "with Boldness", or Fortitude. A Sermon Preached at the Ordination of the Reverend Mr. Penuel Bowen, A Colleague-Pastor of the New-South-Church in Boston, April 30, 1766. Boston: Edes and Gill, 1766.

Early Piety recommended and exemplify'd. A Sermon Occasioned by the Death of Elisabeth Price, An eminently pious Young Woman, Who departed this Life, February 22. 1731/2. In the Seventeenth Year of her Age. Boston: S. Kneeland & T. Green for B. Gray, 1732.

The Earth delivered from the Curse to which it is, at present, subjected. A Sermon Occasioned by the late Earthquakes in Spain and Portugal, as well as New-England; and Preached at the Boston-Thursday-Lecture, January 22, 1756. Published by the general Desire of the Hearers. Boston: Edes and Gill, 1756.

Earthquakes a Token of the righteous Anger of God. A Sermon Preached at the Old-Brick-Meeting-House in Boston, the Lord's-Day after the terrible Earthquake, which suddenly awoke us out of our Sleep in the Morning of the 18th of November, 1755. Boston: Edes and Gill, 1755.

Enthusiasm described and caution'd against. A Sermon Preach'd at the Old Brick Meeting-House in Boston, the Lord's Day after the Commencement, 1742. With a Letter to the Reverend Mr. James Davenport. Boston: J. Draper for S. Eliot and J. Blanchard, 1742.

Five Dissertations on the Scripture Account of the Fall; and its Consequences. London: C. Dilly, 1785.

The Gifts of the Spirit to Ministers consider'd in their Diversity; with the wise Ends of their various Distribution, and the good Purposes it is adapted to serve. A Sermon Preach'd at the Boston Thursday-Lecture, Decemb. 17. 1741. And made publick at the Desire of the Hearers. Boston: Rogers and Fowle for S. Eliot, 1742.

The horrid Nature, and enormous Guilt of Murder. A Sermon Preached at the Thursday-Lecture in Boston, November 19th. 1754. The Day of the Execution of William Wicer, for the Murder of William Chism. Boston: Thomas Fleet, 1754.

The Idle-Poor secluded from the Bread of Charity by the Christian Law. A Sermon Preached in Boston, before the Society for encouraging Industry and employing the Poor. Aug. 12. 1752. Boston: Thomas Fleet, 1752.

Joy, the Duty of Survivors, on the Death of Pious Friends and Relatives. A Funeral Discourse On the Death of Mrs. Lucy Waldo, The amiable Consort of Mr. Samuel Waldo, Merchant in Boston: Who departed this Life August 7th 1741, in the 38th Year of her Age. Boston: S. Kneeland and T. Green, 1741.

A Letter to a Friend, Containing Remarks on certain Passages in a Sermon Preached, by the Right Reverend Father in God, John Lord Bishop of Landaff, before the Incorporated Society for the Propagation of the Gospel in Foreign Parts, at their Anniversary Meeting in the Parish Church of St. Mary-Le-Bow, February 20. 1767. In which the highest Reproach is undeservedly cast upon the American Colonies. Boston: Kneeland and Adams for Thomas Leverett, 1767.

A Letter To a Friend; Giving a concise, but just, Account, according to the Advices hitherto received, of the Ohio-Defeat; and Pointing out also the many good Ends, this inglorious Event is naturally adapted to promote: or, Shewing wherein it is fitted to advance the Interest of all the American British Colonies. To which is added, Some general Account of the New-England Forces, with what they have already done, counter-ballancing the above Loss. Boston: Edes and Gill, 1755.

A Letter to a Friend. Giving a concise, but just, representation of the hardships and sufferings the town of Boston is exposed to, and must undergo in consequence of the late Act of the British-Parliament; which, by shutting up it's port, has put a fatal bar in the way of that commercial business on which it

223

depended for it's support, Shewing, at the same time, wherein this Edict, however unintended, is powerfully adapted to promote the interest of all the American Colonies, and even of Boston itself in the end. Boston: Greenleaf, 1774.

A Letter from a Gentleman in Boston, to Mr. George Wishart, one of the Ministers of Edinburgh, concerning the State of Religion in New-England. Edinburgh, 1742. Reprinted in *Clarendon Historical Society Reprints,* March 1883.

A Letter To the Reverend Mr. George Whitefield, Vindicating certain Passages he has excepted against, in a late Book entitled, Seasonable Thoughts on the State of Religion in New-England; and shewing that he has neither sufficiently defended himself, nor retracted his past Misconduct. Boston: Rogers and Fowle for S. Eliot, 1745.

"Life of the Rev. President Chauncy, Written At the Request of Dr. Stiles." *MHS Colls.,* 1st Ser., X (1809), 171–80.

Man's Life considered under the Similitude of a Vapour, that appeareth for a little Time, and then vanisheth away. A Sermon on the Death of that Honorable & Vertuous Gentlewoman Mrs. Sarah Byfield, The amiable Consort of the Honorable Nathanael Byfield, Esq; Who died Decemb. 21st, 1730. In the 58th Year of her Age. Boston: B. Green, 1731.

Marvellous Things done by the right Hand and holy Arm of God in getting him the Victory. A Sermon Preached the 18th of July, 1745. Being a Day set apart for Solemn Thanksgiving to almighty God, For the Reduction of Cape-Breton by his Majesty's New England Forces, under the Command of the honourable William Pepperrell, Esq; Lieutenant-General and Commander in Chief, and covered by a Squadron of his Majesty's Ships from Great Britain, commanded by Peter Warren, Esq. Boston: T. Fleet, 1745.

Ministers cautioned against the Occasions of Contempt. A Sermon Preached before the Ministers of the Province of the Massachusetts-Bay, in New-England, at their Annual Convention, In Boston; May 31. 1744. Boston: Rogers and Fowle for Samuel Eliot, 1744.

Ministers exhorted and encouraged to take heed to themselves, and to their Doctrine. A Sermon Preached the 7th of November, At the Instalment of the Rev. Mr. Thomas Frink to the Pastoral Care Of the third Church in Plymouth. Boston: Rogers and Fowle for S. Eliot, 1744.

The Mystery hid from Ages and Generations, Made Manifest by the Gospel-Revelation; or, The Salvation of all Men the Grand Thing aimed at in the Scheme of God, as opened in the New-Testament Writings, and Entrusted with Jesus Christ to Bring into Effect. London: Charles Dilly, 1784.

Nathanael's Character display'd. A Sermon, Preach'd The Lord's Day after the Funeral of the Honourable Nathanael Byfield, Esq; Late Judge of the Vice-Admiralty, And One of His Majesty's Council for this Province. Who died at

224

his House in Boston, on the 6th of June, 1733. In the 80th Year of his Age. Boston: n.p., 1733.

The New Creature Describ'd, and consider'd as the sure Characteristick of a Man's being in Christ: Together with some Seasonable Advice to those who are New-Creatures. A Sermon Preach'd at the Boston Thursday-Lecture, June 4. 1741. And made public at the general Desire of the Hearers. Boston: G. Rogers for J. Edwards and S. Eliot, 1741.

The only Compulsion proper to be made Use of, in the Affairs of Conscience and Religion. A Sermon Preach'd at the Old Brick Meeting-House in Boston, September 2d 1739. And Printed at the Desire of many who heard it. Boston: J. Draper for J. Edwards, 1739.

The Opinion of one that has perused the Summer Morning's Conversation, concerning Original Sin, wrote by the Rev. Mr. Peter Clark, in Two Things principally: First, That he has offered that, which has rendered it impossible the doctrine of the imputation of Adam's guilt to his posterity, should be true in the sense it is held by Calvinists. Secondly, That tho' he pretends to be a friend to the Calvinistical doctrine of imputed guilt, yet he has deserted this doctrine and given it up into the hands of its enemies, as it teaches the liableness of all mankind, without exception, to the torments of hell, on account of the first Sin. To which is added, A few remarks on the recommendatory preface by five reverend Clergymen. In a Letter to a Friend. Boston: Green & Russell, 1758.

The out-pouring of the Holy-Ghost. A Sermon Preach'd in Boston, May 13. 1742. On a day of prayer observed by the first Church there, to ask of God the effusion of his Spirit. Boston: T. Fleet for D. Henchman and S. Eliot, 1742.

Prayer for help a seasonable duty upon the ceasing of Godly and Faithful men. A Sermon occasion'd by the death of several worthy Members of the first Church in Boston: Preach'd the Lord's-day following the Anniversary fast, being the sabbath after the funeral of Mr. Jonathan Williams, one of the Deacons of said Church; who departed this life, March 27th. 1737. Aetat 63. Boston: T. Fleet, 1737.

A Reply to Dr. Chandler's 'Appeal Defended:' Wherein His Mistakes are rectified, his false Arguing refuted, and the Objections against the planned American Episcopate shewn to remain in full Force, notwithstanding all he has offered to render them invalid. Boston: Daniel Kneeland for Thomas Leverett, 1770.

"The Right Hand of Fellowship" delivered at the installation of Mr. Joseph Howe at the New South Church on May 19, 1773. Printed in Naphtali Daggett, *The Testimony of Conscience a Most Solid Foundation of Rejoicing.* Boston: Mills and Hicks, 1773.

"Preface" to John Clarke, *Salvation for all Men, illustrated and vindicated as A Scripture Doctrine, in Numerous Extracts from a Variety of Pious and Learned*

Men, who have purposely writ upon the subject. Together With their answer to the objections urged against it. By One who wishes well to all Mankind. Boston: T. and J. Fleet, 1782.

Seasonable Thoughts on the State of Religion in New-England, A Treatise in five Parts. I. Faithfully pointing out the Things of a bad and dangerous Tendency, in the late, and present, religious Appearance, in the Land. II. Representing the Obligations which lie upon the Pastors of these Churches in particular, and upon all in general, to use their Endeavours to suppress prevailing Disorders; with the great Danger of a Neglect in so important a Matter. III. Opening, in many Instances, wherein the Discouragers of Irregularities have been injuriously treated. IV. Shewing what ought to be corrected, or avoided, in testifying against the evil Things of the present Day. V. Directing our Thot's, more positively, to what may be judged the best Expedients, to promote pure and undefiled Religion in these Times. With a Preface Giving an Account of the Antinomians, Familists and Libertines, who infected these Churches, above an hundred Years ago: Very needful for these Days; the like Spirit, and Errors, prevailing now as did then. The whole being intended, and calculated, to serve the Interest of Christ's Kingdom. Boston: Rogers and Fowle for Samuel Eliot, 1743.

A Second Letter To a Friend; Giving a more particular Narrative of the Defeat of the French Army at Lake-George, By the New-England Troops, than has yet been published: Representing also the vast Importance of this Conquest to the American-British-Colonies. To which is added, Such an Account of what the New-England Governments have done to carry into Effect their Design against Crown-Point, as will shew the Necessity of their being helped by Great-Britain, in Point of Money. Boston: Edes and Gill, 1755.

A Sermon, Delivered at the First Church in Boston, March 13th, 1785: Occasioned by the Return of the Society to their House of Worship, After Long Absence, to Make Way for the Repairs that were Necessary. Boston: Greenleaf and Freeman, 1785.

A Sermon Preached May 6, 1767. At the Ordination of the Reverend Simeon Howard, M. A. To the Pastoral Care of the West-Church in Boston. To Which the Charge, and Right-Hand of Fellowship, delivered upon the same Occasion, are added. Boston: R. Draper, Edes & Gill, and T. & J. Fleet, 1767.

"A Sketch of Eminent Men in New-England. In a Letter from the Rev. Dr. Chauncy to Dr. Stiles." MHS Colls., 1st. Ser., X (1809), 154–65.

[With and Thomas Foxcroft.] "To the Reader," preface to Samuel Whittelsey, The woful Condition of Impenitent Souls in their Separate State. A Sermon Preach'd to the Old or first gather'd Church in Boston, On the Lord's-Day, April 4. 1731. Boston: S. Kneeland and T. Green for S. Gerrish, 1731.

Trust in God, the Duty of a People in a Day of Trouble. A Sermon Preached, May 30th. 1770. At the request of a great number of Gentlemen, friends to

*the Liberties of North-America, who were desirous, notwithstanding the re-
moval of the Massachusetts General-Court (unconstitutionally as they judged)
to Cambridge, that God might be acknowledged in that house of worship at
Boston, in which our tribes, from the days of our fathers, have annually
sought to him for direction, previous to the choice of his Majesty's Council.*
Boston: Daniel Kneeland for Thomas Leverett, 1770.

*Twelve Sermons On the following seasonable and important Subjects. Justifica-
tion impossible by the Works of the Law. The Question answered, "wherefore
than serveth the Law"? The Nature of Faith, as justifying, largely explained,
and remarked on. The Place, and Use, of Faith, in the Affair of Justification.
Human Endeavours, in the use of Means, the way in which Faith is obtained.
The Method of the Spirit in communicating the "Faith, by which the Just do
live". The Inquiry of the young Man in the Gospel, "what shall I do that I
may have eternal Life"? With interspersed Notes, in Defence of the Truth; especially in the Points treated on, in the above Discourses.* Boston: D. and J.
Kneeland for Thomas Leverett, 1765.

*An Unbridled Tongue a sure Evidence, that our Religion is Hypocritical and
Vain. A Sermon Preach'd at the Boston Thursday-Lecture, September 10th.
1741. And publish'd at the Desire of the Hearers.* Boston: Rogers and Fowle,
1741.

*The Validity of Presbyterian Ordination asserted and maintained. A Discourse
Delivered at the Anniversary Dudleian-Lecture, at Harvard-College in Cambridge New-England, May 12. 1762. With an Appendix, Giving a brief historical account of the epistles ascribed to Ignatius; and exhibiting some of the
many reasons, why they ought not to be depended on as his uncorrupted
works.* Boston: Richard Draper, 1762.

UNPUBLISHED MATERIALS

For this list I have selected those manuscripts and unpublished materials I have
found most useful in my study of Chauncy's life.

"Arbitral Award" re. Antigua Plantation. April 30, December 31, 1783; July 4,
1785. Massachusetts Historical Society.
Bernhard, Harold. "Charles Chauncy: Colonial Liberal." Unpublished disserta-
tion, University of Chicago Divinity School, 1945.
"The Boston Ministers." Harris Manuscripts, American Antiquarian Society.
Bridge, Ebenezer. Diary. Houghton Library, Harvard University.
Chauncy, Charles. Account with Messrs. R., R., and E. Maitland re Antiguan
Plantation. Massachusetts Historical Society.
——. Deed to William Pepperrell, April 21, 1733. Massachusetts Historical So-
ciety.
——. Letter to Samuel Adams, August 26, 1774. New York Public Library.
——. Letter to Samuel Adams, November 7, 1778. New York Public Library.

227

——. Letter to William Amory, September 13, 1774. Massachusetts Historical Society.

——. Letter to Nathaniel Chauncy, July 14, 1722. Yale University Library.

——. Letter to Nathaniel Chauncy, October 26, 1722. Yale University Library.

——. Letter to Nathaniel Chauncy, June 21, 1731. Yale University Library.

——. Letter to Nathaniel Chauncy, March 13, 1731/32. Yale University Library.

——. Letter to Nathaniel Chauncy, June 16, 1732. Yale University Library.

——. Letter to Nathaniel Chauncy, September 4, 1732. Yale University Library.

——. Letter to Nathaniel Chauncy, January 3, 1732/33. Yale University Library.

——. Letter to Nathaniel Chauncy, June 15, 1743. Boston Public Library.

——. Letter to Nathaniel Chauncy, November 6, 1743. Historical Society of Pennsylvania.

——. Letter to Nathaniel Chauncy, September 3, 1744. Yale University Library.

——. Letter to David Cheesbrough, February 2-4, 1767. Historical Society of Pennsylvania.

——. Letter to Timothy Cutler, September 24, 1742. Boston Public Library.

——. Letter to Thomas Fayerweather, February 15, 1774. Historical Society of Pennsylvania.

——. Letter to William Pepperrell, January 18, 1746. Massachusetts Historical Society.

——. Letter to Richard Price, March 22, 1770. Boston Public Library.

——. Letter to Thomas Prince, January 15, 1733. Massachusetts Historical Society.

——. Letter to Josiah Quincy, Jr., November 4, 1774. Massachusetts Historical Society.

——. Letter to Ezra Stiles, October 1, 1773. Historical Society of Pennsylvania.

——. Letter to Solomon Williams, December 9, 1749. Historical Society of Pennsylvania.

——. Letter to Stephen Williams, February 24, 1778. Historical Society of Pennsylvania.

——. Letter to Shute Shrimpton Yeamans, June 12, 1761. Massachusetts Historical Society.

——. Sermon, November 13, 1776. New York Public Library.

——. Subscription in support of Josiah Cotton in the ministry, May 27, 1731. Massachusetts Historical Society.

Cooper, Samuel. Letter to William Livingston, April 18, 1768. Massachusetts Historical Society.

Cutler, Timothy. Letter to Zachary Grey, November 8, 1734. Photostat in Massachusetts Historical Society.

Eliot, Andrew. Letter to the Rev. William Harris, December, 1767. Houghton Library, Harvard University.

——. Letter to Thomas Hollis, December 7, 1767. Houghton Library, Harvard University.

Gibbs, Norman Brantley. "The Problem of Revelation and Reason in the Thought of Charles Chauncy." Unpublished dissertation, Duke University, 1953.

228

Hoffman, John Maynard. "Commonwealth College: The Governance of Harvard in the Puritan Period." Unpublished dissertation, Harvard University, 1972.

Jones, Barney Lee. "Charles Chauncy and the Great Awakening." Unpublished dissertation, Duke University, 1958.

Lippy, Charles H. "Seasonable Revolutionary: Charles Chauncy and the Ideology of Liberty." Unpublished dissertation, Princeton University, 1972.

Livingston, William. Letter to Samuel Cooper, March 26, 1768. Massachusetts Historical Society.

"Quarter Bill Books," Harvard University Archives.

Rowe, John. Diary. Massachusetts Historical Society.

Tromsness, Clair Eugene. "Isaac Backus: Colonial Apologist for Religious Liberty." Unpublished dissertation, Stanford University, 1964.

University of Edinburg. Doctor of Sacred Scripture degree to Charles Chauncy, 1742. Copy in Yale University Library.

Waldron, William. Letter to Richard Waldron, August 30, 1725. Boston Public Library.

Wheelwright, Jeremiah. Diary. Massachusetts Historical Society.

Wohl, Harold B. "Charles Chauncy and the Age of Enlightenment in New England." Unpublished dissertation, University of Iowa, 1956.

Index

Index

233

Street, 27; Marlborough Street, 107;
Faneuil Hall, 149, 159; harbor, 151; port
of, 153; Bunker Hill, 160-61; Bunch of
Grapes Tavern, 162
—Meetings of ministers: 35, 49, 75, 76, 77,
78, 103-4, 136, 157, 162
—Natural calamities: *1727* earthquake, 10,
28, 29, 38-39, 45, 47, 105; *1755* earthquake, 105; *1722* smallpox epidemic, 18;
1752 smallpox epidemic, 104
—Newspapers, press: effect of Great Awakening on, 36, 46; Boston *News Letter*,
30; Boston *Weekly News Letter*, 75; Boston *Evening Post*, 77, 149-50, 156; Boston *Gazette*, 140
—Schools: Boston Public Latin School: and
Charles Chauncy, 14-15, 18; and John
Taylor, 14-15; and Edward Wiggles-
worth, 18; Boston Grammar School: and
Benjamin Franklin, 15; Charles Chauncy
as inspector of public schools, 35
Bowdoin, James: president of Society for
Propagating Christian Knowledge among
the Indians of North America, 133;
and Hutchinson-Whately letters, 153;
called rebel, 156; first president of
American Academy of Arts and Sciences,
170
Bowman, Joseph, 134
Boyle, John, 149
Braddock, Edward, 105
Bradford, John, 156
Bradford, William, 3
Brewster, Massachusetts, 48
Bridenbaugh, Carl, 134-35, 142, 143
Bridge, Ebenezer, 94
Brookline, Massachusetts, 160
Brownell, George, 15
Brunswick, Maine, 77-78
Buell, Able, 150
Buell, Samuel, 53, 63-64
Bunch of Grapes Tavern. *See* Boston: Loca-
tions
Bunker Hill, battle of, 160-61
Byfield, Nathanael: and Charles Chauncy's
father, 14; Chauncy's affection for, 14;
asks Thomas Foxcroft to call election at
First Church, 24; Chauncy preaches on
death of, 31; mentioned, 99
Byles, Mather: character of, 72; opposition
to Great Awakening, 72; denunciation of,
163; dismissal of, 164

Calvin, John, 4, 5, 122
Cambridge, Massachusetts: and Benjamin
Wadsworth, 23; and Charles Chauncy, 24;
Congregational Church, 24
Canada, 98
Caner, Henry, 130, 131-32
Canterbury, Archbishop of, 13, 128-29
Cape Breton Island. *See* Colonial Wars
A Careful and Strict Enquiry into . . . Free-
dom of Will. See Edwards, Jonathan
Case and Complaint of Mr. Samuel Osborn,
The. See Osborn, Samuel
Catholicism, 50-51, 57, 93, 132, 138
"Caucus Club," 140
Chandler, Thomas Bradbury: and episcopacy
controversy, 134, 142; *An Appeal to the*
Public, 136-38; *The Appeal Defended*,
137, 138; *The Appeal Farther Defended*,
137-38; Charles Chauncy's *Reply* to, 166
Channing, William Ellery: represents Unitar-
ianism, 3; Charles Chauncy considered
follower of, 3; Chauncy's differences
with, 4
Chappel, Noah, 66
Charles I. *See* Kings of England
Charlestown, Massachusetts, 67
Chatham, Lord, 155. *See also* Pitt, William
Chauncy, Charles (Charles Chauncy's great-
grandfather): biography written by Cotton Mather, 9-10; religious views of, 10;
will, 12; characterized, 12, 95; and family
legend of resisting Anglicanism, 128; ac-
cidental burning of his papers, 180
Chauncy, Charles (Charles Chauncy's father):
biographical sketch, 13; death and fun-
eral, 14; Charles Chauncy recalls, 180;
mentioned, 10
Chauncy, Charles
—Ancestry, 9, 14, 95, 128, 180
—Boyhood, 11-15
—And Colonial Wars: 93, 94, 96-99, 104-7
—Education, 16-25
—Episcopacy Controversy: 5, 29, 30, 31, 45,
98, 127-38, 144-45, 151, 166
—Great Awakening: 5, 27, 28, 46-70, 71,
72, 88, 89, 94, 95, 96
—Ministry, 9-10, 24-36, 72, 94, 101, 126,
144, 162, 168-69, 174-81
—Northampton Awakening ("Surprising
Conversions"), 36, 38-46, 70, 71
—Personal life: character, 5, 6, 8, 25; up-
bringing, 11-14; courtships and marriages,

235

34; marries Benjamin Greenleaf, 107;
death, 145

Chauncy, Elizabeth Hurst (Charles Chauncy's
wife): Joseph Sewall's description, 22;
Samuel Sewall as guardian, 26; marries
Chauncy, 27; first pregnancy, 27; relationship to Jane Hirst, 29; second pregnancy, 34; death, 34, 39

Chauncy, Elizabeth Phillips Townsend
(Charles Chauncy's wife): marries
Chauncy, 35; contributes to repair of
Summer Street parsonage, 35; estate of,
101; death, 107

Chauncy, Isaac (Charles Chauncy's grandfather): emigrates to England after graduation from Harvard, 13; Chauncy recalls, 180

Chauncy, Isaac (Charles Chauncy's brother),
14

Chauncy, Mary Stoddard (Charles Chauncy's
wife): marriage to Chauncy, 107-8; and
siege of Boston, 159; provisions for
widowhood, 170; death, 174-75

Chauncy, Nathaniel (Charles Chauncy's
cousin): praised by Jonathan Edwards,
39; mentioned, 75, 180; correspondence
with Chauncy, 88, 89, 111, 121, 122

Chauncy, Sarah (Charles Chauncy's daughter): birth, 34; death of mother, 34; marriage, 107

Chauncy, Sarah Walley, (Charles Chauncy's
mother): marriage, 13; widowhood, 14;
inheritance, 14

Chauncy, Walley (Charles Chauncy's brother), 14

Checkley, John, 20

Checkley, Samuel: George Whitefield visits,
52; and attempt to dismiss Samuel
Mather, 58

Chelmsford, Massachusetts, 94

Christ. See Biblical figures

Church, Benjamin, 156

Church of England: Congregational fear of,
5, 45, 144; Charles Chauncy's distrust
of, 29, 30, 31, 98, 145, 166; Addington
Davenport's defense of, 30; Chauncy inspired by Addington Davenport to study
government of, 31, 136; New England's
fear of, 45, 144, 145; George Whitefield's
ministry in, 46; attempt to establish
bishops in America, 98, 127-38, 145,
151, 166; appoints commissaries to ex-

ercise ecclesiastical jurisdiction, 128; and
separation of church and state, 166, 169

Civil Magistrates Must be Just. See Chauncy,
Charles, Works

Clark, Francis, 14

Clark, Peter, and The Scripture Doctrine of
Original Sin . . . In a Summer Morning's
Conversation, 122

Clarke, John: becomes Charles Chauncy's
associate, 169; and Salvation for all Men,
173-74; and A Letter to Doctor Mather,
174; and funeral ceremony for Mary
Chauncy, 174-75; wants clerical gown
and organ for the meetinghouse, 177;
and return to refurbished First Church,
178; preaches Charles Chauncy's eulogy,
181

Clarke, Samuel, 4

Clinton, George, 164

Coercive Acts, 151, 153-54

Collson, David, 35

Colman, Benjamin: and Charles Chauncy's
ordination, 9-10, 24; and Harvard Corporation, 17, 23; asks Jonathan Edwards
for narrative of surprising conversions,
37-38; and Samuel Osborn controversy,
49, 78; welcomes George Whitefield, 52;
mentioned, 53; and attempt to dismiss
Samuel Mather, 58

Colonial wars:

—King George's War (War of the Austrian
Succession): declared, 93; Charles
Chauncy follows course of, 94; expedi-
tion against Louisbourg, 93, 96-99;
Chauncy's role in, 96-99; campaign
against Cape-Breton Island, 96, 98; effect
on New England economy, 101; Parlia-
ment reimburses Massachusetts for Cape-
Breton expenses, 102; treaty of Aix-la-
Chapelle, 104

—Seven Years' War: begins, 104; engagements at Nova Scotia, 105; at Fort
Duquesne, 105-6, 107; at Crown-Point,
106; at Fort Ticonderoga, 106, 107; at
Lake George, 106, 107; at Fort William
Henry, 107; at Frontenac, 107; at Niagara,
107; at Quebec, 107; at St. Francis, 107

Colonies, Anglo-American, 3

Committees of Correspondence: development, 151; and Hutchinson-Whately letters, 152-53

Common Sense. See Paine, Thomas

237

239

on, 36; visit of George Whitefield, 52; and attempt to dismiss Samuel Mather, 58; Chauncy's friction with Foxcroft during Great Awakening, 72; John Cotton's ministry, 104; Mary Stoddard and, 108; Chauncy's pastorate, 126, 144, 168, 178; and Eli Forbes, 134; mentioned in popular ballad, "The Boston Ministers," 141; Chauncy preaches rival election sermon, 147; and siege of Boston, 162, 163; debate on Massachusetts Constitution held at, 166; considers Ezra Stiles as minister, 169; selects John Clarke as minister, 169; controversy over installing organ, 177; *1786* Declaration of Faith, quoted, 180-81; mentioned, 63, 67, 68, 90, 92, 93, 100, 143

Fiske, Samuel, 76

Five Dissertations on . . . the Fall. See Chauncy, Charles, Works

Flanders, 106

Fleet, Mary, 105

Flynt, Henry: seeks membership on Harvard Corporation, 17; friendship with Charles Chauncy, 19

Forbes, Eli, 134

Fort Duquesne. *See* Colonial wars

Fort Ticonderoga. *See* Colonial wars

Fort William Henry. *See* Colonial wars

Foxcroft, Thomas: and Charles Chauncy's ordination, 9-10, 24; views on *1727* earthquake, 10; becomes pastor at First Church, 23; conducts election of Chauncy, 24; oratory, 25; residences, 27; size of family, 27; salary difficulties, 27, 28, 34, 101; Chauncy's relationship with, 28, 59, 72, 144-45; and centenary of First Church, 29; stroke and its consequences, 34, 35, 36, 39, 168; and Samuel Osborn controversy, 49; pastorate, 58; endorses Peter Clark's *Summer Morning's Conversation*, 122; death and burial, 144-45

France, 164, 173

Franklin, Abiah, 13

Franklin, Benjamin: and secular Deism, 3; and Jonathan Edwards, 3, 6, 8; on Puritan doctrine, 6-7; *Autobiography*, quoted, 6, 7, 12, 15, 54; as Bostonian, 7; on divinity of Christ, 7-8; neighbor of Charles Chauncy, 12; on parents, 13, 99; and Boston Public Latin School, 15; and

New-England Courant, 16; and self-mockery, 96; and Hutchinson-Whately letters, 152-53; and Jane Mecom, 156; and American Philosophical Society, 170; and peace treaty of Paris, 173

Franklin, James, 16

Franklin, Josiah: child-rearing practices, 13; schooling of Benjamin Franklin, 15

French and Indian wars. *See* Colonial wars

Frink, Thomas, 90

Gage, Thomas: and Boston Massacre, 147; Hutchinson writes to, 149; becomes governor of Massachusetts, 154; and closing of port of Boston, 157; advises against coercion, 158; and siege of Boston, 159-60; replaced by William Howe, 161

Gay, Ebenezer, 49

Gee, Joshua: George Whitefield visits, 52; dislike for Samuel Mather, 58; disputes with Charles Chauncy, 59, 76-78, 88, 95; and Samuel Osborn controversy, 78

George II. *See* Kings of England

George III. *See* Kings of England

Germany, 161

Gibbs, Norman Brantley, 109

The Gifts of the Spirit to Ministers. See Chauncy, Charles, Works

Goen, C. C., 89

Gordon, William, 174

"Grand Itinerants, The": nickname for George Whitefield, Gilbert Tennent, and James Davenport, 46-47; and Whitefield's return to America, 88; Whitefield's leadership, 90

Gray, Edward, 35

Great Awakening, The: Charles Chauncy's opposition, 5, 27, 28, 71, 72, 88, 94, 95, 96; phases of, 36, 89, 93, 101; and New England, 46-70; aftermath, 89, 110, 126, 127, 171; and episcopacy controversy, 128; mentioned, 32, 40, 107, 109, 138, 144, 163

Great chain of being, 114-20

Green, Jeremiah, 24

Green, Joseph, 21

Greenleaf, Benjamin, 107

Greenleaf, Elizabeth Chauncy. *See* Chauncy, Elizabeth

Greenleaf, Joseph, 156

Greenough, Deacon, 173

Greenwood, Isaac, 18

241

243

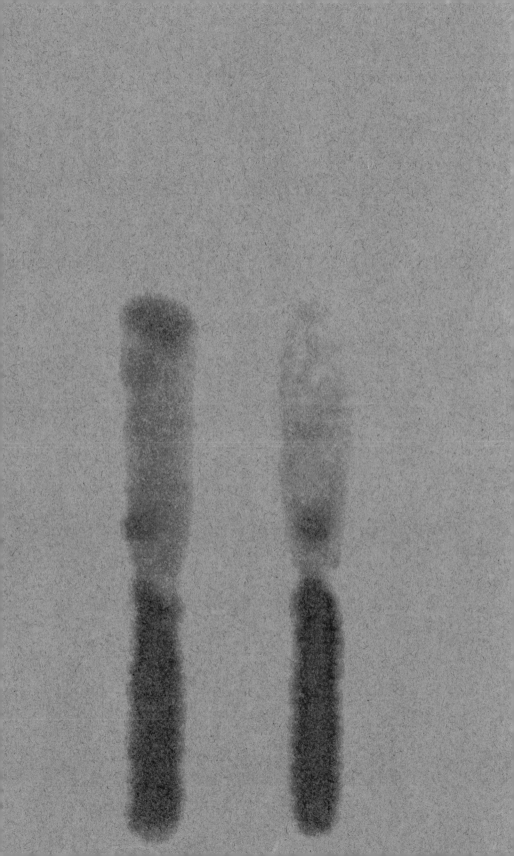

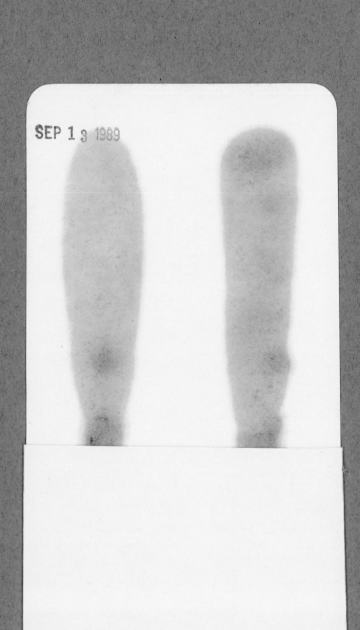

SEP 1 3 1989